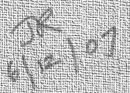

Rishis, Mystics and Heroes of

India

Volume I

Rishis, Mystics and Heroes of

India

Volume I

by

Sadhu Mukundcharandas

Swaminarayan Aksharpith
Shahibaug Road, Amdavad,
India.

Rishis, Mystics and Heroes of India (Volume I)

By Sadhu Mukundcharandas

Inspirer: HDH Pramukh Swami Maharaj

First edition: June 2005

Reprint : September 2006

Cost: 250/-

Copies: 5,000

Sadhu, Mukundcharandas
    Rishis, Mystics and Heroes of India
by Sadhu Mukundcharandas. - Amdavad : Swaminarayan Aksharpith, 2006. -
    xxii, 306p. : col. ill., maps; 25 cm.
    Bibliography : p.290 - 297
    Includes index
    ISBN: 81-7526-296-6 (v.1)
    1. Biography 2. India - Biography
3. Hinduism - Biography I. Title
DDC : 920.054
UDC : 929 (54) : 294.5

Published & Printed by
Swaminarayan Aksharpith
Shahibaug, Amdavad-4, India.

Websites : *www.swaminarayan.org*
        www.akshardham.com
        www.mandir.org
        kids.swaminarayan.org

Contents

Part I - Rishis and Rishi Scientists

Part II—Acharyas of Philosophy

Part IV-Heroes and Heroines

Acknowledgements

We sincerely thank the Vedic scholar Dr. David Frawley (Pundit Shri Vamadeva Shastri) of the American Institute of Vedic Studies for kindly writing the 'foreword' to this book and useful comments in improving the book.

We are also grateful to the following for their contribution:

Sadhu Swyamprakashdas (Dr. Swami), Sadhu Ishwarcharandas,

Sadhu ShriHaridas, Sadhu Shrutiprakashdas (AARSH, Archives, Gandhinagar), Sadhu Vivekjivandas, Sadhu Vivekpriyadas, Sadhu Aksharvatsaldas, Sadhu Shrijiswarupdas & Design Studio Staff.

Dr. Hasubhai Yajnik (Musicologist & author).

Dr. N. M. Kansara (Director AARSH).

The Wellcome Institute Library, London for kindly providing Kawasji's rhinoplasty sketch and printing permission.

Dr. N. M. Chovatia, O. H. Nazar Ayurvedic College, Surat, for kindly providing permission to photograph and print replicas of Sushrut's instruments.

The late Shri Yogendra Prakash Mittal (Delhi), Prakash Panchal (M.D. Ayurveda).

Shri Lalitkumar Singh (Amdavad), for photograph of palm leaf manuscript on back title.

Narharibhai Brahmbhatt and Trilok Brahmbhatt for their untiring efforts in procuring reference books from libraries.

R. L. Patel, Librarian - Gujarat University.

The following libraries for providing reference books:

M. J. Library, B. J. Institute of Research, Gujarat Vidyapith.

Dharmendra Somkunvar – for the following watercolours: Yagnavalkya, Panini, Dhanvantari, Jaimini, Gautam, Patanjali, Nimbarkacharya, Madhvacharya, Vitthalnath, Gopis, Alwars, Kabir, Nanakdev, Surdas, Haridas, Eknath, Gauribai, Tyagraj, Sati Savitri, Brahmanand Swami, Zamkuba, Gopalanand Swami and Ahalyabai.

Sadhana – monthly magazine, Amdavad – for permission to print Raidas's colour painting.

Navnitbhai Kapadia and G. M. Shah (for data entry).

Sadhu Achalmunidas and Mahesh Rangi (for book design).

Note on reprint

Since the inauguration of the Swaminarayan Akshardham in New Delhi in November 2005, this book will also be helpful to teachers and students seeking further details of the rishi scientists depicted in the boat ride exhibition "Sanskruti Vihar". Many of these appear in this book.

- Swaminarayan Aksharpith,
July 2006

Foreword

It is a natural thing for the youth to emulate and seek to follow the example of great people. This inherent attitude of devotion extends to other age groups as well, touching all of us. We look up to those whom our society honors and automatically strive to be like them. Especially important in this regard are great historical personalities, who represent important discoveries, developments or movements in society. Though such individuals may have lived many years ago, their lives have become an example for future generations and they continue to be of interest to everyone. Their life stories help raise our own aspiration to a higher level and provide us with insights how to better fulfill our own deeper potential.

It is often said, and rightfully so, that the youth of today have no real role models to follow. The current social and political leaders seldom have any real character or integrity. In the modern media culture, the youth mainly looks up to entertainers, athletes, business executives or other people successful only in the external world. Such individuals may have skill and talent in certain areas but seldom project the model of a fully realized human being in body, mind and spirit. They do not provide us with real examples to follow in life in order to find real peace and happiness. Emulating them only causes us further distraction, frustration and confusion.

Much of this is not the fault of the individuals so honored as the current state of our society and its values. We live in a commercial age in which outer appearance, wealth, power and prestige is given more importance than inner wisdom, strength or integrity. In yogic terms, our current culture and its role models are rajasic (worldly), not sattvic (spiritual).

Modern history books, following mainly a western view of the world, do have their great historical individuals that students are taught to look up to in modern educational programs. But these personages are largely intellectuals, artists, scientists or politicians, not yogis, saints or sadhus. Their contribution is also more to the outer world than to the

realm of the spirit or to the higher evolution of humanity beyond the body and ego. While they can demonstrate certain special insights, skills or discoveries, they rarely provide the kind of spiritual role models that we really need.

However, many great spiritual role models do exist in the history of India, which is founded recognizing and honoring the wise. Some of these towering personalities are still living today. They are the great gurus of the country, whose lives and teachings are the very life blood of the Hindu heritage. They remain the appropriate people to serve as cultural role models, particularly for those who want to follow a truly spiritual way of life. Some of them are also great scientists, doctors or musicians, showing how we can be successful in all fields of life without losing our inner equilibrium, but they approached their outer work with a yogic vision that made it something more than personal. They reflected some aspect of divinity into our mortal sphere.

Unfortunately, there is little available today on such great spiritual figures of the ages, particularly in a single book. This keeps the powerful influence of these great souls from reaching us today. The current book, Rishis, Mystics and Heroes of India, Vol. I helps remedy this situation, restoring our connection with this great stream of Hindu teachers. It revives the ancient Hindu literature of honoring great souls and their life stories.

Sadhu Mukundcharandas brings us such important life stories of great rishis, yogis, scientists, bhaktas and even kings of old India, extending to figures up to a few centuries ago. He takes many notable examples in a broad panorama of human types and experiences. His book provides us with true teachers to emulate and significant aspects of their lives to contemplate. As Vol. I only, we can expect that it will be followed by additional volumes and including those of more contemporary figures.

Hindu thought tells us that we tend to take on the samskaras or tendencies of the people whom we emulate in

our hearts. If we mainly emulate people of rajasic (egoistic) disposition such as most oler leaders and famous people are today then we become more rajasic or worldly-minded ourselves. If we mainly emulate people of sattvic (spiritual) disposition such as these great teachers are then we become more sattvic or spiritual ourselves. Emulating the right leaders and guides is an important means of character development, without which our personality is likely to remain unsound. It is a way of connecting to God and the Atma or Divine Self within us.

Contemplating such great personalities is part of the principle of 'Satsang' in Hindu thought, the idea of association with the wise. We tend to become like those whom we associate with. It is important that we choose our associations carefully and consciously, if we want to move our lives in the right direction to reduce our karmas and promote the liberation of the spirit. This is true not only for us individually but for our entire culture and civilization. If our society mainly emulates rajasic people such as it does today then our society as a whole must remain rajasic and lead to suffering, violence, unhappiness or mental agitation. While we cannot always change the people around us at a physical level, we can change those that we follow in our thoughts and actions. To contemplate the lives of noble souls is one way to do this.

India has a wealth of such great people, Mahatmas, and from every generation from the Vedic seers to the Mahabharata period to the modern age. Their lives are good examples of how we should live and how we can make our own lives more meaningful. Their teachings remain as a light to guide us forward along our higher path.

Sadhu Mukundcharandas has done a great work bringing the stories of so many great people into a single volume. He has grasped the essence of their experience and presented it to the modern reader for quick and easy understanding. He has covered the ancient rishis of India including in diverse fields as Ayurveda and astronomy. He has gone through the founders

of the main philosophical schools of the country, which remain probably the greatest philosophies of all time. He has given an important place to poets and singers as well. He has brought in several important political leaders and kings, indicating that right action in the outer world was always part of Hindu thought. He has shown the great women of India as well, who have always had their importance as representing the Shakti of Mother India.

Rishis, Mystics and Heroes of India is a good book for the youth to show them a different model of how to make both themselves and the world better. It can be read and studied over a long period of time, a story a day or a week, affording many different facets on how to bring dharma into all that we do. The book is bound to encourage all people to change their lives in a spiritual direction. It affords a deeper vision of the human being and one that is truer to our real purpose in lives, which is to return to the Godhead within all.

I am happy to recommend this inspiring book to all readers, East and West. May the light of all such noble souls awaken in everyone!

- Dr. David Frawley (Pundit Vamadeva Shastri)
Santa Fe, New Mexico, USA.
January 2005.

Preface

A culture's future rests on the strength of its legacy. Preserve this legacy and the future brightens. Destroy it and the future bleakens. Regardless of the present state of affairs the richness of its past can certainly act as a beacon of inspiration both for those in the present and the future. As in other ancient cultures of the world, *Bharatvarsh's* (India's) firmament has scintillated down the ages with a legacy of eminent personalities. Each has played some role in illuminating this cultural firmament. *Rishis, Mystics and Heroes of India* will enlighten readers about the sublime contributions of these personalities.

Secondly, it hopes to induce a sense of pride in young NRIs and those distanced from their motherland, about its rich heritage and antiquity. Raised and educated in a western cultural milieu, the young at home and abroad are little aware about their lofty contributions. This presents two grave problems. The first is that demeaning accounts often radically estrange the young from their culture, to the extent that they develop a strong distaste for everything Indian. The second problem is of historical distortion. For example, Western authors give the earliest date of the *Rg Veda* and *Mahabharat* as 1500 BCE and 500 CE respectively! They quote Max Mueller as authority, who in turn gave his dates without any convincing evidence.

This problem of dating Sanatan Dharma's shastras is discussed and clarified in Part I, Chapter 1, in 'Bhagwan Veda Vyas', the author of the above texts.

The accounts of rishi scientists offer concrete evidence about their scientific discoveries, centuries before the so-called 'first discoveries' by Western scientists in the past few centuries. The evidence dispels the continuing false information disseminated in schools today. The evidence includes the rishis' first accounts regarding gravity, zero, the atom, the earth's rotation on its axis and spherical nature, astronomy, algebra, mathematics, trigonometry, chemistry,

medicine and surgery, music, art, literature, architecture, agriculture and many other fields. Thus young readers may fathom the truth for themselves and remain open-minded about India's original contributions to the world.

The third aim of this book is to provide accounts of characters from the view of *dharma* and *bhakti*, rather than just a shallow account based on *dehabhav* – body consciousness – which is often the bane of Western accounts. In this volume, each character's contribution is discussed in enriching, ennobling, expounding or upholding any ideal or belief of Sanatan Dharma over the ages.

In Part II, the details of philosophy will be of special interest to college level readers, who may wish to understand comparative philosophy of the six main schools of thought in a nutshell.

Personalities in Part III include people who have contributed to Sanatan Dharma by their *bhakti* literature, such as, devotional poems and commentaries, or by their profound saintliness.

The heroes and heroines in Part IV include people who, by their statesmanship and values of *dharma*, continued the struggle against *adharma*, to liberate their kingdoms from oppression and instill values of *dharma* in people.

- Author

Part I-Rishis and Rishi Scientists

Introduction

From time immemorial Bharatvarsh has been graced with sages known as rishis. By performing austerities, meditation and by divine grace they fathomed the secrets of creation. Each rishi gleaned truths of a particular field of knowledge. The rishis imparted two types of knowledge (*vidya*): *para* – spiritual and *apara* – mundane. In this first section we consider nine rishis or rishi-scientists.

Bhagwan Veda Vyas and Yagnavalkya were rishis who fathomed both *para* and *apara vidya* in the Vedas. Panini formulated the intricacies of Sanskrit, the language of the *devas* and rishis. Then follows the three rishi-scientists of Ayurveda; Divodas Dhanvantari, Sushrut and Charak. They revealed to mankind the secrets of longevity, health, medicine and surgery. It is important to realise that these rishis literally 'saw' intuitively and gleaned the truths about the human body, its multiple systems, the medicinal qualities of plants and minerals for treatment and the secrets of holistic health. One who 'sees' intuitively, by his supernormal faculty of vision, is known as a seer and *drushta* in Sanskrit. The rishis possessed spiritual power and omniscience such that through them the sacred texts and knowledge were revealed to man. Many of their observations defied European physicians of the 18th century and continue to baffle those of the 21st century, as we shall see.

The final three rishi-scientists, namely, Varahamihir, Aryabhatta and Bhaskaracharya (II) were geniuses in astronomy, mathematics and algebra respectively. Their original contributions reflect their immense spiritual enlightenment. Of these, Varahamihir may be considered the supremely versatile. He has cited intricate details about a staggering range of topics; secrets impossible to be fathomed in one lifetime single–handedly.

All such rishis then, perfected their body, mind and *atma* to serve as a fine–tuned laboratory. Their inner enlightenment and divine grace added the crowning touch.

1. Bhagwan Veda Vyas

(Redactor of the Vedas)

Bhagwan Veda Vyas is Sanatan Dharma's *adi* (first) *acharya*. He was born on Ashadh Purnima, of Parashar rishi and Satyavati. His dark complexion also rendered him the name Krishna. Further, due to his birth on an island – *dwip* - in the middle of the river Yamuna, conferred the name Dvaipayan. Hence the name Krishna Dvaipayan Vyas. Being a descendent of the Badari family, he is also called Badarayan. He is one among the renowned twelve *chiranjivis* – long lived personalities of Sanatan Dharma - which include: Hanumanji, Bali, Parshuram, Ashwatthama, Krupa, Vibhishan and others.

In the beginning, there existed only one Veda, which Vyasji then simplified and divided into four: Rg, Sam, Yajur and Atharva. "Vyas" means divider. Since he divided the Vedas, he became known as Veda Vyas. For the lay people he then composed eighteen Purans. Through these, in the form of stories, different groups of people were then able to consolidate their devotion to their revered deities.

B – Badrinath

Vyasji then composed the *Itihas* text Mahabharat, to propagate the principles of dharma*, arth, kam* and *moksha*. As he uttered the *shloks*, Ganeshji scribed them. This text is also glorified as the fifth Veda – *panchamo vedaha*. Among the philosophical sections of the Mahabharat, the Bhagvad Gita is considered the crest–jewel. The Gita is contained in the *Bhishma Parva*, Chapters 23 to 40.

Vyas studied under great scholars like Parashar, Vasudev and Sanakadik rishis. He established his ashram in the recesses of the Himalayas, at the confluence of the sacred rivers Saraswati and Alaknanda, near the pilgrim place of Shamyapras. Here he taught the Vedas to four pupils: Paila, Vaishampayan, Jaimini and Sumantu. His sons, born from his thoughts – a phenomenon known as *sankalp putras* – included: King Pandu, father of the Pandavs; Dhrutrashtra, father of the Kauravs; Vidurji and Shukdevji. The latter was the brahmanishth sadhu who expounded *katha* to King Parikshit, to redeem him in seven days.

After composing seventeen Purans and the Mahabharat, he still experienced discontentment at heart. He divulged this to Narad rishi, who is considered to be Bhagwan's 'mind'. Naradji replied, "Though you have written extensively on dharma, *arth*, and *kam*, you have not dealt with *moksha* and the knowledge of the self. This is not possible without Bhagwan's manifest form. Today, he manifests as Shri Krishna. Therefore, compose a sacred text narrating Shri Krishna's glory and which will inspire bhakti in the hearts of devotees. This is the only work left for you. Only by glorifying such divine episodes will your unhappiness be alleviated. There is no other way."

Vyasji then composed the eighteenth mahapuran, the Shrimad Bhagvatam, also known as Satvati Shruti – the Veda of the Vaishnavs. He then experienced peace at heart.

Veda Vyas also composed the *Vedant Sutras*, also synonymously known as *Uttar Mimamsa, Brahman Mimamsa, Brahman Sutra, Badarayan Sutra, Vyas Sutra* and *Sharirak Sutra*.

Vyasji was wedded to asceticism all his life. He embodied the ideals of asceticism such that Shri Krishna regarded him as the supreme ascetic: *munināmapyaham vyāsah* among the ascetics I am Vyas (Gita 10/37). He was endowed with omniscience. With his divine power he saw events of the past, present and future. On several occasions he used his *divya chakshu* (divine sight) to try to prevent the conflict that eventually culminated into the Mahabharat War. He advised Dhrutarashtra to discipline his Kaurav sons when they decided to attack the Pandavs during their forest exile. Finally during the battle, Vyas and Narad intervened, appearing between the converging missiles released by Arjun and Ashwatthama, to prevent collision. Known as *brahmastra,* these missiles threatened to annihilate the world. Vyas ordered both to recall them. Arjun did. Ashwatthama could not. Therefore, Shri Krishna cursed the latter, as did Vyas. He was the spiritual preceptor of both the Pandavs and Kauravs. He advised them about dharma and was the knower of dharma.

Dating the Shastras

Sanatan Dharma's fundamental belief is that the Vedas are *sanatan* – eternal – and *apaurusheya* – not composed by any human entity. At the beginning of every cosmic cycle of Brahmā, Paramatma utters the divine words through Brahmā's mouth. Later, at various periods different rishis, through divine grace, realised these divine words, known as *sakshat* darshan. They then imparted their realised knowledge orally to their pupils. In this manner the tradition was handed down the ages. Later, this knowledge was scribed using letters. Mankind is graced with Vedic knowledge through this five–fold manner: (i) eternal existence of Vedic knowledge (ii) vocalisation of Vedic knowledge (iii) darshan (realisation) of Vedic knowledge (iv) the propagation of this 'heard' Vedic knowledge and (v) the compilation by scribing of Vedic knowledge.

At the end of Brahmā's cosmic period, the Vedic knowledge in its gross *(sthul)* form apparently disappears, only to reappear in Brahmā's next cycle of creation. Hence, in reality, the Vedas are eternal and so in Bharatvarsh's true tradition and belief the question of dating hardly arises.

Hence the dates and periods attributed by Western so–called intellectuals and Indians swayed by them are totally preposterous; an insidious attempt to ridicule the sacred and eternal heritage of Bharat. Even their interpretations of the true and sacred meanings of the shastras are flagrantly warped and often shallow. Without the bona fide guru's guidance this is but natural. Though many claim to have studied the texts in Sanskrit, they had not grasped the basics. Most copied their predecessors or Indian scholars whose thinking and bent of mind was also 'colonialised'. The most notorious among the Europeans was Max Muller, who, solely on whim, extremely reluctantly placed the dating of the Rg Veda at 1200 BCE, and the Upanishads at a mere 800 to 600 BCE!

By astronomical observations of planetary movements the exact date of the beginning of *Kali–yug* has been verified.

3

From this, by simple arithmetic, the date of the Mahabharat and *Brahma Sutras* can be calculated.

1. *Kali–yug*: 3,102 years BCE – on 20 February at 2 hours 27 minutes and 30 seconds. The astrologer, Bailey, concurred, "The calculation of the Brahmins is so exactly confirmed by our own astronomical tables that nothing but actual observation could have given so correspondent a result." (*Theology of the Hindus* by Count Bjornstjerna, p.132.)

   This amounts to 3102 + 2005 (CE) = 5,107 years.

2. The Mahabharat War: began 36 years prior to the start of *Kali–yug* (or when 36 years of *Dwapar–yug* remained).

   This means 5,107 + 36 = 5143 years ago.

3. Shrimad Bhagvatam: its first discourse was related by Shukdevji to King Parikshit 30 years after Shri Krishna's departure (Padma Puran, Uttarkhand, 198–71.) i.e. 30 years into *Kali–yug* – 3082 BCE.

4. From this it can be inferred that Vyasji composed the Shrimad Bhagvatam prior to 3082 BCE. And, as mentioned earlier, the Mahabharat was written after the Bhagvatam, since the Gita (part of Mahabharat, Bhishma Parva. Ch. 23 to 40) also mentions the Brahma Sutras and vice–versa. They can both be contemporaneous or within a short period of each other, post 3082 BCE (c. 5084 years ago).

Hence the periods assigned to the writing of the Brahma Sutras by Western and Eastern scholars listed below, can be seen to be wholly ludicrous!

A.B. Keith	–	200 BCE
Jacobi	–	250 to 450 BCE
Frazer	–	400 BCE
Max Muller	–	300 BCE
Hiriyanna	–	480 BCE
Dasgupta	–	200 BCE

Veda Vyas and Bhagwan Swaminarayan

Bhagwan Swaminarayan has upheld Veda Vyas and the shastras written by him as supremely authoritative. Of the eight shastras that He cites in the Shikshapatri (93–95) and Vachanamrut Vartal–18 as authoritative, five are by Vyasji: four Vedas, Vedant Sutras, Shrimad Bhagvatam, Vidurniti (Mahabharat, Udyog Parva 33–40) and Bhagvad Gita.

He praises Vyasji in eleven Vachanamruts: Gadhada I–39, Kariyani–6, Loya–4, 9, 18, Gadhada II–6, 9, 21, 64, Vartal–18 and Gadhada III–10. In Gadhada II–21, He cites the essence of all Vyasji's works – that for the liberation of the *jiva*, understand Bhagwan as the creator, sustainer and destroyer of the cosmos. In Vartal–18 and Gadhada III–10 He lauds Vyasji as the greatest of all acharyas; even greater than Shankar, Ramanuj and all others, because all of them have based their beliefs and established their *sampradays* on Vyasji's works, whereas Vyasji does not need to rely upon anyone else to be authoritative. To a Vedanti (in Gadhada I–39) and a scholar of the Madhva Sampraday (Gadhada III–10), He emphatically commands them to quote from Vyasji's shastras to clarify certain beliefs. To the Madhvi scholar, He further requests reference from the Bhagvatam because, "It is the essence of the Vedas, Purans and Itihas shastras," and also from the Gita, which is the more authoritative part of the Mahabharat. Too overwhelmed by Bhagwan Swaminarayan's logical reasoning, both scholars failed to answer Him!

A Sanksrit scholar-*paramhansa* of Bhagwan Swaminarayan, Swami Shatanand, composed 108 auspicious names of Bhagwan Swaminarayan in the *Janmangal Stotras*. Of these, the 99th name is Vyassiddhantbodhakah – the expounder of Vyas's principles.

Finally, in the Swamini Vato (1/35), Aksharbrahma Gunatitanand Swami cites Vyasji's essence and principle after his deep reflection of his texts:

Ālodya sarva shāstrāni vichārya cha punaha punaha,
Idamekam sunishpannam dhyeyo Nārāyano Harihi.

– after repeatedly reflecting on all the shastras, I have arrived at one principal – that life's goal is to attain Bhagwan Narayan.

In remembrance and glory of Veda Vyas as the first and foremost acharya and guru of Sanatan Dharma, the festival of Guru Purnima is celebrated annually on Ashadh Punam, also known as Vyas Purnima, when one's spiritual guru is offered *pujan*.

Eighteen Purans

1.	Brahma	10.	Brahmavaivart
2.	Padma	11.	Ling
3.	Vishnu	12.	Varah
4.	Shiv	13.	Skand
5.	Brahmand	14.	Vaman
6.	Narad	15.	Kurma
7.	Markandeya	16.	Matsya
8.	Agni	17.	Garud
9.	Bhavishyottara	18.	Bhagvat

(Total 400,000 *shloks*)

2. Yagnavalkya Rishi
(Promulgator of Shukla Yajur Veda)

A *brahmanishth* rishi of the Upanishadic period, Yagnavalkya rishi, was a profound scholar, invincible in debates. *Yaagna* is derived from *yagna*, symbolising Vishnu and *valkya* means 'knower of the Vedas'. He is also referred to as Vajsani, Brahmarath and Devarath in other *shastras*. He obtained his wisdom from three gurus: Darshan *shastras* from Udalak rishi, *Vedic* shastras from Vaishampayan rishi and Yog shastra from Hiranyanabh Kaushalya rishi. Vaishampayan was his maternal uncle. (Mahabharat. Shanti Parva. 323–16,17).

According to the Skand Puran, his father Brahmarath and mother Sunanda lived in Chamatkarpur – today's Vadnagar in north Gujarat. A reference is also cited of another Chamatkarpur, in eastern India on the banks of the Ganga. Yagnavalkya possessed scholarly acumen from childhood. While he studied Rg Veda from Shaakalya, a king named Supriya arrived to observe austerities during *Chaturmas* – the four holy months of the monsoon. By his request Shaakalya sent a pupil everyday to perform a *yagna* for him. While Yagnavalkya performed the *yagna*, he was on the verge of sprinkling the rice grains and water on the king. But the latter, on impulse, requested him to do so on a dry log nearby. After complying, Yagnavalkya left. Shortly the king was astonished to see green leaves sprout on the dead wood. Therefore the king requested Shaakalya to send Yagnavalkya again the next day. Yagnavalkya refused on the grounds that the king was too egotistical. This angered the guru, who then commanded Yagnavalkya to return the knowledge he had imparted. Yagnavalkya promptly complied by vomiting the knowledge. He then left the guru. The other pupils, assuming the form of *tetar* birds (partridges) licked the 'knowledge'. This branch of knowledge came to be known as Taittiriya. Yagnavalkya then studied under Vaishampayan. A slightly different version in the Skand Puran cites that Yagnavalkya studied Yajur Veda under

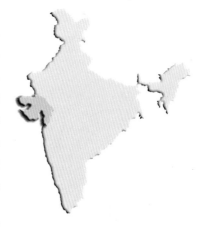

P – Patan
V – Vadnagar
A – Amdavad

Vaishampayan. During this period, a group of rishis decided to convene a scriptural conference on Mount Meru and also invited Vaishampayan. They stipulated that any invitee who failed to attend would incur the great sin of *brahmahatya* – killing a Brahmin. For some reason, Vaishampayan could not attend. Thus the sin befell on him. He then instructed all his pupils to perform *prayashchitt* – atonement - for the sin. Out of compassion for the pupils, Yagnavalkya proposed that he alone would observe atonement. The guru considered this as unruly and insulting. Angered, he ordered Yagnavalkya to return the knowledge he had imparted. He again vomited the knowledge. The pupils then assumed the form of *tetar* birds and scooped up the 'knowledge'.

Then vowing not to adopt a guru on earth, he worshipped Surya *deva*. The Sun deity granted him wisdom, which became known as the *Vaajasaneya* branch of the Shukla Yajur Veda. This seer's cogent rendering of profound philosophy in the Bruhadaranyak Upanishad attests to his immense erudition. From Surya *deva* he also obtained *brahmavidya* knowledge of Brahman (Paramatma). Yagnavalkya's disciples included stalwart rishis and others such as Katyayan, Shataanik, Janmejay (III) and Devarati Janak, king of Mithila.

Once King Janak performed a *yagna* in which he gifted immense riches to rishis and Brahmins. After the *yagna* he ordered that one thousand cows be prepared, all with five gold coins hung from each horn. He then humbly proposed to the rishis that he would gift these cows to whoever was declared the greatest *brahmanishth* among them. Yagnavalkya promptly stood up and instructed his disciple, Saamshrava, to take the cows to their ashram! This caused a furore among the rishis. They were not prepared to accept him as a *brahmanishth* so easily. Therefore the king's priest, Ashwal, stood up and barked, "Do you consider yourself the greatest?"

"I am the dust of the feet of the greatest *brahmanishth*," replied Yagnavalkya humbly. "Yet," he calmly added, "I want these cows so I have taken them."

Incensed, Ashwal entered into a debate, rattling off a series of questions which Yagnavalkya answered. In the end, accepting defeat, Ashwal sat down humiliated. Other rishis, too, pitted themselves against Yagnavalkya, but failed to dent his overwhelming prowess.

Finally a female rishi stood up. She was Vaachaknu rishi's daughter, Gargi. Well versed in Vedic wisdom, she was often invited to such debates. With her sharp intellect she often defeated stalwart rishis. She fired off a series of vexing questions concerning the elements in the cosmos. Finally she blurted out, "What is Brahmalok immersed in?"

"Beware Gargi!" warned Yagnavalkya. "You dare to ask who is above Brahman (the Ultimate Reality)? Beware of the limits of your questions, otherwise you will lose your head!"

Gargi realised her folly. In the excitement of firing a volley of questions she got carried away. Sheepishly, she sat down. By now the whole assembly was blinded by Yagnavalkya's scriptural luminescence. For quite some time a chilling silence prevailed. Then Gargi stood up again, with two extremely abstruse questions in her mind.

"O Yagnavalkya! What is that which is above Swarg, below Earth, between Swarg and Earth, that which is itself Swarg and Earth, and that which is known as the past, present and future?"

"O Devi! That is *akash* (space),' replied Yagnavalkya.

"O Yagnavalkya! What is that *akash* immersed in?"

Essentially she was questioning the ultimate support of *akash*, of creation itself. Being a *brahmanishth*, Yagnavalkya was not ignorant of this profound element.

He replied, "O Gargi! You are asking about Aksharbrahma." He then elaborated on its metaphysical nature. Hearing this Gargi vociferously hailed, "I proclaim Yagnavalkya as the greatest *brahmanishth*!"

Yagnavalkya was married to Maitreyi, who was a *brahmavadini* (versed in the Vedic texts) and Katyayani. Once, Yagnavalkya decided to renounce samsara. Therefore he distributed his wealth equally to both wives. However, Maitreyi questioned him, "Does one attain *amrut (moksha)* with these material objects? What shall I do with something that does not grant *amrut*? I crave for your spiritual wisdom."

These words of wisdom pleased him immensely. He replied, "Maitreyi, the husband is not loved because he is a husband. He is lovable only because of the *atma*. A wife, children, wealth, deities, heaven, happiness are all lovable only because of the *atma*. One should realise that *atma*. By realising the *atma* the whole universe is realised."

Maitreyi then accompanied Yagnavalkya into the forest. She performed austerities, offering worship to Surya *deva*. By his grace she gained the wisdom of Shukla Yajur Veda.

Yagnavalkya gifted the world many texts. He performed the great task of clarifying and restructuring the Krishna Yajur Veda. The texts which have survived are: (1) *Saangashatapath Brahman*, (2) *Yagnavalkya Shiksha*, (3) *Manahaswar Shiksha*, (4) *Bruhad Yagnavalkya*, (5) *Bruhadyangiya Yagnavalkya*, (6) *Yog–vishayak Granth* and (7) *Yagnavalkya Smruti*.

Bhagwan Swaminarayan has accepted the latter text (see details below) in the Shikshapatri (93–95), as one of the eight shastras He favours. After the Vasant festival in the spring of 1827, He held a *katha* and expounded on the Yagnavalkya Smruti for one month in Gadhada (Dave 2003 VI:199).

Yagnavalkya Smruti

Regarded as a Dharmashastra, the Yagnavalkya Smruti contains 1003 Sanskrit couplets in *anushtup chhand* : a type of poetic metre. It is categorised into three sections:

1. *Āchār*: of 13 chapters, on dharma, marriage, *shrāddh*, edible/inedible foods, purity of wealth.

2. *Vyavahār*: of 25 chapters, on general conduct, types of crimes, criminal law, four stages of court procedure, purity of goods and punishment for adulterating market goods and fraudulent weighing, details of partnership in business, family planning, adoption of children and codes for widows.

3. *Prāyashchitt*: of 14 chapters, on dharma in exigencies, atonement for mistakes and sinful acts, *sutak* – rituals of purity after birth and death, destiny of a *jiva* after death to hell or heaven (since Yagnavalkya was a *brahmanishth* rishi he could observe a *jiva's* transmigration). Of the three principal *Smrutis* of Sanatan Dharma Parashar, Manu and Yagnavalkya – the latter attained eminence over the ages, primarily due to the Vignaneshwar *Mitakshara* commentary. During Muslim and colonial rule, the Yagnavalkya Smruti was a standard manual for court procedures, rather than Manu Smruti, since contradictions existed in certain sections of the latter. The Yagnavalkya Smruti's lucidity, concision and precision is laudable.

3. Panini

(Sanskrit Grammarian)

Regarded as an unequalled Sanskrit grammarian, Panini was the son of Aj Rishi and Daakshi, in Vishwamitra's lineage. Dates vary about him; Katyayan assigns him a date of 1600 BCE.

D – Delhi
L – Lahore

Mentally retarded when young, he was expelled from his *gurukul*. The guru showed him the absence of the line of intelligence on his palm. Pained by this, he carved a crease with a knife! He then stomped off to the Himalayas to perform austerities to please Shankar (Shivji). Pleased with his endeavour, the latter granted him the knowledge of Sanskrit grammar. Thus becoming a stalwart scholar, he composed the famed *Ashtadhyayi* – of eight chapters and 3996 *shloks*. His other works include: *Ganpaath, Dhatupaath, Linganushasan, Shiksha Sutra* and the *Jambuvatijya*, the latter being a poetic work.

He categorised the Vedic literature into two: *Dhrushta*, which include the four Vedas, and *Procta*, which include: *Brahmana, Kalpa* and *Sutra*. Other scholars before him, such as Shakalya, Vaabhravya, Galav and Shaakataayan had written Sanskrit grammar texts. But they lacked in many ways. Panini collated all the words up to his period, etymologised them and assigned a set of rules. His brevity, meticulousness and thoroughness collectively rendered his text a greater importance, value and usage. It has remained standard and unsurpassed. Patanjali rishi wrote a commentary on his grammar. Bhattoji Dikshit also wrote one, the famous Siddhant Kaumudi.

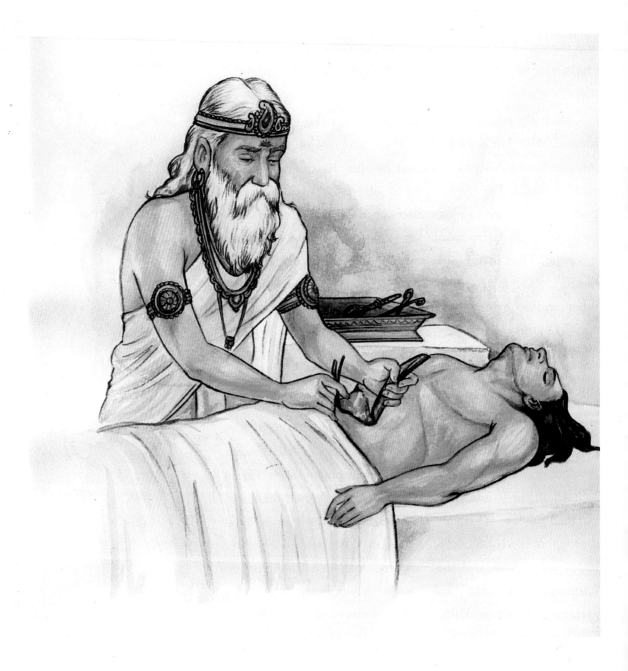

4. Divodas Dhanvantari

(Father of Surgery)

Born in 1000 BCE, Kashiraj Divodas Dhanvantari is hailed as the Father of Surgery in Ayurveda, the oldest and the most holistic medical science in the world. It forms a part of the Atharva Veda, one of the four Vedas.

Ayurveda means 'science of longevity', derived from the Sanskrit root *ayus,* meaning longevity and *vid*, meaning knowledge. Ayurveda originated from Brahmã, the Creator. He created Ayurveda before creating man, as an *upa*–Veda – subsidiary of the Atharva Veda – in one thousand chapters containing 100,000 *shloks*. He taught this to Daksh, who then revealed it to Ashwini Kumars, the celestial twins and physicians of the devas. They transmitted it to Indra, who revealed it to the rishis of Ayurveda. Three important rishis of Ayurveda are: Dhanvantari, Sushrut and Charak.

The name Dhanvantari first appears in the ancient Hindu shastras as the twelfth avatar of Vishnu during the *Samudra Manthan* – churning of the ocean. Of the fourteen gems that sprung forth, one was Bhagwan Dhanvantari, who emerged with an urn of *amrut* the divine nectar which delivered its drinker from death, to attain immortality. He is also known as the original, *Adi* Dhanvantari, the celebrated physician of the devas.

A – Ayodhya
V – Varanasi (Kashi)

The second, down to earth Dhanvantari, was Kashiraj Divodas Dhanvantari, the King of Kashi. He was the first surgeon of Ayurveda. His teachings and surgical techniques were compiled by his foremost pupil, Sushrut, in the Sushrut Samhita which has survived over the ages. *Samhita* means compendium. Some of his teachings, too, were compiled in works, now lost, by his other pupils, namely, Aupadhenava, Aurabhra, Bhoja, Galava, Gargya, Gopurarakshita, Kankayana, Nimi, Paushkalavata and Vaitarana. He is also the founder of the school of surgeons which came to be known as Dhanvantariyas.

One of Kashiraj Dhanvantari's ancestors categorised the vast range of Ayurveda into *ashtang* – eight faculties:

(1) *Kayachikitsa*   – internal medicine
(2) *Kaumarabhrtya*   – paediatrics
(3) *Bhutavidya*   – psychiatry
(4) *Salakyatantra*   – oto–rhino–laryngology & ophthalmology
(5) *Salyatantra*   – surgery
(6) *Vishatantra*   – toxicology
(7) *Rasayantantra*   – rejuvenation
(8) *Vajikarantantra* – revitalisation

According to Dhanvantari, the fifth faculty, Salyatantra, was the oldest of all faculties of Ayurveda. Only after the formation of the school of surgery did the school of physicians emerge, heralded by Bhagwan Punarvasu Atreya. The latter recognised Dhanvantari as a high authority of surgery. A contemporary medical treatise, Agnivesh Samhita, also mentions that specialisation in surgery had reached such a stage that general practitioners referred all cases needing surgical treatment to specialists in surgery. In this *Samhita,* Divodas Dhanvantari details the formation and development of the human embryo by Dhanvantari, which correlates with the vivid description given by Sushrut in his *Samhita*.

A proficient surgeon, Dhanvantari laid great emphasis on the study of anatomy using cadavers. The Sushrut Samhita cites a lecture on anatomy. Jurgeon Thorwald, in his *Science and Secrets of Early Medicine* (1962), averred, "Certainly this was the oldest lesson in dissection known to history." Dhanvantari meticulously described the preparation of a dead body by first disembowelling and then placing it in a stream or body of running water for seven days. He advocated preceptors to demonstrate surgical techniques in detail to their pupils, in addition to their mastery in other branches of medicine. "Otherwise," he asserted, "a well read pupil, but not initiated in the practice of medicine or surgery, is not competent to take in hand the medical or surgical treatment of a disease."

In the absence of PVC or the foam materials available to trainee surgeons today, Dhanvantari creatively improvised an astonishing array of natural objects for practicing surgical procedures:

Technique	*Objects used for practice*
• Incision (cuts) *Chhedya*	Gourd, watermelon, cucumber
• Excisions (removal) *Bhedya*	Bladder of a dead animal, puncturing a leather pouch filled with fluid.
• Scraping *(Lekhya)*	Piece of skin with hair
• Venesection *(Vedhya)* (puncturing a vein)	Vein of a dead animal, lotus stem
• Probing & Stuffing	Wormeaten wood, bamboo. Eshya reed, mouth of a dried gourd
• Extraction *(Aharya)*	Withdrawing seeds from the kernel of a bimbi *(Aegle marmelos)*, bilva *(Cephalandra indica)* or jack fruit, teeth from jaws of a dead animal
• Secreting or evacuating fluids *(Visravaniya)*	Surface of Shalmali *(Bombax malabaricum)* wood covered with beeswax.
• Suturing *(Sivya)*	Pieces of cloth, skin or hide
• Bandaging	Limbs of a full–sized doll stuffed with linen
• Repairing a severed ear–lobe	Soft severed muscle or flesh, stem of lotus or lily
• Cautery & applying caustics	Piece of soft flesh
• Inserting a syringe or injecting enemas in bladder region or ulcerated channel	Inserting a tube into a lateral fissure or pitcher full of water or mouth of a gourd
	(Sushrut, Sutrasthan 9/2,3).

The advantage of such experimental practice, according to Divodas Dhanvantari, was that an intelligent physician would never lose his presence of mind in professional practice. Divodas's methods, as compiled by Sushrut illustrates his emphasis and insistence on discipline and high standard of training expected from a student training in surgery.

In addition to these innovative practices he also devised ingenious instruments, cited in the Sushrut Samhita, for skilled surgery. He devised twenty sharp and 101 blunt instruments, in addition to special tables for use in major operations. Thorwald comments on these surgical instruments of ancient India, "The vast variety of Indian surgical instruments which have come down to us from the first millennium A.D. suggest that surgery had developed to an extraordinary extent in early India" (see photographs of replicas on p. 28).

Some of the surgical procedures include lithotomy – removal of stones, skin grafting and rhinoplasty – repairing a mutilated nose (see sketch and details on p. 28–29). The latter two earned him the title "Father of Plastic Surgery." However, recent scholars have conferred the title to his pupil Sushrut, probably because it was first penned in his *Samhita*, since Dhanvantari had no written treatise to his credit. A German scholar, Jurgeon Thorwald, in his book *Science & Secrets of Early Medicine – Egypt, Mesopotamia, India, China, Mexico & Peru* (1962), has observed that his method for rhinoplasty, which used a flap from the cheek was adopted and practiced by Gasparo Tagliacozzi, professor of surgery at Bologna, in the sixteenth century. "There is scarcely any doubt that this method... which seemed to emerge out of nothing (in Europe), ... had its roots in early India ... Nowhere else in the whole world of antiquity do we find any precedent for that conception," observes Thorwald. He added that in 1814, a newspaper account from India inspired Joseph Constantine Carpue, a pioneer of modern plastic surgery to restore a nose. This was the first attempt in Europe then. Carpue was greatly impressed by such successful operations performed by Indian village surgeons exactly as described thousands of years ago in the *Sushrut Samhita* (ref. details and sketch on pp. 28-29).

Regarding lithotomy, Dhanvantari gave a detailed description of the removal of stones from the bladder and urethra by perineal incision (*Sushrut Samhita, Chikitsasthan* 7/14). Yet according to medical historians of Europe, the founders of the

"The surgical instruments of the Hindus were sufficiently sharp indeed as to be capable of dividing hair longitudinally."

– Dr. Mrs. Manning
(British surgeon)

"Modern art of Lithotomy" were Giovanni de Romain and Marios Santos of Italy, in the late 15th and early 16th centuries. However, Thorwald doubts this and asserts that these men learned their methods from India. "Now that the texts of the *Sushrut Samhita* are available of at least 2000 years before the time of these Italians," Thorwald observed, "it was found that they contained an exact description of bladder surgery."

Dhanvantari also made contributions in the fields of physiology and anatomy, *dravya vignan* – pharmacology and material medica - and *chikitsa vignan* – therapeutics. One of his important contributions has led modern scholars to also call him a molecular biologist. He gave a complete theory of drug-composition, molecular structure, physico-chemical properties and therapeutical actions of food and drugs. He based these concepts on the Nyaya system of *paramanus* (atoms) and *anus* (molecules). In physiology, he was the first in the world to cite the haemopoetic, or blood forming factor in the *yakrut* – liver – known as *ranjakpitta,* and the role of both the liver and spleen in the formation of blood. He was also the first to prescribe raw goat liver for treating anaemia and *naktāndhya* (night blindness). Acharya Vaghbhatt, a later proponent of Ayurveda, in the fifth century CE, described a similar factor occurring in the stomach with identical functions. In 1926, Minot and Murphy showed that liver was the most effective ingredient in the treatment of anaemia. Ricks in 1948, and Smith, a few years later, described an amorphous red–principle from proteolysed liver, to be effective in pernicious anaemia in very small doses - now known as Vitamin B12. Vaghbhatt's factor was re–discovered by Castle in 1929, in the stomach and was named Castle's Intrinsic Factor.

Many such original discoveries can be listed which originated in ancient India, attributable to Dhanvantari and his followers. The few examples discussed remind us that these stalwarts of Ayurveda practiced an astonishingly scientific, sophisticated and advanced art of medicine as early as the third and second millennium BCE. Several millennia later, so called "modern medicine" is retreading their beaten paths.

"The vast variety of Indian surgical instruments which have come down to us from the first millennium suggest that surgery had developed to an extraordinary extent in early India."

– Jurgeon Thorwald
Science and Secrets of Early Medicine (1962

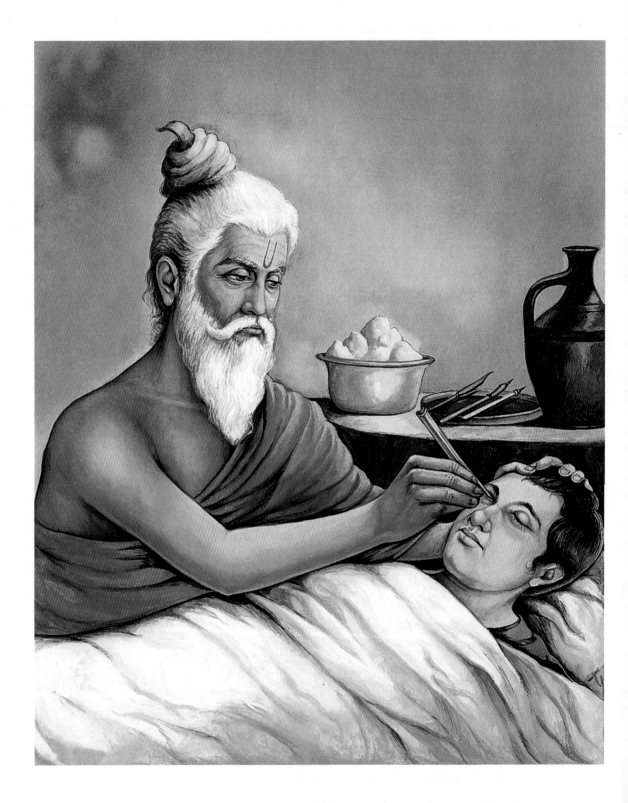

5. Sushrut

(Father of Cosmetic Surgeory)

Sushrut compiled the knowledge and teachings of his guru Divodas Dhanvantari, King of Kashi, in the Sushrut Samhita. It was common for surgeons then to be associated with kings, as has been cited in the Rg Veda, Mahabharat, Sushrut Samhita and Kautilya's *Arthashastra*. Sushrut and his descendants are said to pre–date Panini, the great Sanskrit grammarian. Patanjali in his Mahabhashya and Katyayan in the *Varttika* also mention Sushrut. However scholars ascribe Sushrut's true period to 1000 BCE (Sharma 1999: 87).

During his era, surgery formed a major role in general medical training. It was known as *Shalya–tantra* – *Shalya* means broken arrow or sharp part of a weapon, and *tantra* means manoeuvre. Since warfare was common then, the injuries sustained led to the development of surgery as a refined scientific skill.

Apart from being a treatise primarily on surgery, the Sushrut Samhita encompasses the other seven Ayurvedic faculties. Sushrut also details surgical procedures in other specialised branches which warrant surgery, such as obstetrics, orthopaedics and ophthalmology. To consider an example of

V – Varanasi (Kashi)

the latter, he describes a method of removing cataract, known today as 'couching'. This was routinely practised by Ayurvedic surgeons in India over the ages until the late half of the twentieth century. For successful surgery Sushrut induced anaesthesia using intoxicants such as wine and henbane *(Cannabis indica)*. This led A.O. Whipple in his *Story of Wound Healing* (1965), to comment, "Sushrut must be accepted as a pioneer in some form of anaesthesia." The depth of his expositions in such a variety of faculties reflects his brilliance and versatility. He asserted that unless the surgeon possessed knowledge of the related branches, he does not attain proficiency in his own field.

Like his guru Dhanvantari, Sushrut too, considered the

अर्धचन्द्रानन शस्त्र
Half-Moon Scissors

सनिग्रह संदंशयंत्र
Pincer-like forceps with
handles.
For splinter removal
from: skin & muscle-
tissues

वृधिपत्रशस्त्र-अश्रिताग्र
Curved Bistoury
To puncture & drain
internal abscess esp. in
bladder or urethra

knowledge of anatomy obligatory for a surgeon to be skilled in his art. This necessitated dissecting cadavers. Alongwith anatomy, Sushrut gives details of human embryology in *Sharirsthan*, which are mind–boggling. This is all the more astounding when we bear in mind that such detailed observation is today only possible using microscopy, ultrasonography and X–rays. To cite just one example, he mentions that the foetus develops seven layers of skin, naming each layer and the specific diseases which may affect that layer in adult life! (Sharirsthan IV–3). He was also aware of diseases by genetic inheritance. He mentions many congenital defects acquired from parents and those resulting from indulgences of the mother during pregnancy. Therefore he advises her to avoid exertion for the perfect development of the foetus. For instance, she should avoid physical exertion, daytime sleep, keeping awake late into the night, extreme fasting, fear, purgatives, travelling on a vehicle, phlebotomy and delaying the calls of nature (Sharirsthan III.11).

Sushrut's era, as all down the ages, involved warfare. This meant injury from weapons such as arrows often embedding as splinters – *shalya*. He has categorised two types of symptoms for splinters - general and specific - from which a diagnosis can be made, of the type of splinter and its exact depth. He further details the different symptoms for different splinters of bone, wood, metal embedded in skin, muscle, bones, joints, ducts, pipes or tubes. He then prescribes fifteen different procedures for removing loose splinters. Two notable methods for problematic splinters though seemingly extreme, are highly effective and innovative. If a splinter is lodged in a bone and fails to budge, its shaft should be bent and tied with bowstrings. The strings should be tied to the bit of the bridle of a tame horse. While holding the patient down, the horse should be slapped or hit with a stick so that it jerks its head. In doing so, the splinter is forced out! If that fails, one could pull down a strong branch of a tree and tie the splinter to it. One then lets go of the strained branch, which will draw out the splinter!

Besides splinter injuries, Sushrut also deals with trauma. He describes six varieties of accidental injuries encompassing almost all parts of the body:

Name of Injury	Type of Injury
Chinna	Complete severance of a part or whole of a limb
Bhinna	Deep injury to some hollow region by a long piercing object
Viddha prana	Puncturing a structure without a hollow
Kshata	Uneven injuries with signs of both *chinna* and *bhinna,* i.e. a laceration
Pichchita	Crushed injury due to a fall or blow
Ghrsta	Superficial abrasion of the skin

Besides trauma involving general surgery, Sushrut gives an in–depth account and treatment of twelve varieties of fractures and six types of dislocations, which would confound orthopaedic surgeons today. He mentions principles of traction, manipulation, apposition and stabilisation, as well as post–operative physiotherapy!

Being a genius and a perfectionist in all aspects of surgery he even attached great importance to a seemingly insignificant factor such as scars after healing. He implored surgeons to achieve perfect healing, characterised by the absence of any elevation or induration, swelling or mass, and the return of normal colouring. He went as far as prescribing ointments to achieve this, managing to change healed wounds from black to white and vice versa!

He also prescribed measures to induce growth of lost hair and to remove unwanted hair. Such minute detailing reflects his deep insight, rendering him the first surgeon in world history to practice a holistic approach in treating surgical patients. According to Sankaran and Deshpande, "No single surgeon in the history of science has to his credit such masterly contributions in terms of basic classification, thoroughness of the management of disease and perfect

शल्य-निर्घातनी
Hammer
To mobilise a foreign object lodged in multiple directions of tissues

एकताल यंत्र
Pick-lock like instrument
For removal of object logded in: ears, nose, blood-vessel or fistula

सर्पास्यशस्त्र
Polypus
Excision of nasal/ear/ rectal polyps.

तरक्षुमुखस्वस्तिक यंत्र
Hyena Forceps
To hold bones during
bone surgery to extract
foreign objects.

नसा-नलिका
Nasal Insufflator
For insuflation of
powder in nasal cavity

understanding of the ideals to be achieved" (1976:69). To Sushrut health was not only a state of physical well–being, but also mental, brought about and preserved by the maintenance of balanced humours, good nutrition, proper elimination of wastes and a pleasant, contented state of the body and mind.

Finally, from the patient to the surgeon. He gave a definition of an ideal surgeon embodying all possible requisites, which has yet to be improved upon even today. "He is a good surgeon," he declares, "who possesses courage and presence of mind, a hand free from perspiration, tremorless grip of sharp and good instruments and who carries his operations to success and the advantage of his patient who has entrusted his life to the surgeon. The surgeon should respect this absolute surrender and treat his patient as his own son."

Sushrut's excellence in surgery and original insights in all branches of medicine render him the most versatile genius in the history of medical science. His contributions have withstood the test of over three thousand years. In the absence of sophisticated instruments available to us today, his profound observations then may be attributed to two factors: grace of a stalwart guru, Dhanvantari, and divine revelation through personal sadhana – meditation. These observations of an ancient rishi, today continue to intrigue researchers at the Wellcome Institute of the History of Medicine in London and other similar institutions in Europe, USA and India.

Sushrut's Surgical Instruments

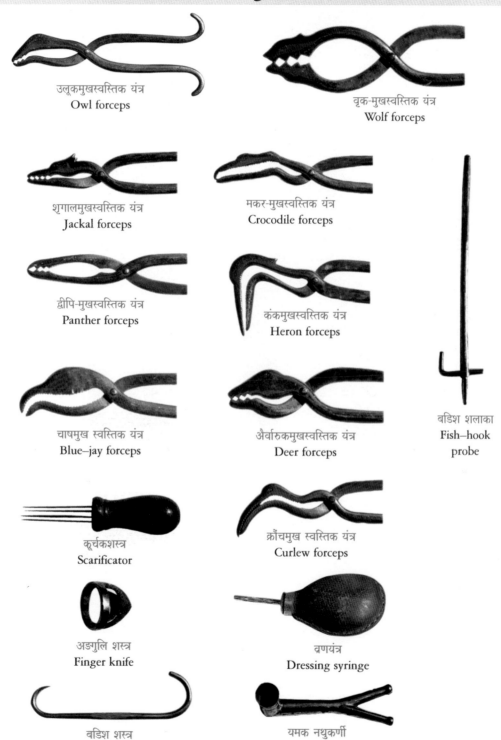

उलूकमुखस्वस्तिक यंत्र
Owl forceps

वृक्-मुखस्वस्तिक यंत्र
Wolf forceps

शृगालमुखस्वस्तिक यंत्र
Jackal forceps

मकर-मुखस्वस्तिक यंत्र
Crocodile forceps

द्वीपि-मुखस्वस्तिक यंत्र
Panther forceps

कंकमुखस्वस्तिक यंत्र
Heron forceps

चाषमुख स्वस्तिक यंत्र
Blue–jay forceps

अैर्वारुकमुखस्वस्तिक यंत्र
Deer forceps

बडिश शलाका
Fish–hook
probe

कूर्चकशस्त्र
Scarificator

क्रौंचमुख स्वस्तिक यंत्र
Curlew forceps

अङ्गुलि शस्त्र
Finger knife

व्रणयंत्र
Dressing syringe

बडिश शस्त्र
Sharp hook

यमक नथुकर्णी
Nasal speculum

Courtesy: Dr. N. M. Chovatia, O.H. Nazar Ayurvedic College, Surat.

Painted by J.Wales, Bombay, and   Engraved from ye Original Picture by W.Nutter.

A SINGULAR OPERATION.

1. Figure of the Skin taken from the forehead.   4. The Septum of the new nose.

2. and 3 form the Alæ of the new nose.   5. The slip left undivided.

The Plate of wax
when flattened.

666. The Incision into which the edge of the skin is engrafted.

The Plate of wax in the form of
the Nose.

COWASJEE A Mahratta of the Cast of Husbandmen. He was a bullock driver with the English Army, in the War of 1792; and was made a prisoner by Tippoo, who cut off his nose, and one of his hands. In this state he joined the Bombay Army near Seringapatam, and is now a pensioner of the H.E.I. Company. For above 12 months he remained without a nose, when he had a new one put on by a Mahratta Surgeon, a Kumar near Poona. This operation is not uncommon in India, and has been practised for time immemorial. Two of the Medical Gentlemen, Mr. Thos. Cruso, and Mr. James Findlay, of the Bombay Presidency have seen it performed, as follows. A thin plate of wax is fitted to the stump of the nose, so as to make a nose of a good appearance; it is then flattened and laid on the forehead. A line is drawn round the wax, which is then of no further use, and the operator then dissects off as much skin as it covered, leaving undivided a small slip between the Eyes. This slip preserves the circulation till an union has taken place between the new and old parts. The Cicatrix of the stump of the nose is next pared off, and immediately behind this raw part an incision is made thro' the skin, which passes round both Alæ, and goes along the upper lip. The skin is now brought down from the forehead, and being twisted half round, its edge is inserted into this incision, so that a nose is formed with a double hold above, and with its Alæ and Septum below fixed in the incision. A little Terra Japonica is softened with water, and being spread on slips of cloth five or six of these are placed over each other, to secure the joining. No other dressing but this cement is used for four days. It is then removed, and cloths dipped in Ghee (a kind of butter) are applied. The connecting slip of skin is divided about the 25th day, when a little more dissection is necessary to improve the appearance of the new nose. For five or six days after the operation the Patient is made to lie on his back, and on the 10th day bits of soft cloth are put into the nostrils to keep them sufficiently open. This operation is always successful. The artificial nose is secure and looks nearly as well as the natural one, nor is the scar on the forehead very observable after a length of time. The Picture, from which this Engraving is made, was painted in Jany. 1794 ten months after the operation.

Published Jany. 1st 1795 by James Wales of Bombay, at Mr. R.Cribbs, Carver & Gilder 288 Holborn, London. **see details opposite**

Reconstructive Surgery in India

In 1792 Tippu Sultan's soldiers captured a Maratha cart–driver named Cowasjee (Kawasji) in the British army and cut of his nose and an arm. A year later, a *kumbhar* (potter) *vaidya* in Puna reconstructed Kawasji's nose. Two British surgeons in the Bombay Presidency, Thomas Cruso and James Findlay witnessed this skilful procedure and noted the details. In October 1794, this account was published in *The Gentleman's Magazine* of London, describing it as an operation 'not uncommon in India and has been practiced for time immemorial'! This procedure, similar to that cited in the Sushrut Samhita, ultimately changed the course of plastic surgery in Europe and the world. It was different from Sushrut's, in that Kawasji's graft was taken from his forehead. Sushrut grafted skin from the cheek. To aid healing, he prescribed the use of three herbs and cotton wool soaked with sesame seed oil in dressing the graft. After the graft healed, he advocated cutting off the tissue joined to the cheek (Sutrasthan 16/18).

Regarding cosmetic surgery, Sushrut could also reconstruct ear lobes and enumerates fifteen ways in which to repair them. Guido Majno in *The Healing Hand: Man and Wound in the Ancient World* (1975), notes that, "Through the habit of stretching their earlobes, the Indians became masters in a branch of surgery that Europe ignored for another two thousand years." Sushrut meticulously details the pre–and post–operative procedures. After stitching, for example, he prescribes dressing the lobe by applying honey and ghee, then covering with cotton and gauze and finally binding with a thread, neither too tightly nor too loosely. Torn lips were also treated in a similar manner (Sutrasthan 16/2–7, 18, 19).

1 Figure of the skin taken from the forehead
2 and 3 form the Ala of the new nose.
4. The septum of the new nose.
5. The slip left undivided.
6.6.6. The Incision into which the edge of the skin is engrafted.

Cowasjee A Mahratta of the Cast of Husbandmen. He was a bullock driver with the English Army in the War of 1792; and was made a prisoner by Tippoo, who cut off his nose and one of his hands. In this state he joined the Bombay Army near Seringapatam and is now a pensioner of the H.E.I. Company. For above 12 months he remained without a nose, when he had a new one put on by a Mahratta Surgeon a Kumar near Poona. This operation is not uncommon in India, and has been praised for time immemorial. Two of the Medical Gentlemen Mr. Thomas Cruso and Mr. James Findlay, of the Bombay Presidency have seen it performed, as follows. A thin plate of wax is fitted to the stump of the nose, so as to make a nose of a good appearance; it is then flattened and laid on the forehead: undivided a small slip between the eyes. This slip preserves the circulation till an union has taken place between the new and old parts. The cicatrice of the stump of the nose is next pared off, and immediately behind this raw part an incision is made thro' the skin which passes round both ala, and goes along the upper lip. The skin is now brought down from the forehead, and being twisted half round, its edge is inserted into this incision, so that a nose is formed with a double hold above, and with its ala and septum below fixed in the incision. A little Terra Japonica is softened with water, and being spread on slips of cloth five or six of these are placed over each other to secure the joining. No other dressing but this cement is used for four days. It is then removed, and cloths dipped in Ghee (a kind of butter) are applied. The connecting slip of skin is divided about the 25th day, when a little more dissection is necessary to improve the appearance of the new nose. For five or six days after the operation the patient is made to lie on his back, and on the 10th day bits of soft cloth are put into the nostrils to keep them sufficiently open. This operation is always successful. The artificial nose is secure and looks nearly as well as the natural one, nor is the scar on the forehead very observable after a length of time.

The picture, from which this Engraving is made, was painted in Jan. 1794, ten months after the operation. Published Jan. 1st 1795 by James Wales of Bombay, at Mr. R. Cribbs, Carver & Gilder 288, Holborn, London.

6. Charak
(Physician of Ayurveda)

Hailed as India's most outstanding ancient medical practitioner, Charak's work reveals just how far ahead of his time he was. Around 4000 years ago, the rishi Agnivesha compiled an Ayurvedic treatise, the Agnivesha Samhita, guided by his guru, the rishi Atreya Punarvasu. Down the ages it underwent interpolations. Around 800 BCE, Charak rishi redacted the Agnivesha Samhita, which became renowned as the Charak Samhita. Its fame spread beyond Bharatvarsh's borders. By 987 CE it had been translated from Sanskrit to Persian, and from Persian to Arabic. Al–Beruni's chief source of medicine was the Arabic edition by Ali Ibu–Zain. The famous Arabian physician, Serapion, often quoted Charak in his own medicinal treatise, as *Sharaka Indianus*. Avicenna in the 9th century also referred to Charak.

Northern India

Char means 'to move about'. Therefore he was a peripatetic teacher, who practiced and propagated his knowledge by travelling constantly to relieve the suffering masses. There are no details about his birthplace parentage in the *Samhita*. Scholars contend that he predated Patanjali (200 BCE) and Buddha (500 BCE).

The Charak Samhita

This voluminous text on therapeutics consists of 120 chapters categorised in eight sections:

The Charak Samhita		
1	Sutrasthan	30 chapters on food, diet, physicians and quacks, philosophy and pharmacology
2	Nidansthan	8 chapters on diagnosis of diseases
3	Vimansthan	8 chapters on specific determination of taste, nourishment, general pathology and medical studies
4	Sharirsthan	8 chapters on physiology and anatomy, including embryology

5	*Indriyasthan*	12 chapters on prognosis of diseases
6	*Chikitsasthan*	30 chapters on treatment of diseases
7	*Kalpasthan*	12 chapters on pharmaceutics
8	*Siddhisthan*	12 chapters on *Panch* Karma (further general therapy)

A few of these sections, namely 6,7 and 8, were lost and therefore written anew by Acharya Dhrudhbal in the 12th century.

Besides medicine, Charak mentions all the other branches of medicine, leaving the details of surgical interventions to the surgeon. Charak's detailed and monumental medical compendium has deeply impressed many allopathic physicians. Dr. George Clarke of Philadelphia observed, "As I go through Caraka, I arrive at the conclusion that if physicians of the present day would drop from the pharmacopoeia all the modern drugs and chemicals and treat their patients according to the methods of Caraka, there will be less work for the undertakers and fewer chronic invalids in the world."

Philosophy

Charak firmly believed in rebirth. He describes in detail the role of invisible factors which determine events in one's present life. He attributes some diseases and their curability to actions of previous lives. He attributes the following enigmas to *punarjanma* – theory of reincarnation: dissimilarity of children to their parents, difference in fortune of children of the same parents, occurrence of events for which there is no tangible cause in the present life, appearance of auspicious and inauspicious birth-marks, likes and dislikes for specific vocations and recall of events in past births (*Sutrasthan* 11/30). Charak posits that the life-span of an individual is pre-ordained. However strong actions in the present life may to some extent lengthen or shorten it.

Human body

It is composed of the *Panch Mahabhuts* – five principle elements: earth, water, light, wind and space. The body's constitution is based on the three *doshas* or humours: *vatta, pitta* and *kapha*. When their equilibrium is disturbed disease sets in. Vitiated *vatta* can lead to eighty types of diseases, *pitta,* forty and *kapha,* twenty. The three *doshas* affect the seven *dhatus* – body tissues and ultimately *ojas* – vital energy or the finest essence in the body. Factors which affect the constitution of an individual include: genetic inheritance, the mother's health in pregnancy, race, family, geographical location, time and age.

Over 2000 years before Harvey, the concept of blood circulation was well known to Ayurveda. Charak described the heart as the controlling organ of blood circulation, though he did not mention its chambers. The body, he said, is composed of *dhamanis* – big and small vessels which supply nutrition to tissues and remove waste products from them.

Disease

As mentioned above, an imbalance of the three humours and vitiation of the *dhatus* led to disease. Charak refuted the theory that germs were the only causative factors for disease. He believed that various germs – he described twenty disease – causing germs – may flourish in the body only if favourable conditions prevailed. Therefore, despite the presence of germs, none would thrive in the absence of a soiled environment.

He prescribed a system of *Mahakashāya,* each having ten herbal preparations for various diseases (*Sutrasthan* 4/13). For example, he prescribes the following ten for relieving physical exertion: grapes, dates, *charoli*, *bor*, pomegranate, figs, *falsa*, sugar cane, barley and *sathi* rice (*Sutrasthan* 4/40).

Interestingly, Charak even reveals the attributes of a person who will not suffer from disease: one who has a healthy diet and lifestyle *(hitkar ahar–vihar)*, who thinks deeply before performing an action *(samikshakari)*, who is detached from all worldly objects *(vishayānāsakta)*, is a donor *(dātā)*, who regards

Concept of health

Charak attaches importance to the digestive fire – agni – to maintain vitality, energy and ojas. He describes the digestive process and its end products, which are remarkably similar to those described by Western science. Charak contends that when the digestive fire is vitiated either decreased or increased – disorders result. To rectify agni he prescribes medications.

all creatures with equanimity *(samah)*, always speaks the truth *(satyapar)*, who forgives and does not punish even those who commit a bad act on him *(kshmāvān)* and who associates with pious people *(āptopasevi)* *(Sharirsthan 2/45)*.

This was Charak's and Ayurveda's unique approach to understanding and treating diseases. Charak treated the patient as a whole rather than just the disease. In addition to medications, he stressed the importance of diet, *dincharya* – daily activity – and *rutucharya* – seasonal activity – in the holistic, long–term health of an individual. Primarily he laid emphasis on prevention of disease rather than cure.

Epidemics

Charak discusses epidemics which he calls *Janapada uddhawmsha* – that which destroys a locality *(Vimansthan 3)*. He lists four contributing factors: corrupt air, water, locale and time. He was aware of water–borne diseases, for which he rightly recommended drinking boiled water during the monsoon. This reflects his scientific genius. Fascinating is his account of visible *krumis* – parasites. More astonishing is his description of microscopic *krumis* in the blood. In the absence of the microscope, his account of microbes would probably confound and awe microbiologists today. He says, "They are very minute and can be observed with a *yantra* (did he possess a microscope or foresee it?). They are round in shape, without feet (protozoa?). Some are so minute that they are totally invisible and copper coloured"! *(Vimansthan 7/9)*. He was the first to identify and name such microbes. Further, he revealed the typical symptoms they produce, "raising one's hairs, itching, needle–like piercing pain and a current–like effect." Such accuracy, without a microscope is only possible by a *brahmanishth* seer – one who has realised Brahman. This would enable him to observe the minutest functions of the body right down at the cellular level.

Charak also averred that the root cause of epidemics was mankind's unrighteousness – *adharma*. Those who lose their dharma are abandoned by the deities.

The Physician

Charak laid great emphasis on the physician's integrity and having total control of the senses *(indriyas)*, including observance of *brahmacharya* (Sutrasthan 29/6). Aware of man's innate weaknesses, he advises physicians not to enter a house of a female patient nor examine her in the absence of her husband or guardian. To Charak, medical practice was, "not for self, not for the fulfilment of any desire or gain, but solely for the good of suffering humanity." A physician "who fails to enter the inner body of the patient with the lamp of knowledge and understanding, can never treat diseases." According to Charak, the physician should, above all, be compassionate (*Sutrasthan* 10/25).

Though Charak redacted Agnivesha's work, he contributed his own original and accurate observances, which have prevailed for over two millennia. His theories, methodology of treatment and the patient's holistic management ranked as the most effective in the world during his period. These were later translated, borrowed and practised by Arab, Persian and Chinese physicians.

Akin to Sushrut, Charak's excellence and genius as Ayurveda's stalwart physician can be attributed to two factors: an enlightened guru and personal sadhana. This endowed him with a phenomenal ability to document the medicinal qualities of thousands of plants and minerals during his lifespan, without experimentation.

Hospitals

Charak showed how to plan, construct and equip hospitals, including mental and obstetric hospitals (*Sutrasthan 15/1–7*). He gives minute details on accommodation, bathrooms, toilets, disinfection, medicines, equipment and security. He even considers cooling rooms in the summer and warming them in winter. The hospitals also included a section where healthy people could undergo rejuvenation therapy such as Panch Karma thrice a year (*Chikitsasthan 1,1,24*).

Rejuvenation Therapy

To curtail the effects of aging and for convalescing patients, Charak prescribed therapies for strength, greater resistance to disease, sharpness of memory and intelligence and longevity. The most important 'herb' for this is the Amlaka fruit (Embelica officinalis), from which the extremely popular Chyavanprash is made. He also prescribed vitalisers to replenish vital fluids of health (Chikitsasthan 1/7–8). He describes two types of rejuvenating therapies – one for implementing indoors and one for outdoors. For the former, he gives special instructions for the type of house to be built. Today this rejuvenation therapy involving Panch Karma may prove useful in treating poor AIDS patients.

Charak also prescribes aphrodisiacs to cure impotency. Despite this, he firmly advocates abstinence, or brahmacharya, for increasing health and longevity: brahmacharyamāyushyānām (Sutrasthan 11/35).

7. Aryabhatta
(Astronomer & Mathematician)

Aryabhatta, the greatest astronomer and mathematician of ancient India, first gave theories that were 're–discovered' many centuries later by scientists of the West. He was the first to gift algebra to the world. He cites his date of birth in Kusumpura, eastern India, with astonishing accuracy in his famous work, *Aryabhatiya*: "When sixty times sixty years and three–quarter–*yugas* had elapsed (of the current *yuga*), twenty–three years had then passed since my birth."

This means that in the Kali year 3600, he was twenty–three years old. The Kali year 3600 corresponds to 499 CE. Therefore Aryabhatta was born in 476 CE, the year when Buddhagupta, the Gupta King ascended the throne in Pataliputra modern Patna, in Magadha (modern Bihar). Magadha was an eminent centre of learning in ancient India; housing the famous University of Nalanda.

P – Patna

A special observatory existed for studying astronomy in this university. Aryabhatta was designated as 'Kulapati', meaning head of a university. Therefore, in all likelihood, he was a Kulapati of the Nalanda University during the end of the 5th and in the early 6th centuries.

Since the *Aryabhatiya* contains little else about Aryabhatta, not much is known about his education or personal life.

He wrote at least two works, namely, *Aryabhatiya* and Aryabhatta–siddhanta. The latter has not survived, but is known through references in later works. He wrote the former at the age of twenty–three in 499 CE. It deals with both astronomy and mathematics.

Aryabhatta's contribution to mathematics

1) Value of π as 3.1416 to four decimal places. Remarkably it is the same as we use today! Yet he calls this value *aasanna*, meaning approximate. In 825 CE, the Arab mathematician, Mohammed Ibna Musa acknowledged the

origin of Pi's value, "This value has been given by the Hindus."

2) The sine–table. He gives two methods for computing the table.

3) Theory of solving indeterminate equations of the type:

    i) $N = ax+b = cy+d = ez+f = ...$

    ii) $(ax \pm c)/b$ = a whole number.

4) Theory of earth's rotation. It was well–known that the Earth is spherical. The period of one sidereal rotation of the Earth in *Aryabhatiya* is given as 23 hours 56 minutes 45.1 seconds. The modern value is 23 hours 56 minutes 45.091 seconds!

Aryabhatta determined the length of the solar year from the heliacal risings of some bright stars at an interval of 365 and 366 days :

$$\text{The year according to the } Aryabhatiya = \frac{1,577,917,500}{4,320,000}$$

$$= 365.2586805$$

$$= 365 \text{ days, 6 hours, 11 min., 29.64 secs.}$$

This value of the solar year is nearer to the true value than that of Ptolemy.

5) Astronomical constants. Based on his own observations, they differ from those of other astronomers and are more accurate than of previous astronomers.

6) Theory of planetary motions. The epicycles of the planets given by earlier astronomers, including Ptolemy, are fixed in value. Those given by Aryabhatta vary from place to place and yielded better results.

7) Divisions of time:

	Manu Smruti & Suryasiddhanta	Aryabhatta
1 Kalpa =	1000 *yugas*	1008 *yugas*
1 Manu =	71 *yugas*	72 *yugas*
1 Yuga =	4,320,000 years	4,320,000 years

Both systems divided the *yuga* into 4 smaller *yugas*, but Aryabhatta took them to be of equal duration, naming them quarter–yugas, the duration of each being 1,080,000 years.

His division was simpler and more scientific.

8) Celestial latitude of planets. He gave the correct method for calculating this, for both the superior and inferior planets.

9) Radian measure in minutes. It is probably the earliest text on astronomy to use the radian measure of 3438´, for the radius of the circle. Later Indian astronomers adopted and used this method.

10) Theory of eclipses. He was the first astronomer ever to describe the true theory of the cause of the lunar and solar eclipses; that they were due to the shadow of the earth and moon. He revealed that the moon was inherently dark but was illuminated by the sun.

In the 7th century, Bhaskar wrote the first commentary on the *Aryabhatiya*. In glowing terms, he praised his knowledge, "None except Aryabhatta has been able to know the motion of the heavenly bodies. Others merely move in the ocean of utter darkness of ignorance."

The *Aryabhatiya* also reached the Arabs. Translated by Abul Hasan Ahwazi, they misinterpreted the title, *Arajbahara* or *Arajbahaz*; whose meaning they took as, 'one thousandth part.'

The *Aryabhatiya* placed Aryabhatta at the forefront of the genius mathematicians and astronomers of India, whose texts were studied like shastras over the ages. His original contributions in algebra, trigonometry and astronomy rank him the first on many counts in the history of science. His revelation of the earth's rotation, and orbit around the sun was 1000 years prior to Copernicus's heliocentric theory. Many such primers have rendered Aryabhatta immortal in the scientific legacy of India and the world.

> *"Aryabhatta is the master who, after reaching the furthest shores and plumbing the inmost depths of the sea of ultimate knowledge of mathematics, kinematics and spherics, handed over the three (sciences) to the learned world."*
> — *Georges Ifrah.* (1998). *The Universal History of Numbers from Prehistory to the Invention of the Computer. London: The Harvill Press, p. 447.*

The Aryabhatiya

It is written in 121 stanzas and divided into four parts known as *paada*.

Part I: *Gitikaa–paada*. 13 stanzas. Gives the basic definition and astronomical parameters and tables, longer units of time (*kalpa, manu* and *yuga*) circular units (sine, degree & minutes) and linear units (*yojan, nru, hasta* and *angula*); states the number of rotations of the earth and the revolutions of the sun, moon and planets; their orbits, diameter and epicycles, and a table of sine–differences.

Part II: *Ganita–paada*. 33 stanzas. Deals with mathematics – geometrical figures, their properties and mensuration; problems of the shadow of the gnomon; series, interest; and simple, simultaneous, quadratic and linear indeterminate equations; the arithmetical methods for calculating the square–root and cube–root and the method of constructing sine tables.

Part–III: *Kaalakriya–paada*. 25 stanzas. Deals with units of time and determination of the time positions of the sun, moon and planets. Gives the divisions of the year (month, day, etc.) and of the circle; explains the motion of the sun, moon and planets by means of eccentric circles and epicycles; and gives the method for computing the true longitudes of the sun, moon and planets.

Part IV: *Gola–paada*. 50 stanzas. Deals with the motion of the sun, moon and planets in the celestial sphere. Describes the method of automatically rotating the sphere once in twenty–four hours; describes the motion of the celestial sphere as seen by those on the equator and by those at the poles; and gives rules of spherical astronomy. Also deals with the calculation and graphical representation of the eclipses and the visibility of the planets.

The Aryabhatta–Siddhanta

Aryabhatta's second work, the Aryabhatta–siddhanta, was popular and studied throughout India. Its popularity peaked in the 7th century not only as a textbook on astronomy but also as a reckoner for everyday calculations of marriage times and other special ceremonies. A later astronomer, the renowned Brahmagupta (628 CE) was impressed to the extent that he wrote its abridged edition under the delightful title *Khaanda–khaadayaka*, meaning 'food prepared with sugar–candy.' In some parts of India it is consulted even today. From this work arose a new school of astronomy, the 'Aryabhatta–Brahmagupta School'. The principal exponents of this school later wrote commentaries on the *Khaanda–khaadayaka*. Brahmagupta utilised the *Aryabhatiya* in writing his *Brahma–sphuta–siddhanta*. Pruthudakaswami (860 CE) of Kannauj in Uttar Pradesh gave the same rule for calculating the volume of a celestial sphere as given by Aryabhatta.

8. Varahamihir
(Astrologer & Astronomer)

Denoting both Astronomy and Astrology, Jyotish is one of the oldest sciences with its roots in the Vedas. And in the history of India's Jyotish, Varahamihir's name outshines all others. Excelling all his predecessors of Indian astronomy, he was aware of gravity over a millennium before Newton.

The son of a Brahmin named Adityadas, Varahamihir, was born in Kapitthaka, later migrating to Avanti (Ujjain). Both father and son were ardent disciples of the Sun, as the names imply. He was born in 499 CE and passed away at the age of 88 in 587 CE. Therefore, he lived a little later than Aryabhatta, probably being his younger contemporary.

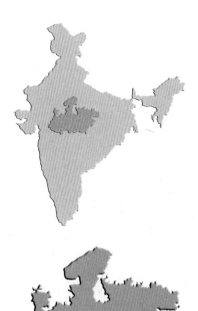

I – Indore
U – Ujjain

His works known to scholars today include: *Panchasiddhantika, Vivahpatal, Bruhajjatak, Laghujatak, Yatra* and *Bruhatsamhita*, written in this order. Each of these works was written after thoughtful study of the entire relevant literature written before him. He not only presented his own observations in brief, but embellished them in attractive poetic and metrical styles. The usage of a large variety of metres is especially evident in his *Bruhajjatak* and *Bruhatsamhita*. Possessing a broad outlook in obtaining knowledge, he was well versed in the use of Greek astrological literature, as is evident from Greek terms in the *Bruhajjatak*.

His *Panchasiddhantika* is a text on astronomy dealing with the five *siddhantas* – systems of ancient astronomy. These comprise the *Paitamaha, Vasishtha, Romaka, Paulish* and the *Saura*. If it were not for him, the details of these five ancient systems would have been lost.

As the names indicate, the *Vivahpatal* and *Yatra (Yogayatra)* deal with the auspicious times for marriage and for journeys, respectively.

The *Bruhajjatak* deals with individual horoscopes in 25 chapters. It is still regarded as the most authoritative work on the subject. The *Laghujatak* is an abridgement of the *Bruhajjatak*.

The *Bruhatsamhita* is Varahamihir's most celebrated work, which he wrote last. The encyclopaedic contents, of 106 chapters and 4000 *shloks*, fall into two categories – *anga* and *upanga*. The former includes everything based on planets, asterisms and the signs of the zodiac. The major portion of *upanga* deals with architecture, sculpting, geography, iconography and iconometry, auspicious and inauspicious characteristics of men and animals such as elephants, horses, dogs, goats, etc., omens, groundwater channels (see box on p.46), *anga vidya (samudrik)*, characteristics of the *khadaga* (sword), manufacture of cosmetics and perfumes, science of precious stones, *Vrukshayurveda* (botany) and others. These provide important details of life during his times.

Scholars credit Varahamihir as being the earliest datable authority on Vastuvidya – science of architecture. There did exist older authors and works on Vastuvidya, to whom Varahamihir extends his indebtedness. However, their works have been ravaged by time. In the *Bruhatsamhita*, his brief account of residential and mandir architecture, sculpture, plasters and furniture, reflect his immense versatility and erudition.

His depth of knowledge in astronomy was profound. Another point worth mentioning is that he regarded the shape of the earth, a debated issue then, as spherical' "All things which are perceived by the senses are witness in favour of the globular shape of the earth, and refute the possibility of its having another shape."

The famed Arab Indologist, Abu al–Raihan ibn Ahmad Al–Biruni (973–1048 CE), or Al–beruni as he is commonly known, frequently referred to two Indian astronomers–astrologers in his observations; Varahamihir and Brahmagupta. Himself the court astrologer of Mahmud of Ghazni, Al–beruni lauded Varahamihir as 'an excellent astronomer' whose 'foot stands firmly on the truth' and who 'speaks out the truth.'

Besides veracity, his poetic excellence, humility and meditative insight contributed to his rishi–like personality.

His poetic creativity in Sanskrit has rendered him one of the 'jewels' of Sanskrit literature, alongside giants such as Dhanvantari and Kalidas. In his writing, his request to those who would follow him, to improve the deficiencies in his work reflects his humility, the mark of a truly noble intellectual. Finally, his uncanny methods of locating groundwater veins could not possibly have all been discovered in a human lifetime solely as a result of physical digging. This is especially so for those sources located at depths of 25 to 75 heads. More likely, such revelations sprang from his meditative insight, similar to the rishis of Ayurveda.

Vastuvidya (Architecture)

Vastu means dwelling, *vidya* – knowledge of. In the Bruhat Samhita, Varahamihir meticulously describes the science of house–building (LIII), mandir architecture (LVI) and *shilpa* – sculpture (LVIII). He cites the types and dimensions of dwellings for the different members of society; from palaces for kings and princes, to officers, royal astrologers, preceptors, physicians and lay citizens. He gives details of twenty types of mandirs. He even stipulates the type of flowers and trees to be grown near dwellings to augur auspiciousness.

The sheer depth of other details reflects his genius, versatility, profound insight and realisation.

Varahamihir's Methods of Locating Groundwater

When chronic water scarcity hit rural areas of Gujarat in the mid-1980s, hydrologists scrambled in search of cheaper methods of locating groundwater sources, rather than the expensive hit-or-miss method of drilling borewells. It was then that scholars browsing through the *Bruhat Samhita* discovered astonishingly simple and sure-fire methods. A few are listed below to depict Varahamihir's incomparable depth of knowledge in a field diametrically different from Jyotish.

1. If there is a termite hill in the easterly direction, near a Jambu tree (Black plum *Syzygium Cumini*), then to its right, sweet water will be found two heads deep (3.54.9). ('One head deep' is the distance from the ground to the fingertips of a person standing with arms fully raised overhead.)

2. Sweet water which will not dry up, will be found $3\frac{1}{4}$ heads deep, three arm-lengths in the southerly direction from a *nagod* tree *(Vitex negundo)*, shading an ant–hill (3.54.14).

3. In a dry area, if there is a *khakhra* tree (Flame of the forest *Butea monosperma*) growing next to a *bor* shrub (Jagged jujube *Zyzyphus jujuba*), then to its west, water will be found $3\frac{1}{4}$ heads deep. As a sign, one head deep, a white, non–venomous snake *(dundubh)* will be found (3.54.17).

4. One arm–length away from any tree under which a frog lives, water will be found $4\frac{1}{2}$ heads deep (3.54.31).

5. Water will be found five heads deep, seven arm–lengths away from a snake's mudhill found in a southerly direction from a *kotha* tree (wood apple *Feronia elephantum*). Here, one head deep, a multi–coloured snake will be found. The soil will be black, the stone hard, white soil further below, then a west–flowing vein

will be found. Further deep, a north–flowing vein will be found (3.54.4–1,42).

6. Red, pebbled soil renders water bland, almond–coloured soil adds salt to the water, yellowish–white soil makes it salty. And where there is brown soil, sweet water will be found (3.54.104).

In further *shloks*, Varahamihir even details methods of fracturing hard rock, which one may encounter when digging deep. He advocates heating the rock by lighting a fire and then splashing limestone water, buttermilk *(chhas)*, etc.

After obtaining water, he thoughtfully gives astonishing details on the method of constructing ponds to store water for long periods. He even gives the direction of the pond's walls to minimise evaporation by winds! In the absence of heavy road rollers, common today, he advises trampling the ground by elephants or horses to compact the bottom of a pond (3.54.118).

Varahmihir's nadika yantra (water clock)

Varahamihir was the first to devise a simple ingenious water clock. It was a bowl made from copper or a coconut shell with a small hole at the bottom, placed in a larger water vessel. The hole's size allowed water to sip in, sinking the bowl about once every half an hour; 60 times in 24 hours. Every time it sank a *zalar* (gong) was sounded and a bead moved in a type of abacus, indicating the total time.

9. Bhaskaracharya (II)

(Genius in Algebra)

Bhaskaracharya's work in algebra, arithmetic and geometry catapulted him to fame and immortality. His renowned mathematical works, *Lilavati* and *Bijaganita,* are considered to be unparalleled, reflecting his profound intelligence.

Bhaskaracharya was the first to discover gravity, five hundred years before Newton. His works fired the imagination of Persian and European scholars, who through research on his works earned fame and popularity.

Bhaskar, son of Maheshwar, was born in the Saka year 1036, 1114 CE, in Vijjadavida, in the Sahyadri Hills, now in Maharashtra. Being a mathematician, Maheshwar taught him mathematics. From the time of Aryabhatta (I), mathematics began to be incorporated into astronomy, which also required knowledge of geometry, trigonometry, arithmetic and algebra. Later, Bhaskar's son, Lakshmidhar, and grandson, Changadev, also became renowned astronomer–mathematicians. The latter was the royal astrologer of the Yadav King Singhana of Devagiri.

M – Mumbai

Bhaskar has cited details of his family in the Goladhyaya section of his first work, *Siddhantshiromani*, which he wrote at the age of thirty–six, in 1150 CE. These details are corroborated by two stone inscriptions in mandirs, one in Patan and the other in Behal. Though his family of scholars were attached to royal courts as astrologers, there is no reference to him being a royal astrologer.

The *Siddhantshiromani* is a large text divided into four sections: (1) *Patiganit*, also known as *Lilavati*, named after his daughter, (2) *Bijaganit,* (3) *Grahaganit* and (4) *Goladhyaya*.

The *Lilavati* deals with arithmetic and geometry (see details below).

Lilavati

Parikarmashtak	addition, subtraction, multiplication, division, squaring, cubing, extraction of square and cube roots. Then follow in sequence:
Shunyaparikarma	operations with zero
Vyastavidhi	method of inversion
Ishtakarma	unitary method
Sankraman	finding a and b when a + b and a − b are known, i.e. the method of elimination
Vargasankraman	finding a and b so that a^2+b^2-1 and a^2-b^2-1 may be perfect squares
Mulgunak	problems involving square roots, i.e. those leading to quadratic equations
Trairashik	rule of three
Bhandpratibhandak	barter
Mishravyavahar	mixtures
Shrenivyavahar	series
Ankapash	permutations and combinations
Kuttak	indeterminate analysis

Bhaskar's model and inspirer was Brahmagupta (598 CE) the author of *Brahmasphuta Siddhanta* and a contemporary of Bhaskar I. He pays homage to his master at the beginning of his *Siddhantshiromani*. Bhaskar improved upon Brahmagupta, with a thoroughness that eclipsed his master's works.

Bijaganit

Bhaskar's Bijaganit is a systematic and complete treatise of Hindu algebra till modern times. His greatest expertise was his ability to solve problems of indeterminate equations of the second degree. For these problems, he gave both algebraic and geometrical solutions.

ghanarnashadvidham	fundamental operations with positive and negative quantities
shunyashadvidham	with zero
varnashadvidham	with symbols
karanishadvidham	and surds
kuttak	indeterminate simple equations
vargaprakruti	indeterminate equations of the second degree
ekavarnasamikaranam	equations on one unknown
madhyamaharanam	solving quadratic equations by completing the square
anekvarnasamikaranam	equations with more than one unknown
bhavit	equations of higher degrees with more than one unknown and solutions of equations involving products of the unknowns

The *Grahaganit* and *Gola* chapters deal with astronomy of heavenly bodies, based on the *Suryasiddhant*. In the third chapter, *Bhuvankosh* (the universe), he explains the situation of the earth, unsupported in space, and how beings exist on the surface of the spherical earth. He then deals with the circumference, surface area and volume of the earth, using pi as 3.1416.

The fifth chapter considers the mean motions of the sun, moon and planets. The sixth or eighth chapter, *Triprashavasana*, shows how to know the time for sunrise, the relative length of the day and night in different seasons and at different latitudes. It also teaches how to know the latitude of a place.

The next three chapters deal with eclipses. The following chapter, *Yantradhyaya*, details astronomical instruments used for observing heavenly bodies. However, at the end, he suggests that intelligence is a better tool than all instruments.

Siddhantshiromani achieved fame since it contained everything about Indian astronomy. The period between Aryabhatta I and Bhaskar II is considered the golden age of Indian Jyotish, due to the advent of many treatises on astronomy. However, all these were eclipsed by Bhaskar's works, because of his brilliant exposition and analysis. His thorough treatment left no room for further improvement. The subsequent treatises were generally all commentaries on Bhaskar's works.

It seems that his mental faculties were still in peak condition in his old age, for at the age of sixty–nine he composed his second treatise, the *Karanakutuhal*, in 1183–4. This dealt with astronomical calculations. It is used even today in many parts of India to make calendars. Of Bhaskar's works that others later chose to write commentaries on, the most popular was *Lilavati*. Over twenty have been discovered.

During and after Bhaskar's period decadence set in. It affected all cultural and literary fields as wave after wave of foreign hordes began to destroy and desecrate the land. His works reached beyond India. One source claims that the *Lilavati* was translated into Persian in 1577 and the *Bijaganit* in 1665. Another claims that Akbar had the former translated into Persian by Abu Fazl in 1587; the *Bijaganit* being completed by Attaullah Rushudee in 1634. More recently, Colebrooke also translated both these texts into English (1817).

The *Lilavati* is so highly acclaimed that it outshines all Bhaskaracharya's works. One school of mathematics opines that a person adept in the *Lilavati* can even compute the exact number of leaves on a tree!

Bhaskar was the last of the stalwart astronomer – mathematicians of ancient India.

Bhaskaracharya's Noteworthy Contributions to Mathematics

1. Calculating the correct volume of a sphere by dividing it into pyramids with their apexes at the centre and bases on the surface of the sphere.

2. Calculating the correct surface area of a sphere by cutting the surface into concentric rings and into lenticular strips and then adding up their areas. Though it is not exactly clear, researcher, Prof. P.C. Sengupta, supposes it as a sort of differentiation–integration.

3. His mathematics of the zero is noteworthy, for claiming that any quantity divided by zero is infinity - termed *khahar*.

4. The implied concept of the infinitesimal.

5. Anticipating differentiation to calculate the instantaneous motions of planets.

Part II-Founders of Philosophy

Introduction

Sanatan Dharma's six principle systems of philosophy are known as *Shad Darshans*. *Shad* means six and darshan means 'that which is seen'. Hence the founders and proponents of these systems are known as *Daarshaniks* – those who literally 'saw' or realised their beliefs. This is the point of divergence of Western philosophers. Did they truly realise and practice their philosophy? Did it lead to realisation of the Divine or some form of spiritual enlightenment? Moreover, did these philosophies help the common man, in solving life's common problems? The issues remain moot.

The founders of the *Shad Darshans* were rishis. Endowed with saintly attributes and enlightened by their sadhana, they formulated their own principles. Each *Darshan* has some practical application in a person's life, as we shall see. The six *Darshans* are Nyaya-Vaisheshik, Samkhya-Yog, Purva Mimamsa and Uttar Mimamsa. The latter is commonly known as Vedant, propounded by Bhagwan Veda Vyas.

After considering these rishis, we examine the Acharyas. These were ascetics of the highest order. Hence, Part II examines the lives of *Daarshaniks*, who contributed to the realm of attaining Paramatma and left a vibrant and rich legacy after their departure. Each wrote a commentary (*bhashya*) on the Upanishads, Brahma Sutras and Bhagvad Gita, collectively known as the *Prasthantrayi*. Each *acharya* derived his own school of thought: Shankar's *Advait*, Ramanuj's *Vishishtadvait*, Nimbark's *Dvaitadvait*, Madhva's *Dvait* and Vallabh's *Shuddhadvait*. The latter's son, Vitthalnath, completed his father's unfinished *Anu Bhashya* commentary.

The ultimate goal of these schools of thought was to realise the *atma* and Paramatma. All the *acharyas* greatly emphasised bhakti towards Paramatma. With the exception of Shankar, this bhakti was to be offered by the aspirant considering himself as the servant – *das*-of Paramatma.

10. Kapilmuni

(Samkhya Darshan)

The principle founder of Samkhya Darshan, Kapilmuni was born of Vishvapati and Rohini, daughter of the demon King Hiranyakashipu (Svetashvatara Upanishad 5/2). Scholars are not at a consensus about his time period. However they propose the composition of the Samkhya sutras around 600 BCE. There's little else known about him. Many scholars contend that he is the same Kapilmuni cited in the Bhagvatam, born of Kardam rishi and Devahuti who lived at Bindu Sarovar in north Gujarat.

However the latter was *seshvarvadi* – believer in Parabrahman, while the former was *nirishvarvadi* – not believing in Him but not denying His existence either.

There's little information available about Indian seers generally, since they were disinclined to note their personal details. Therefore in this chapter and others that follow, there will be a greater discussion on their contribution to philosophical thought. In our culture, Samkhya Darshan's contribution to philosophical knowledge is foremost.

Samkhya Darshan

One of the oldest Indian philosophies, Samkhya Darshan deals with the process of cosmic evolution. It attempts to harmonise the teaching of the Vedas through reason. Initially Samkhya was mixed with Vedant. It was Kapilmuni who gave it an independent form, as a separate Darshan. As such he is regarded as the first *acharya* of Samkhya shastra.

Samkhya is a Realistic, Dualistic and Pluralistic Darshan. It is Realistic in that it believes the world (*jagat*) to be real, in contrast to Vedant, which believes that the world is unreal and it evolved from the real (Brahman). It is Dualistic, since it accepts two entities which are totally different, independent and perfect (*purna*), namely (i) *Purush* (*jiva*) and (2) *Prakriti* (Nature). It is Pluralistic since it believes in manifold Purushs, not just one.

Aim of Samkhya

Samkhya's aim is to attain complete knowledge of the

It is believed that initially there were 537 Samkhya sutras in six chapters. These are not available today. However based on these sutras, Vijnanbhikshu wrote Samkhyapravachan bhashya in the 16th century CE and 22 sutras in Tattvasamassutra, which are not available either. In the absence of these, the only available Samkhya text is Ishvarkrishna's Samkhyakarika (1st century CE). All the details of Samkhya Darshan are based on this text. Many commentaries have been written on this. The most important are: Maathar's Maatharvrutti, Gaudapaad's Gaudapaad Bhashya and Vachaspati Mishra's Samkhyatattva Kaumudi.

difference between Purush and Prakriti. It is the ignorance of the difference between the two that has led the Purush or *jiva* to be eternally bound. When the *jiva* attains knowledge that, 'it is separate from Prakriti and is eternally pure,' it attains *mukti* (liberation) from Prakriti. Hence Samkhya places greater emphasis on complete knowledge rather than *sadhana*, as expounded by Patanjali's Yog Darshan. In fact, commentators of Samkhya such as Shridhar Swami, Ramanuj, Vijnanbhikshu and others, give the meaning of Samkhya as *atmatattva* and *atmajnan*.

Bhagwan Swaminarayan supports Samkhya's belief of attaining such knowledge. In Vachanamrut Gadhada I-12, He says, "When one understands the nature of the causes of the entire creation, specifically Purush, Prakriti, *kāl*, the 24 elements including *mahatattva* etc., then one is liberated from the bondage of one's inherent *avidya* and the 24 elements evolved from it."

Kapilmuni's contribution

Kapilmuni extracted the essence from the Vedas and Upanishads and gave a well-classified account about the 25 principles *(tattvas)*. Samkhya's aim is to acquire *vivek* – to discriminate between *purush* and *prakriti* through knowledge of the 25 *tattvas*.

Through this knowledge any person in any stage can attain *mukti*. Kapil classified these *tattvas* into four categories:

Form	No. of tattvas	Name
(1) Keval Prakriti (only cause, no effect)	1	Pradhaan, Avyakta, Mul Prakriti
(2) Keval Vikriti (only effect)	16	Five *jnan indriyas* – eyes, nose, tongue, skin, ears. Five *karma indriyas* – speech, hands, feet, genitals, anus. Five *Mahabhuts* – earth, water, light, wind, space. mind

(3) Prakriti – Vikriti (both cause & effect)	7	*Mahatattva, Ahamkar, Panch tanmatra* (sight, smell, taste, touch and sound).
(4) Niether Prakriti, nor Vikriti (neither cause nor effect)	1	Purush
Total	25	

Kapil's concept of cosmic evolution is depicted below.

Cosmic Evolution in Kapil's Samkhya

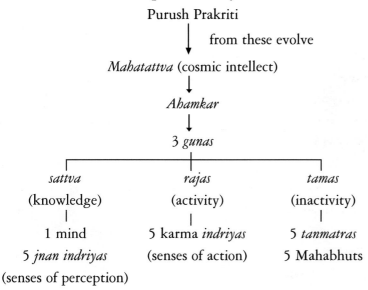

Samkhya's logical and cogent elaboration had an effect on all the later Darshans. Though Vedant and its acharyas heavily condemned Samkhya, they have accepted and used its 25 *tattvas* to explain cosmogenesis in their own way.

Samkhya and Swaminarayan Darshan

In the Vachanamrut (Gadhada I–52 and Vartal 2), Bhagwan Swaminarayan advocates understanding Bhagwan's form with a combined correlative study of four shastras, namely, *Samkhya, Yog, Panchratra* and *Vedant*.

Aksharbrahma Gunatitanand Swami stipulates, "Without Samkhya one cannot eradicate the five *doshas*: avarice, lust, anger, attachment and ego. And without Samkhya one cannot fully consolidate one's *satsang*. Therefore to remain happy, one should inculcate Samkhya" (Swamini Vato 1/2).

11. Kanad
(Vaisheshik Darshan)

Kanad rishi is the founder of Vaisheshik Darshan, one of the six schools of Indian philosophy. He lived in Prabhas Patan, northern Gujarat. Scholars date him to about 600 BCE. By *gotra*–name, he is called Kashyap, descendant of Kashyap. His other names include Kanabhuk, Kanachara, Kanabhaksha, Kanasin and Kanavrat, which indicate his association with *kana* meaning grain or particles of food. This reflects his extreme asceticism, living on particles of food. *Kana* also means 'atom', while Kanabhaksha means 'atom–eater', referring to his atomic theory. This is also supported by other epithets, Pailuka and Pailukantha, in which the root *pilu* designates *anu* or atom. Thus, Kanad rishi was the first propounder of the atomic theory; about 2500 years prior to John Dalton (see box p.64). In the *Nyayakundali*, the scholar Shridhar, notes that the rishi existed on scattered grains left over from harvests in the fields or byways. Another reference by a Chinese, H. Ui, mentions that he begged for food at night much like an owl. Hence, he was also known as Uluka, a name by which he is referred to in other texts. Other scholars, Gunaratna and Rajshekhar, note that Shivji appeared to the rishi as an owl and imparted the tenets of Vaisheshik. In the concluding *shlok* of *Padarthdharmasamgraha*, Prashastapad venerates Kanakbhuk, who composed *Vaisheshik Sutras* after propitiating Shivji through his supramundane power of meditation and practice of Yog (*yogachar*). Since this Yog system is similar, if not identical to Paashupat Yogashastra, some authorities also attribute this to Kanad.

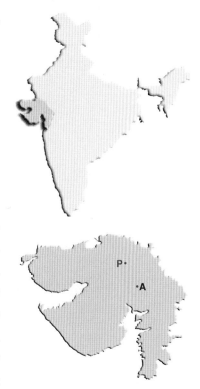

P – Patan
A – Amdavad

Vaisheshik Darshan

This Darshan cites several references to the Vedas and Vedic literature. Since Kanad accepts Vedic authority and deals with characteristics of deities, *yagna*, objects used in *yagna*, the self and so on, he cannot be termed a *nastik*, as some have. A *nastik* is one who does not accept (1) the existence of Paramatma as the creator of the universe, (2) authority of the Vedas or (3) existence of *parlok* heaven.

To use the articles appropriate to a rite requires knowledge of their qualities. Therefore, Kanad systematically treated this on a broader basis, with frequent references to the Vedas, Brahmanas, Vedic rites and rituals. Therefore, Vaisheshik Darshan, along with the other five, is regarded as one of the six *astik darshans* of Indian philosophy, and is the oldest.

Vaisheshik Sutras consists of ten chapters, each of two daily lessons known as *ahaniks*. The total number of Sanskrit *shloks* is 370. Several commentaries have been written on this system:

1) *Prashastapad Bhashya*, also known as *Padarthdharmasamgraha* by Vyomacharya.
2) *Upaskara* by Shankar Mishra.
3) *Kiranavali*, a commentary by Udayanacharya.
4) *Kandali*, a commentary by Shridharacharya.
5) *Setu*, a commentary by Padmanabh Mishra and
6) *Kiranavali Bhaskar*, a commentary by Padmanabh Mishra

Other references of Kanad's *sutras* are cited in the *Samkhya Sutras, Vayu Puran, Padma Puran, Devi Bhagvatam*, Mahabharat, Shrimad Bhagvatam and others. Vaisheshik Sutras also precedes Vyas's *Vedant Sutras*, since the latter has critically commented on Kanad's theories.

Kanad & Law of Causation

Satya Prakash, in his *Founders of Sciences in Ancient India* (1965:319), avers that the greatest discovery of human thought is the realisation of a link between cause and effect. Scientific inquiry obligates searching for a cause of a particular phenomenon. In the history of science, Kanad was the first rishi–scientist to explore a relation between cause and effect. This was later developed upon by the Samkhya and Vedant schools.

In the tenth chapter of *Vaisheshik Sutras*, Kanad gives *shloks* relating to the nature of the cause. The *sutra* refers to three kinds of causes:

1. *Samavayi Kāran* – inherent cause
2. *Asamavayi Kāran* – non–inherent or formal cause, and
3. *Nimitta Kāran* – instrumental cause.

The first two are always uncommon – *asādhāran* – while *nimitta* is of two kinds – *sādhāran* and *asādhāran*. *Sādhāran* includes eight causes: Paramatma, His knowledge, desire, His action, space, time, unseen *(adhrushta)* and prior existence *(pragbhav)*. *Asādhāran* causes are innumerable.

Kanad's Predicables

Philosophy seeks to know all things. Over the ages, every thinker in every culture has attempted to classify things suited to his thought. In the history of philosophy, categories of classification have been made of things, words, ideas or forms of thought. However a comprehensive theory of classification can never be possible. Kanad's classification of predicable or category is considered 'eminently satisfactory'.

In Kanad's view the objective world has a real existence independent of the cogniser. The *padārths* (substances) exist even if the cogniser does not cognise them. According Kanad there are six *padarths* (categories) called *dravya* (substance), *guna* (quality), karma (action), *sāmānya* (universal/generality), *vishesh* (particularity) and *samavāya* (inherence) and to these six, later on, *abhāva* – non-existence as seventh category *(padarth)* is added. It is *dravya* or substance that is of nine kinds, namely earth, water, light air, *ākāsh* (ether), time, space, mind and *atma*. Of these the first four are composed of eternal and indivisible *anus* – atoms. Kanad's *Anu* or Atomic Theory (see below) is deep–rooted in Indian philosophy. Other schools, such as, Buddhism, Ajivakas, Jainism, Naiyayiks, Ayurveda and others also accept it. Uttar Mimamsa and Purva Mimamsa, two of the six Darshans have many similarities with Vaisheshik. The two Mimamsa teachers, Prabhakar and Shaliknath, have used Vaisheshik *shloks* and tenets in their works. The latter wrote a commentary on the *Padarthdharmasamgraha* of Prashastapad.

Badarayan's Brahma Sutras, as well as commentators and sub–commentators on the Brahma Sutras such as Shriharsh and Chitsukh, among others, have commented on Vaisheshik, albeit in refuting it. The Samkhya Sutras mention Vaisheshik, while the *Yuktidipika*, a commentary on the *Samkhya Karika* also comments on it.

The Nyaya and Vaisheshik Darshans are kindred philosophies – *samaan tantras*. Vatsyayan's *Nyayabhashya* and Uddyotkara's *Nyayavarttika* are partial to Vaisheshik concepts. The relationship between the two systems deepened and eventually coalesced into a single school.

Kanad's system exercised immense influence in the philosophical firmament of ancient Bharat, leading proponents of their own thoughts either to adopt the concepts or take great pains in refuting them. T.N. Colebrooke, the eminent historian acknowledged Kanad's contribution, "Compared to the scientists of Europe, Kanad and other Indian scientists were the global masters in this field."

Kanad Rishi's Atomic Theory and Characteristics of Atoms

About 2500 years before John Dalton, Kanad rishi conceptualised the Atomic Theory. He defined *anu*, also known as *paramanu* (atom), as the ultimate particle, of each of the following four, of the nine *padārths* – earth, water, fire and air. Kanad also mentions in great detail the chemical reactions *(paka)* that occur in earthly *paramanus*, and motion – which persists even during *pralay* (destruction of the universe) in the form of atomic vibration.

The important characteristics of *paramanus* are:

1 They are eternal and indivisible (*Vaisheshik Sutras* (VS). IV. i.4).

2 They cannot produce anything by themselves, otherwise their eternal nature would involve a continuous process of production (*Kandali*, pp.31–32).

3   Each of the four kinds of *paramanus* possesses its specific attributes of: smell, touch, taste and colour. Thus the earthly *paramanu* has smell, the aerial has touch, the watery has taste and the fiery has colour (VS. IV. i.3).

4   They are imperceptible by any of the sense *indriyas*. For example, to fathom magnitude and manifested touch, they cannot be felt by the organ of touch (*sparsh*), and so forth (VS. IV. i.6). This does not mean that a sense organ does not come in contact with *paramanus* for they are perceived by yogis (*Upasak* commentary by Shankar Mishra. VIII. i.2).

5   The attributes inherent in the *paramanus* are also eternal except in the case of the earthly *paramanus* (VS. VII. i.3).

6   The *paramanus* are the ultimate material cause (*upādān kāran*) of the universe (*Nyayavarttika* of Udyotkara. IV. i.24).

7   They are both collectively and individually imperceptible (*Nyaya Lilavati* by Vallabhacharya, p.8).

8   They possess quiddity (*antyavishesh*) which differentiates one *paramanu* from another (*Prashastapad Bhashya* p.131, Kandali pp.33–4).

9   A *paramanu* possesses both the smallest and shortest possible dimensions (*Kanad Rahasya*, pp.72–73).

10 The dimensions of the *paramanus* are known as *parimandal* and are eternal (VS. VII i.19–20).

12. Jaimini
(Purva Mimamsa)

Jaimini rishi is the propounder of Purva Mimamsa, one of the six *astik* Darshans. *Purva* means previous or former. *Mimamsa* means examination or investigation. In contradistinction to Purva Mimamsa, there exists Uttar Mimamsa, better known as Vedant, propounded by Badarayan. *Uttar* means final or subsequent. Purva Mimamsa is also simply known as Mimamsa.

Jaimini was born in the Kautsa family and was a Rutvij priest during Yudhishthir's Ashwamedh Yagna. He was present with other seers while Bhishma lay on the bed of arrows. He also performed the Snake Yagna for Janmejay. Finally, the *Saamvidhan Brahman* cites him as a pupil of Vyas, who imparted to him the Sam Veda. He was also a pupil of Langli.

Jaimini's works include: *Jaimini Samhita, Jaiminiya Brahman, Jaimini Shrautsutra, Jaiminiyopanishad, Jaimini–bhagvat, Jaimini–bharat, Jaimini Gruhyasutra, Jaimini Sutrakarnika, Jaimini Stotra* and *Jaimini Smruti*. He was also the guru of Panini (c.1600 BCE), who systematised Sanskrit grammar. Jaimini's son was Sumantu.

From the foregoing information it can be seen that an uncertainty exists about Jaimini's period and exact identity. One uncertainty concerns the identity of Vyas. For a rishi named Vyas also appears as Jaimini's fourth descendant: Jaimini–Paushpindya – Parasharyayam – Badarayan (Vyas). Is this Badarayan Vyas the author of the Mahabharat and the *Vedanta Sutras (Brahma Sutras)*? The enigma is compounded by the fact that Jaimini and Badarayan cite each other's references in their *sutras*. So it is difficult to fathom who existed first! Hence, scholars are divided about Jaimini's period. One scholar places him a 100 years after the Mahabharat (c.3000 BCE) probably due to his presence before Bhishma and in Yudhishthir's *yagna* mentioned earlier. Other scholars assign him a period of around 500 BCE based on the

B – Badrinath

greater affinity of the *Mimansasutras* to the *Kalpasutras*.

The only other detail about Jaimini's 'life' is about his death, which was caused by a wild elephant!

Now we will consider his life's work, the *Mimansasutras*, which is the first systematic treatise on Mimamsa.

Mimamsa Darshan

The earliest commentary on Jaimini's *sutras* is by Shabar Swami (c. 200 CE). In turn this was commented upon by Prabhakar (c. 650 CE), Kumaril Bhatt (c. 700 CE) and Murari Mishra (c. 1200 CE).

Prabhakar's work is known as *Bruhati*, while Kumaril Bhatt wrote five treatises: *Bruhat–tika, Madhyam–tika, Shlokvartik, Tantravartik* and *Tuptika*. Three *sampradays* arose, named after these three commentators.

Opinions vary about the exact number of *Mimansasutras*, ranging from 2500 to 3000; in twelve to seventeen chapters. A thousand topics have been discussed in these *sutras*. Through these *sutras*, Jaimini discusses the real meaning of the Vedas. The first *sutra* says: *Athāto Dharmajignāsā* after this begins the desire for knowing dharma. From this, his *sutras* are also known as *Dharmamimansa*. He defines dharma as an act or set of actions enjoined by the Vedas which is simultaneously conducive to human well–being (Mimamsasutras 1.1.2). This Darshan deals primarily with *yagnas*, rites and rituals enjoined by the Vedas. Mimamsa attaches greater importance to the ordained acts of the *yagnas* than to the deities to whom they are offered. Mimamsa considers the Vedas as entirely authoritative and *apaurasheya* – not written by any human agent. Mimamsa does not postulate Paramatma as the author of the Vedas, for they are self–revealed, self–valid and eternal.

Jaimini held *shabda* (word, testimony) as self-authentic – *svatah pramān* - and therefore all knowledge as self-valid.

The purpose of comparison in Nyaya, using the analogy of the *go* (cow) to *gavaya* (wild ox or nilgai) was to reveal the denotation of a word. However, for the *mimansak*, the purpose is to glean the similarity between two objects. Therefore, the urbanite who entered the forest and saw the *gavaya* remembered what the forest dweller had told him; that the *gavaya* is similar to the *go*. From this he concluded that the *go* is similar to the *gavaya*.

In the early stages, Mimamsa considered *swarg* (heaven) as man's ultimate aim for which Vedic *yagnas* were to be performed. However, the later *mimansaks* upheld *moksha* as the final human goal. Similarly, Jaimini, as well as Shabar and Kumaril, his commentators, remain mute about the existence of the omniscient, omnipotent and all merciful Paramatma. However, later exponents such as Khandadev and Gagabhatt have discussed this, averring that Purva Mimamsa has nothing new to add about Paramatma and *moksha*, to what has been thoroughly discussed in Uttar Mimamsa. Moreover, it is not Mimamsa's aim to deny Paramatma's existence but to explain the truth about Vedic rites and rituals.

Finally, the principles of interpretation formulated by Jaimini in the *Mimansasutras* are absolutely necessary for the accurate understanding of any *Dharmashastra*. Just as grammar is necessary in understanding language and literature, so is semantics. Jaimini's sutras fulfil this requirement.

Mimamsa Darshan's salient contribution

This Darshan's important philosophical contribution lies in its *Gnanmimamsa*. Its belief in the six *pramāns* is also accepted by Vedant. Its greatest contribution is that it relentlessly countered the tremendous castigation of the Vedas by *nastiks*, namely, Charvak, Jain and Buddha schools of thought. Towards this end Kumaril Bhatt's commentaries and efforts were the most successful and laudable. These saved the Vedas and the veracity of Vedic rites – *Karmakand*. Though Samkhya–Yog and Nyaya–Vaisheshik are considered *astik* Darshans, they have almost negligibly depended on the Vedic *shrutis*; wholly depending on their own texts to propound their thoughts. The composition of the *Mimamsasutras* is firmly based on the Vedas. Additionally, the expositions and commentaries of the sutras to establish the veracity and validity of their school of thought are also based on the Vedic *Shrutis*.

Hence, among the *astiks*, who believe in the validity of the Vedas, Mimamsa's contribution is greater and more important than the previous four Darshans. Mimamsa has also deeply reflected and examined the Law of Karma - karma, karma's form, types of karmas and the intrinsic relation between karma and its fruit, etc. - and *Karmashastra* - *yagna*, yagna rites and their stipulated rituals and implementation.

13. Gautam
(Nyaya Darshan)

The son of rishi Deerghatama and grandson of Angira Rishi, Gautam was born in the Himalayas. He is also known as Akshapad Gautam; Akshapad being his personal name and Gautam depicting his *gotra* – family name from the sage Gotama. Details of his life are unknown. Only his philosophical contributions have remained with us.

Akshapad or Gautam, not to be confused with, Gautam the Buddha, was the first authority to systematise the *Nyayashastra* in the form of *shloks*; Nyaya being one of the six *astik* Darshans of Sanatan Dharma. *Nyaya* in Sanskrit means 'analysis'. Nyaya is a system of logical realism or syllogistic reasoning. *Nyayashastra* is also called *Hetushastra, Tarkavidya* and *Vādvidya*.

Some scholars attribute Gautam's period to around 350 CE. However S. Dasgupta in his *History of Indian Philosophy* (1975: 279) mentions that according to Goldstucker, Nyaya existed in some form as early as the 4th century BCE, on the basis that Patanjali (200 BCE) and Katyayan (4th century BCE) knew about Nyaya. Mahadevan, too, assigns 4th century BCE in his *Outlines of Hinduism* (1971: 100).

Nyaya Darshan

Nyaya propounds the existence of an external world independent of all thinking minds and then attempts to establish this through logical reasoning. In the first *shlok* Gautam states that salvation is the summum bonum and ultimate goal of a spiritual aspirant and this highest perfection is possible through a proper understanding of sixteen *padārths* or categories of reason, which are listed later. However, the first topic that every Indian philosophy deals with is the problem of knowledge, of which there are two main aspects:

1. What are the means of valid knowledge?
2. What is valid knowledge or truth?

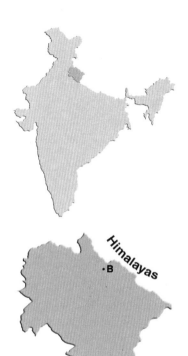

B – Badrinath

71

1. The means of valid knowledge

The means of valid knowledge are called *pramāns*. The number of *pramāns* varies with different systems. In the Nyaya system there are four means of valid knowledge: *pratyaksh* (perception), *anumān* (inference), *upamān* (comparison) and *shabda* (verbal testimony). Similar to Ramanuj Vedant, Swaminarayan Darshan believes in only three: *pratyaksh, anuman* and *shabda*.

Perception

This is knowledge arising from contact of the sense–organ with its object. There are exceptions to this in which there may be no sense activity. For example, Bhagwan knows all things without the aid of any sense–organ. The yogis perceive distant objects, and past and future events without sense–contact with them. However, sense–contact is necessary in all normal perception of external objects.

Inference

Anumān literally means 'after–knowledge'. It is the most important principal in Nyaya. While perceptual knowledge is instantly perceived, inferential knowledge is arrived at through steps. The classic example in Nyaya is:

1. The hill has fire *(pratijna)*
2. Because it has smoke *(hetu)*
3. Whatever has smoke has fire e.g. a hearth *(udāharan)*
4. This hill has smoke which is invariably associated with fire *(upanaya)*
5. Therefore this hill has fire *(nigāmāna)*

Inference is knowledge acquired through means of other knowledge. The above is an example of Akshapad's five–membered syllogism *pratijna, hetu, udāharan, upanaya* and *nigamāna*. Western or Aristotelian syllogism consists of only three parts two premises (or presumed conditions) which form the basis of the arguments, and the conclusion or inference derived from the premises, which follows logically and concludes the argument. This system gives deduction alone, whereas Akshapad's has the advantage of combining induction and deduction. Therefore this disproves the supposition that

Aristotle influenced Akshapad's Nyaya.

Comparison

Upamān, the third means of valid knowledge, resorts to knowledge of similarity. The result is the knowledge of the relation between a name and the object denoted by it. For example, an urbanite ignorant of the word *gavaya* (wild cow or nilgai) learns from a ruralite that it is a forest animal similar to the cow. The urbanite then visits a forest and sees the animal called *gavaya*. Recalling the information from the ruralite, he now knows that the animal he sees is the denotation of the name *gavaya*.

Testimony

The final *praman* of valid knowledge is *shabda* testimony of a trustworthy person (*āpta*). He is trustworthy if he is competent in his topic and conveys the information correctly. Hence, the value of *shabda* as *pramān* depends on the excellence of its source. Also, every word has the power (*shakti*) to signify a meaning. According to the Naiyayika, this power is determined by Paramatma's will *Ishwar Sanket*. It is Paramatma who wills 'from this word, this concept should be known.'

Testimony may be of the Veda (*Vaidik*) or of worldly speech (*laukik*). Since the Vedic statements are of Paramatma, their testimony is perfect and infallible. *Laukik* words are not so, only being valid if they are uttered by a trustworthy authority.

2. What is valid knowledge?

Having considered the means of valid knowledge, we consider what valid knowledge is. According to Nyaya valid knowledge or truth is that which agrees or corresponds to the nature of its object. Akshapad maintained that the logical method of ascertaining truth was by applying the sixteen categories (*padarths*) of thought and reasoning that we mentioned earlier:

1.   means of knowledge (*praman*)
2.   objects of inquiry (*prameya*)

3. doubt *(samshay)*

4. purpose *(prayojan)*

5. examples *(drushtant)*

6. established principles *(siddhant)*

7. syllogistic premise *(avayava)*

8. confutation *(tarka)*

9. decisive ascertainment *(nirnay)*

10. discussion *(vād)*

11. arguing constructively and destructively 'splitting hairs' *(jalpa)* in which both arguing parties wish to win the debate

12. mere destructive argument of the opposition *(vitanda)*, but not consolidating one's stance

13. fallacious reason *(hetvabhasha)*, in *vitanda*

14. quibbling *(chala)*

15. futile objections *(jati)*

16. vulnerable points *(nigrahsthan)*, of which there are twenty–two. If one or the other party inadvertently displays his ignorance in a statement or establishes the opposite, then he loses the debate.

Gautam's Nyaya Darshan in many respects is complementary to and almost in perfect agreement with Vaisheshik. With the synthesis of Vaisheshik's metaphysics and Nyaya's epistemology (theory of knowledge) the two later merged. The epistemology and logic of Mimamsa, Samkhya and Yog also show direct or indirect influence of Nyaya. Charak, too, in his *Charak Samhita*, used many of Nyaya's categories. The Jains developed their own logic from Gautam's system. Commentaries on the *Nyayasutras* include: Vatsyayan's *Nyayabhashya*, Uddyotakara's *Nyayavartika*, Vachaspati Mishra's *Tātparyatika* and Udayan's *Tātparyaparishuddhi*. Nyaya came to be regarded as the science of definitions whose importance began to be realised in modern European philosophy.

Moreover, Nyayashastra reached beyond India's borders. A reference is given to Gautam, the debator, in the *Khorda Avesta* (Yasht.13). There are also manuscripts of new logic in the Arakanese. Buddhist logic, being a branch of the Brahmanic stream, crossed northern India, reached Tibet and China to be preserved, studied and commented upon by scholars. In India, Akshapad Gautam's deep impact is such that it is traditional to begin the study of philosophy with a foundation in Nyaya.

Nyaya Darshan on the existence of Paramatma

Nyaya's salient feature is that it seeks to prove Paramatma's existence. The principal arguments put forth by Udayan in his *Tātparyaparishuddhi* are:

1. The world which is an effect requires an efficient cause. This cause must be equal to the task of creating the world both by knowledge as well as power. That is Paramatma.

2. There is orderliness in the created world. Natural phenomena do not constitute a chaotic mass. They reveal an intelligent design. As the originator of this design, as the controller of the physical order, Paramatma must exist.

3. Just as there is a physical order, there is a moral order too, which dispenses justice in accordance with deservingness. There must be one responsible for this as the moral governor. He is Paramatma.

4. There is also a negative proof. No atheist has so far proved the non–existence of Paramatma! No *pramān* can be offered to show that Paramatma does NOT exist.

Paramatma in the Nyaya system belongs to the class of *atmas*. He is Paramatma, as distinguished from *jivatma* or individual *atma*. He is the efficient cause of the universe and not its material cause. He is the prime mover of the primary atoms, which by coming together in different ways constitute the things of the physical world. Guided by past karmas of the *atmas*, Paramatma creates, protects and destroys the universe and re–creates it.

14. Patanjali

(Yog Darshan)

There are three rishis named Patanjali. One, a grammarian, wrote the *Mahabhashya* commentary on Panini's *Ashtadhyayi*. The second, an Ayurveda acharya, wrote a commentary on the Charak Samhita. It is the third Patanjali, who is famed for his *Yogsutras*, commonly known as *Patanjal Yog Darshan* or *Yog Shastra* (Chitrao 1964:382-385). He is also regarded as an avatar of Sheshnag, the divine serpent. Yet some scholars believe that the latter and the grammarian are the same person. Others even identify him with the physician.

Yog Darshan has been famed since very ancient times. It is cited in the Yajnavalkya Smruti. The Rg Veda, Upanishads, Puranas and Smruti texts have expounded on Yog or Yog sadhana. The Bhagvad Gita gives clear guidance on Yog and that is why it is also named a Yogshastra. Every chapter ends with: *Brahmavidyāyām Yogshastre*. However, it was Maharshi Patanjali who gave Yog Darshan a concise form in his *Yog Sutras*. Veda Vyas (3000 BCE) wrote a commentary on it. Modern scholars give varying dates for the composition of the *Yog Sutras*: 100 BCE, 200 BCE, 450 BCE and 3000 BCE.

Patanjali's Yog Darshan

The word 'Yog' is derived from the Sanskrit root *yuj* which means 'to join', 'to merge'. The association of the *jivatma (atma)* with Paramatma is Yog – *yuj samyoge*.

The Yog that has become vogue in recent decades, especially in the West, is *hatha* Yog, commonly mispronounced yoga. This concerns itself with perfecting physical health and purity with the aid of 84 *asans* (postures) and pranayam (control of *pran* through breath). Patanjal Yog, also known as Raj Yog, focuses on controlling the mind by the will and the gradual suppression of the *chitta–vrutti*: *yogashchittavruttinirodhaha (1/2)*

Raj Yog aims to eliminate all sources of disturbance to the mind, whether external or internal and makes it accessible and responsive to the spiritual reality within the *atma*. Patanjal Yog offers a way of extracting man from his nature, in which the mind, life and body are imprisoned. This state of *atma*–realisation is the fruit of Patanjal Yog, which he divides into eight limbs – *angs*. Therefore, it is also known as Ashtang Yog (see below).

The treatise of 195 *sutras* is divided into four books: *Samadhipaad, Sadhanapaad, Vibhutipaad* and *Kaivalyapaad*.

Patanjal Yog was often combined with other systems of *atma* or Paramatma realisation. The basic principles of purification, orientation and concentration remained, while incorporating other techniques and powers. Even the objectives were widened. This was the case with tantrics, who developed their own Yog systems, such as, *Kundalini, Laya,* Mantra, etc., in which they incorporated the essentials of Ashtang Yog. It was these Yog systems that Buddhists took abroad to Tibet, China and Japan, where they underwent modification.

Patanjali's Ashtang Yog

1.	*Yam* (constraints)	This step comprises five factors: i. *Ahimsa,* ii. *Satya* (truth), iii. *Asteya* (refraining from taking what belongs to others), iv. *Brahmacharya* (eight–fold celibacy), v. *Aparigrah* (detachment).
2.	*Niyam* (injunctions)	This step also comprises five factors: i. *Shauch* (purity), ii. *Santosh* (contentment), iii. *Tapas* (austerities), iv. *Swadhyay* (study of shastras), v. *Ishwar Pranidhan* (bhakti and *upasana* of Paramatma).
3.	*Asan* (postures)	To master a posture *(asan)* in which one is stable and comfortable *(Sthirasukhamāsanam–2/46).* The right *asan* is one in which the body remains stationary for a considerable period without restlessness.

4.	*Pranayam* (control of pran)	Pran is the vital air or life force; *āyām* means 'the spread of'. Pran, mind and body are interlinked. Regulation of pran induces steadiness in the body, controls the wavering mind and promotes serenity in the body. Pranayam also purifies subtle nerve channels known as *nadis*. This promotes flow of pran in the body. This rectifies all irregulated currents, thus harmonising the system.
5.	*Pratyahar* (withdrawal of senses)	This is the control of the senses (eyes, ears, nose, tongue and skin) by the mind, and diverting them inwards from their respective objects. These five steps of *yam, niyam, asan,* pranayam and *pratyahar* are the *bahirang* – external limbs of Yog. The remaining three are *antarang* – internal limbs.
6.	*Dharana* (concentration)	This means concentrating the mind on the object of meditation. The word 'concentration' used for *dharana* has a different meaning in the science of Yog compared to Western psychology. In the latter, the mind cannot be made to remain fixed on any object for any considerable time. It is just a controlled movement of the mind within a limited field. Concentration in Yog psychology begins with the controlled movement of the mind and can reach a state in which all movements cease. The mind becomes one with the essential nature of the

		object concentrated upon and can move no further. The main endeavour in *dharana* is keeping the mind continuously engaged on the object and to bring it back on track immediately when concentration breaks.
7.	Dhyan (meditation)	This is an extension and intensification of *Dharana*. This is the uninterrupted flow (of the mind) towards the object of meditation. When the *sadhak* succeeds in completely eliminating all distractions and concentrating on the object uninterruptedly for as long as he wishes, he masters the stage of dhyan. Therefore the only difference between *dharana* and dhyan is the occasional appearance of distractions in the former.
8.	Samadhi (trance)	This is an advanced stage of dhyan. It is a state in which only the consciousness of the object of meditation remains and not of the mind itself.

Dharana, Dhyan & Samadhi

Dharana, dhyan and samadhi can be understood better symbolically:

A	= Object of meditation
B, C, D, E, F	= Distractions
(A)	= Object of meditation & mental self–awareness

1. Ordinary thinking: (A) (B) (C) (D) (E) (F)

2. *Dharana*: (A) (B) (A) (A) (C) (A) (A) (B) – distractions decrease

3. Dhyan: A (A) A (A) (A) A (A) (A) (A) – distractions cease & mental self–awareness decreases

4. Samadhi: A A A A A A A – Total cessation of mental self–awareness. Object of meditation alone remains in field of consciousness.

Cautionary note on Patanjali's Pranayam

Pranayam is generally misconstrued to mean either regulation of breath or as a deep breathing exercise. Pranayam is the regulation of pran and not the breath. Pran is a highly specialised kind of composite energy. It does not just exist or flow in the gross physical body but in the subtler *pranmay kosh*, which interpenetrates the gross physical body and works in conjunction with it. Pran flows along well–marked channels into every organ and part of the body, vitalising them in different ways. Its specific functions in different organs and areas of the body have led to its different names. It is the control of this pran and not breathing, which is the aim of pranayam. Breathing is only one of the several manifestations of its action in the physical body. This close connection between pran and breathing enables the *sadhak* to manipulate *pranic* currents by manipulating breathing.

The secret of controlling and manipulating pran through breathing can only be obtained from a competent guru. To practice pranayam by merely reading books is dangerous and may lead to health disorders, insanity or even loss of life (Taimni, 1972: 260). Pranayam should only be practiced under the strict supervision of an adept master, with prior practice of the other Yog disciplines of *yam, niyam* and *asan*.

Powerful effects

Inhalation, retention and exhalation are termed *purak, kumbhak* and *rechak,* respectively. As the duration of the practice of pranayam increases, the *sadhak* increases the period of *kumbhak*, under the guru's guidance. This then leads to startling and powerful experiences. Shri Aurobindo practised pranayam for up to six hours per day. He observed that, "Pranayam makes one's intellect sharper and one's brain quicker." He initially wrote about 200 lines of poetry a month. After practising pranayam, he could compose 200 lines in only half an hour! He remarked, "I felt as if my brain was encircled by a ring of electricity... poetry came like a river and prose like a flood..." (Diwakar 1976: 111–112).

Effects of mastering	
ahimsa	wild animals become tame in the *sadhak's* presence
satya	events transpire according to the *sadhak's* speech i.e. whatever he utters occurs
asteya	despite not wishing for them, he acquires immense riches
brahmacharya	he attains power, increasing virtues, and is able to instill knowledge in his disciples.
aparigrah	gains knowledge of his past, present and future births and their purposes
shauch (external)	the *sadhak* comes to revile his body His desire for attaining pleasure from those of other's ceases. He realises that his body is similar to that of others.
shauch (internal)	his intellect becomes pure, *chitta* attains pleasantness, concentration, control over the senses and becomes eligible for *atmadarshan*
santosh	unlimited happiness
tapas	physical obstacles cease and the yogi attains *siddhis* (mystical powers) such as *anima*, *lagima*, etc., ability to hear and see long distances
swadhyay	attains vision of or meets his *Ishtadeva*,

	rishi or *siddha* guru and they also help him in auspicious endeavours
Ishwar pranidhan	attains *sampragnat* samadhi – and if he wishes, he also acquires knowledge of events at long distance, across time and after death
asan	transcends the pain and discomforts of the dualities of cold-heat, hunger-thirst, etc…
pranayam	the *chitta* becomes pure and the *sadhak* then becomes eligible to practice *dharana*
pratyahar	attains supreme control over his *indriyas*
dharana dhyan samadhi	attains supernormal abilities known as *vibhutis* such as: strength of an elephant, *par kaya pravesh*, walking on - water, a cobweb, a light ray and in air, language of all creatures, etc.

Source: Shah 1995: 241-247.

Patanjal Yog and Swaminarayan Darshan

According to Bhagwan Swaminarayan, one who realises Aksharbrahma and then remains engrossed in Paramatma's *murti* is said to have attained *nirvikalp* samadhi (Vachanamrut Gadhada I-40).

He also advocates realising Paramatma with the collective knowledge from the four shastras - Samkhya, Yog, Vedant and Panchratra (Vachanamrut Gadhada I–52). He further points out that the Yog shastra considers Paramatma who has a definite form, as the twenty-sixth element, while *jiva-ishwar* is the twenty–fifth. And one should meditate on Bhagwan realising one's *atma* to be distinct from those elements (Yog *Sutras* 1/24–27).

As mentioned earlier, Patanjal Yog's ultimate aim is to control the *chitta–vrutti* (mind). However, in the Vachanamrut (Vartal–12, 20 and Gadhada III–1), Bhagwan Swaminarayan – who mastered Ashtang Yog in the Himalayas at the age of fourteen – points out that control of *chitta* is not the final aim of sadhana to attain Paramatma. He reveals that even after controlling it and achieving samadhi – the final fruition of Ashtang Yog – the seeds of *vasana* remain. This *vasana* can hinder samadhi and bring a *sadhak* (person endeavouring) out of samadhi. True samadhi, also known as *nirvikalp* samadhi, is achieved when the *chitta* detaches itself from all other desires except Paramatma (becomes *nirvasanic*) and attains Yog (union) with Him. The *sadhak* is then said to have mastered Ashtang Yog, without having resorted to Ashtang Yog (Gadhada I–25). As an example, Bhagwan Swaminarayan cites the Gopis, whose *chitta* became engrossed solely in Shri Krishna.

To become desireless – *nirvasanic* – Bhagwan Swaminarayan advocates *satsang* and bhakti. Shri Krishna also advocates *satsang* in preference to all other endeavours, including Ashtang Yog in the Bhagvatam (11.12.1,2). *Satsang* means obeying the *brahmanishth* and *shrotriya* Satpurush. Bhakti involves the process of becoming *brahmarup* (Shikshapatri 116) and offering intense devotion to Paramatma, with a full–fledged realisation of His *mahatmya* – greatness and glory (Shikshapatri 103). This path is known as *Ekantik* bhakti and *Ekantik* dharma and is a more practical and easy method of attaining moksha and realising Paramatma, than through Patanjali's Ashtang Yog.

During His period, by His Divine powers, Bhagwan Swaminarayan graced countless devotees and animals, birds and fish with *krupa* samadhi. In this state they had His darshan in the divine resplendence of Akshardham, as well as in the form of other avatars - a phenomenon unique in the history of Sanatan Dharma. His third spiritual successor, Shastriji Maharaj, too, graced samadhi to devotees in Amdavad, which was witnessed by many and verified by a Polish visitor in India, Morris Friedman. He then published his findings in the local news media.

Patanjali's Yog Sutras

Ahimsāpratishthāyām tattsannidhau vairatyāgah 2/35
When harmlessness and kindness are mastered by the yogi,
there is a complete absence of enmity, both in men and
animals.

•

Satyapratishthāyām kriyāfalāshrayatwam 2/36
When a yogi masters truth in mind, speech and body, all
his actions bear supreme fruit and they affect all living
creatures.

•

Brahmacharyapratishthāyām viryalabhah 2/38
When a yogi masters brahmacharya he gains strength in
body and mind.

•

*Sattvashuddhisaumanasyaikāgrayendriyajayātmadarshanayogyat
wāni cha* 2/41
From purity of mind and body, a yogi attains mental
goodness, concentration, control over the senses and fitness
to contemplate upon the *atma* and Paramatma.

•

Santoshādanuttamasukhlābhah 2/42
By perfecting contentment the yogi attains supreme
happiness.

•

Samādhisiddhirishwarpranidhānāt 2/45
By greater devotion to Paramatma a yogi attains samadhi.

•

Sthirsukhamāsanam 2/46
An *asan* is that posture in which the yogi is steady and
pleasant.

15. Shankaracharya

(Advait)

The founder of Advait Vedant philosophy, Bhagvadpad Shankar was born on Vaishakh *sud* 5, Samvat 844 (788 CE) in Kaladi, a village in Kerala. His father, Shivaguru, was a Nambudri Brahmin, and mother was named Aryamba. Prior to Shankar's birth, the childless couple fervently prayed to Shivji in a mandir at Tirucchur. Shivji blessed the couple that he himself would be born as their son. Hence, the child was named Shankar.

From birth Shankar exhibited astounding intelligence. By the age of two he studied the Purans and other texts. At the age of five he was given *yagnopavit* samskar (sacred thread), and sent to study at the guru's ashram. By the age of eight he had studied the Vedas and other shastras. Noting the boy's ascetic inclination, his mother decided to arrange an early marriage. However Shankar, not the least interested in mundane life, requested her permission to become an ascetic. She refused, saying that there was nobody except him to look after her. Shankar respected her decision, yet yearned to become an ascetic and embark on his mission to save Sanatan Dharma. One morning, soon after, when both went to bathe in the nearby Churna river, a crocodile grabbed his leg. He cried out to his mother that if she willingly gave permission for his *samnyas*, the crocodile would release him. Horrified at the thought of him being killed in such a hideous manner, she reluctantly granted permission. The crocodile instantly released him.

He then set off in search of a true guru. After meeting many sadhus, he arrived at the cave of Bhagvadpad Govind, disciple of the famous Gaudapad, on the banks of the Narmada. Shankar stood at the entrance of his cave. When Govindpad opened his eyes after emerging from samadhi, he asked the child, "Who are you?"

Shankar respectfully replied by composing ten Sanskrit shloks. Their essential import was, "I am not the earth, nor water, nor fire, nor wind, nor space. I am *chidanandrup* Shiv; I am pure consciousness, the *atma*."

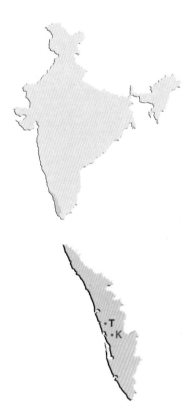

T – Thrissur
K – Kaladi

Delighted with the reply, Govindpad initiated him as his disciple. When Shankar requested a *diksha* mantra, Govindpad imparted four mantras, one from each Veda:

Rg Veda	*Pragnānam* Brahman	Knowledge is Brahman
Yajur Veda	*Aham brahmāsmi*	I am Brahman,
Sam Veda	*Tattvamasi*	You are that Brahman
Atharva Veda	*Ayamātmā* Brahman	This *atma* is Brahman.

After imparting him wisdom, Govindpad commanded him to go to Kashi to write commentaries on the *Prasthantrayi – Brahma Sutras, Upanishads* and Gita. This he accomplished at the remarkably young age of sixteen. Attracted by his supreme erudition, countless ascetics became his disciples. Of these, four were prominent: Sanand, Mandan Mishra (Sureshwar), Totakacharya and Hastamalak.

Once in Kashi, on his way to the Vishwanath mandir for Mahadev's darshan, Shankar politely requested a raggedly dressed *chandal* (low *varna* man) with four dogs to move aside. The man replied whether he should move the body or the *atma*? "If it is the body, your body and mine are of the same composition, of flesh, blood and bones. If it is the *atma*, then the *atma* is the same in everyone." This reply startled Shankar. He realised that this man was none other than Shiv himself and the four dogs were the four Vedas. He prostrated instantly. He expressed this divine realisation – *sakshatkar* – of Vishwanath by composing a pentad verse known as *Manish Panchakam*. When he raised his head, the *chandal* and the dogs had vanished!

On another occasion, on the banks of Ganga in Kashi, Shankar heard a scholar vociferously repeating a grammatical rule. He advised the pundit that on his death, the rule would not help him. It would be wiser to chant the holy name of Govind. Shankar versified this (in thirty–one shloks) in the famed melodious and devotional bhajan known as *Mohamudgara*, with the opening stanza *Bhaj Govindam...* – "Worship Govind, worship Govind, worship Govind, O fool! When the appointed time (death) arrives, grammar rules surely will not save you." 'Grammar rules' signifies mundane knowledge and possessions and *bhaj* means service – offering love and devotion to Paramatma by total surrender. This essentially means *navdha* bhakti. In the *Vivekchudamani* (31) he also says that among the ways of moksha, bhakti holds the supreme position:

Mokshakāranasāmagrayām bhaktireva–gareeyasi

Shankar's total life works of *stotras* and commentaries amount to about ninety, the prominent being: *Saundaryalahari, Vivekchudamani, Shivanandlahari, Govindashtak, Vishnusahasranam Bhashya,* etc. In the famous *Gurvashtakam Stotras* he emphatically advocates surrender to a true guru to attain *brahmapad* – realising Paramatma. In the eight shloks he declares that: health, wealth, women, fame, power, material pleasures, donations or being sinless, all amount to nought if one does not accept refuge of a guru who has realised Paramatma.

Consolidating Sanatan Dharma

During his short lifespan of 32 years, Shankar unflaggingly travelled throughout Bharat, at least twice. In all the principal sacred places, he debated and defeated Shaiv, Vaishnav, Shakta and Vama Marg pundits who had propagated falsities about Vedic injunctions and deities and misguided people onto the path of sensual pleasures. In addition to these debates, by his commentaries, he also defeated the Buddhist and Jain pundits whose corrupt practices and *shunyavād* had nearly choked Sanatan Dharma's pristine ideals and glory. With supreme logic and erudition he outwitted the deluded.

By his incessant travels, debates and teachings throughout Bharat, he re–united Bharat's people, saving them from ignorance, superstition, blind faith and fanaticism. To ensure that his efforts survived over the ages, he established four monastic orders in the four corners of Bharat – Jyotir Math in Badri–Kedar (north), Govardhan Pith at Jagannath Puri (east), Shrungeri Math at Shrungeri (south) and Sharda Pith at Dwarka (west). The head of each is also known as

Shankaracharya. This tradition established by *Adi* Shankar is so sound that 1200 years of tumult and foreign incursions have not dented it. On the contrary it flourishes vibrantly.

An incident in his life concerning a debate with a stalwart scholar named Vachaspati Mandan Mishra, throws light about the great erudition of women then and the spirit of integrity. When Shankar proposed a debate with Mandan Mishra the question arose of who would preside as judge. Mandan suggested his wife, Bharati. Shankar agreed. In the debate, Shankar defeated Mandan. Without feeling hurt about her husband being defeated, Bharati declared Shankar as victorious. However, as Mandan's wife, she was his *ardhangna* – half body. Therefore Bharati would only consider him to be a true victor provided he defeated her in a debate as well. Shankar agreed, with Mandan presiding as judge! Shankar defeated Bharati and Mandan declared him victorious.

Shankar's Advait & Bhagwan Swaminarayan

Shankar's Advait Vedant – non dualism (or absolute monism) – believes that this world is an illusion (maya); only Brahman (Parabrahma) is the ultimate Reality and the *jiva* is not different from Brahman:

Brahman satyam jaganmithyā jivo brahmaiva nāparaha.

Shankar believes in *jivanmukti*, achieved solely by knowledge – *jnan marg* – when the *jiva* realises, "I am He." 'He' denotes Brahman – the highest Reality.

Unlike Shankar, who believes in only one reality, Bhagwan Swaminarayan believes in five eternal realities: *jiva, ishwar, maya, Brahman* and *Parabrahma*. His philosophy is known as *Swaminarayan* Darshan. He also accepts *jivanmukti*, in which the *jiva* becomes *Brahmarup (Aksharrup)* by association with the manifest form of Aksharbrahma. The liberated *jiva*, known as *Akshar mukta*, then offers bhakti to Parabrahma–Purushottam – the Supreme Reality. The *mukta* does not become Aksharbrahma, nor merges with him. Additionally, the *swami–sevak* relationship always prevails between Purushottam and the *mukta* and between Purushottam and Aksharbrahma.

In Vachanamrut Gadhada I–42, Bhagwan Swaminarayan summarises Shankar's philosophy and highlights its true import by clarifying misinterpretations of later scholars. He says that Vedantists regard the moral do's and don'ts (*vidhi* and *nishedh*), *swarg* and *narak*, disciples who attain them and the guru, as false. However, Shankaracharya commanded his disciples to keep a staff and a gourd, to recite the Gita, *Vishnusahasranam*, to perform Vishnu's *pujan*, for the young to respect the elders, and to beg alms from pious Brahmins.

Shankar's principle that, 'There is only Brahman and besides that everything including, *jiva, ishwar,* maya, etc., are false,' is only meant for one who has attained the *nirvikalp* state. One who has not realised this state, who performs all worldly activities, believes them to be real and yet negates *vidhi* and *nishedh*, is a *nastik*.

Bhagwan Swaminarayan further clarifies, "...it was because of the apprehension that such a *nastik* nature may creep into people's hearts that Shankaracharya composed *Bhaj Govindam* and many other shloks praising Vishnu. He also composed shloks extolling Shivji, Ganapati, Surya and many other deities. After hearing these shloks, all deities appear to be *satya*."

"Vedantis also claim, 'Everything is pervaded by Brahman.' However just as the Gopis developed affection for Shri Krishna, similarly, all women develop affection for their husbands and men for their wives. Yet they do not attain what the Gopis attained; instead, they attain dismal *narak* (hell). Therefore, the prescribed moral do's and don'ts are indeed true, not false. Whosoever falsifies them will be consigned to *narak*."

16. Ramanujacharya
(Vishishtadvait)

Ramanuj was a great sadhu of the Sri Vaishnav tradition
of South India. He founded the Vishishtadvait philosophy after
writing his *SriBhashya* commentary on the *Brahma Sutras*. He
was born in 1017 CE, in Sriperumbudur, a village thirteen miles
southwest of Chennai. Considered as an incarnation of
Lakshman, Ramanuj exhibited astonishing intelligence from
childhood. At sixteen he married. Around this time he became
a pupil of Yadavprakash of Kanchi. However the guru rigidly
believed in non–dualism *(Advait)* – not accepting Paramatma
with form. Endowed with bhakti, Ramanuj ardently believed
in Paramatma having a form. This often led to differences of
opinion between the guru and pupil. Once Yadavprakash
interpreted Chhandogya Upanishad's description of
Paramatma's eyes, *kapyasam*, as the red posterior of a monkey.
Tears of grief rolled down Ramanuj's cheeks. He then gave the
true meaning: Paramatma's eyes are like the lovely lotuses
(kapih) blossomed by the sun.

After several such differences, Yadavprakash instructed his
other disciples to drown Ramanuj in the Ganga. However
Govind, Ramanuj's cousin, divulged the plot to Ramanuj. The
latter then walked away into the forest at night. A few days
later he met a couple who were bird hunters, who led him to
the outskirts of Kanchi. Here the couple requested him to
fetch some water from a well. When he returned, the couple
had vanished without trace. It dawned on him that they were
Bhagwan Varadaraj (Vishnu) and consort Lakshmidevi – the
consecrated *murtis* at Kanchipuram. Thereafter Ramanuj
always used water from that well in his daily puja rituals.

In Kanchi, Ramanuj met and associated with a mystic
named Kanchipurna. The latter was a realised devotee of Sri
Varadaraj, and was highly venerated by the people of Kanchi.
Around this time, Yamunacharya, the head of the Srirangam
Math, lay on his deathbed. He had heard about Ramanuj's

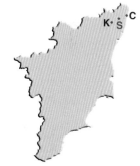

C – *Chennai*
S – *Sriperumbudur*
K – *Kanchi*

brilliance and so wished to bequeath his seat to him. For this purpose he sent one of his disciples. However when Ramanuj reached Srirangam, Yamunacharya had just passed away. Ramanuj fainted. After recovering he vowed to fulfil the mystic's three wishes to offer respects to Veda Vyas and Parashar rishi, pay tribute to Nammalvar and write the *Sri Bhashya* to explain the Vishishtadvait philosophy.

At the age of 32, Ramanuj took *samnyas*. On this occasion, as divinely commanded by Varadaraj, Kanchipurna addressed him as *Yatiraja* – king among ascetics. Realising Ramanuj's greatness and after debating with him, Yadavprakash – the former guru – accepted him as guru! Ramanuj commanded him to write a Vaishnav text. Then aged 80, Yadavprakash wrote the *Yatidharmasamucchya*.

Ramanuj continued studying, as well as travelling throughout India. He preached the path of bhakti and *prapatti* – absolute devotion and surrender to Paramatma. He visited the Sharda Math and obtained a copy of the *Bodhayan–Vritti*, an Advait commentary on the *Brahma Sutras*. Then with his disciple, Kuresh, he made his way towards Srirangam. When the mandir authorities found the book missing, they chased him and took the book back. However while the book was with them Kuresh had read and memorised it! Later he scribed it. After reading this, Ramanuj composed the *Sri Bhashya*, which refuted Bodhayan's Advait doctrine and propounded *upasana* and bhakti. This doctrine came to be known as *Vishishtadvait* – qualified monism.

During this time in Tamil Nadu, there reigned the Chola king Koluttunga I, also known as Rajendra Chola. He was a staunch Shaivite. To those who didn't accept Shaivism, he imposed the death penalty. Hence Ramanuj, then about 78, fled to Mysore in Karnatak. This changed the religious history of South India. By his preachings, thousands of Jains became Vaishnavs. The Hoyshala king, Bittideva, a Jain, also accepted Sri Vaishnavism. Ramanuj renamed him Vishnuvardhan, who then built the magnificent mandir of Keshav at Belur. Ramanuj also stayed in Melukote, where he restored and consecrated a mandir dedicated to Selvapillai (Narayan) in 1099. Here he founded a *math*, known as *Yatiraja Math* (king of ascetics) the name by which followers adored him. Two decades later, in 1118, he returned to Srirangam. He continued composing Sanskrit texts and established 74 Piths in different parts of the country to propagate the Vishishtadvait philosophy. This effectively reduced the influence of the Advait philosophy propagated by Shankar. At the grand age of 120, in 1137, he passed away and departed to Shridham.

Ramanuj composed nine Sanskrit works: *Vedarth Sangrah, Sri Bhashya, Gita Bhashya, Vedant–deep, Vedant–sar, Sharnagati Gadya, Srirang Gadya, Sri Vaikunth Gadya* and *Nitya Granth*. In the first text he elaborated the flaws in the teachings of Advait, *Bhed–abhed* and Shaivism.

Ramanuj's greatest contribution to Sanatan Dharma was that he re–established and consolidated the path of bhakti and *sharnagati* to Parabrahma. Though Shankar had advocated bhakti in his *Bhaj Govindam stotras*, his later followers misled people by propounding only the path of *jnan* – knowledge. They brushed aside the observances of *vidhi* and *nishedh*. Falsely regarding themselves as Brahman, they indulged in material pursuits, without fear of the fruits of their sinful karmas. This culminated in spiritual decadence at the individual and societal levels.

Ramanuj and Bhagwan Swaminarayan

Bhagwan Swaminarayan's guru, Ramanand Swami, was given Vaishnavi *diksha* by Ramanujacharya in a divine form in a dream. The *acharya* then commanded Swami to teach Vaishnavism in the north.

In the Shikshapatri, Bhagwan Swaminarayan has favoured Ramanuj's Vishishtadvait (121) and considered his *Sri Bhashya* and *Gita Bhashya* as authoritative for acquiring *adhyatmic* (spiritual) knowledge (100). During Bhagwan Swaminarayan's *Kalyan Yatra*, He specially visited Srirangam, Sriperumbudur and met Jiyar Swami in Totadri. He accepted Vishishtadvait's

Tattvatraya (three eternal realities) – *jiva, jagat* (maya) and *ishwar*. However, He differentiated Aksharbrahma from Parabrahma and believed in five eternal realities. His philosophy is known as Swaminarayan Darshan.

Since Vishishtadvait was favoured by Bhagwan Swaminarayan over all other philosophies, it is of importance to consider the similarities and differences between Vishishtadvait and Swaminarayan Darshan.

Ramanuj's Vishishtadvait

1. Three eternal realities – *jiva (chit)*, *jagat (achit* or maya) and *Ishwar* (Parabrahma).

2. Parabrahma is independent and yet controller of both *chit* and *achit*.

3. Shri Vishnu, Shri Narayan, Shri Vasudev, Shri Krishna, are all considered as Parabrahma.

4. Parabrahma has five forms: *Para, Vyuh, Antaryami, Vibhav* and *Archa*.

5. Paramatma's divine abode is Vaikunth. It is not a separate reality. It is made of pure *sattva* and is a divine playing field. It does not accompany Bhagwan wherever He incarnates. Vaikunth does not uphold infinite universes.

6. Vaikunth comprises divine gardens, rivers, mountains, fauna and divine objects to fulfil desires.

7. The gender factor prevails in Vaikunth. Lakshmi and Narayan are a divine couple. Additionally Vaikunth has *muktas* eternally liberated from maya, such as Vishwaksen and Garud.

8. Vaikunth is not Bhagwan's *sevak*. Nor does it serve Bhagwan in any other form. The *jiva* does not have to become one with it for mukti. Nor is it needed to realise Bhagwan's glory. Lakshmiji helps the *jiva* to attain Parabrahma, but she is not *dhamrup*. There is no reference to the need of becoming *Lakshmi–rup*. In Vaikunth, she only recommends the *mukta* to be accepted by Parabrahma. She accompanies Bhagwan

on earth, but later He does not remain manifest through her.

9. At the time of death, only the gross body is shed. Bhagwan does not arrive to collect the *jiva*. Only *muktas* arrive to take the *jiva*. When he passes through other abodes on the *Archimarg*, the devas of those abodes honour him. He then bathes in the river Virja, when he sheds his subtle and causal body. He then attains a four–armed divine body of pure *sattva* by divine touch. Vaikunth's *muktas* then bring him to the divine throne of Lakshmi–Narayan, where Lakshmi recommends him to Narayan, who then accepts him.

10. Creation occurs only by Bhagwan's wish. Lakshmiji or a *mukta* does not play a direct or indirect part in it.

11. Besides having Bhagwan's darshan, the *mukta* assumes other forms: a *mugat* (crown), *paduka*, wisp, etc. to serve Paramatma. Apart from Paramatma's bliss, the *mukta* avails of the other divine forms of enjoyment.

12. There is no specific injunction of becoming *brahmarup* to offer bhakti. Bhakti is mainly offered to Paramatma's *antaryami* or *archa (murti)* forms.

13. Dual *upasana* of Lakshmi and Narayan is offered on earth and in Vaikunth, – *upasana* is always of four *charan* (feet).

14. The *sanchit* karmas of a bhakta are removed only at the time of death. Until death both the *sanchit* and *prarabdha* karmas remain.

15. Spiritual fulfillment (*purnakampanu*) is not in attaining or realising Paramatma manifest. The *archa* and *antaryami* forms are offered puja and bhakti. The bhakta's craving of, 'when shall I reach Paramatma's abode and have His darshan?' remains.

16. *Videha* mukti only. i.e. liberation only after shedding the physical body.

Swaminarayan Darshan

1. Five eternal realities: *jiva*, *ishwar*, maya, Aksharbrahma and Parabrahma.

2. Parabrahma is independent and yet controller of *jiva*, *ishwar*, maya and Aksharbrahma.

3. Parabrahma Purushottam is Bhagwan Swaminarayan who transcends all, including Lakshmi Narayan.

4. Parabrahma has four forms: *Para*, *Antaryami*, *Archa* and *manushya* – *vigrahdhari* – manifestation as human form. While residing in Akshardham, Parabrahma Himself manifests as a human, but not as other avatars or *chaturvyuh* forms.

5. Paramatma's divine abode is Akshardham. It is an individual reality, separate from the other four realities. It is the ideal *sevak* (servant) of Purushottam. It incarnates wherever Parabrahma incarnates in human form. It is also the support and beholder of infinite universes as *chidakash*.

6. Akshardham does not have any such divine objects. It is composed totally of divine *chidakash* (light).

7. Akshardham has only divine, liberated *muktas*, devoid of gender. Only Parabrahma and Aksharbrahma eternally transcend maya. There are no *nitya muktas* who are eternally above maya.

8. Aksharbrahma serves Purushottam as His ideal Bhakta. It is obligatory to become *Akshar–rup* to offer devotion to Purushottam. For this, Aksharbrahma in the form of the ever present *Param Ekantik Satpurush* is a necessary medium to help the *jiva* transcend maya and to instill in it the knowledge of Parabrahma's glory and greatness. He is the gateway and key to mukti and attaining Parabrahma. He is also the ideal of bhakti and *seva*. After incarnating on earth, Parabrahma manifests through Aksharbrahma.

9. Either Parabrahma alone, or with Aksharbrahma and *Akshar muktas*, arrives in a divine vehicle to take the

jiva at the time of death. At death, the *jiva* sheds both the gross and subtle bodies and attains a divine human form, with two hands, made of Akshar *tattva*.

10. Creation begins when one *Akshar mukta* pairs with *Prakriti*, after Aksharbrahma – who is inspired by Parabrahma – looks at him in Akshardham.

11. In Akshardham, the *mukta* does not assume any other divine object to serve Bhagwan. His bhakti, *seva* and *kainkarya* (servant) *bhav* are all encompassed in Bhagwan's divine and incessant darshan. Here the *mukta* enjoys Bhagwan's divine bliss.

12. Bhakti is advocated along with the three factors of dharma, *jnan* and *vairagya*. It should be offered by becoming *brahmarup*. Moreover, it is emphasised to offer bhakti to the *pratyaksh* and visual form either to Bhagwan Himself or His Satpurush.

13. After becoming *Akshar–rup,* bhakti and *upasana* are offered on earth and in Akshardham to only Parabrahma, i.e. *upasana* is of only two *charan* (feet).

14. The *sanchit* karmas of a bhakta are dissolved by *sharnagati, upasana* and unflinching *nishtha* in Bhagwan or His Satpurush, in addition to offering *seva* and bhakti by their commands. To cleanse these karmas, the bhakta does not have to wait till death. Only the *prarabdha* karmas remain. These too, are resolved by Bhagwan's wishes i.e. His wish becomes the bhakta's *prarabdha*. (Vachanamrut Gadhada III–13).

15. *Purnakampanu* is through attaining and realising Bhagwan manifest – either Himself or through His Satpurush. The belief that one is not redeemed or become spiritually fulfilled until one does not have the darshan of Bhagwan in His *dham* is strongly negated.

16. *Videha* mukti and for some *jivan* mukti. *Jivan muktas* are *nirvasanic*, have become *brahmarup* and have realised Parabrahma while still alive.

17. Nimbarkacharya
(Dvaitadvait)

R – Raichur
B – Bellary

The founder of the Dvaitadvait (Bhedabhed) school of Vedant philosophy, Nimbarkacharya, was also known as Nimaditya and Niyamanand. He was born a Telugu Brahmin in the village of Nimba or Nimbpura in the Bellary district of Karnatak. Scholars give different dates for his life period. From an analysis of Nimbark's *bhashya*, whose style in several places resembles that of Ramanuj's *bhashya*, it is apparent that he certainly lived after Ramanuj. One reference cites that Devacharya, a disciple and contemporary of Nimbark was 36 years younger than Ramanuj (1017–1137). Therefore Nimbark's period is considered between 1028 to 1125 CE. Also it disproves the assumption by some scholars that Nimbark post–dated Madhvacharya, since the latter's period is 1199 to 1279 CE. Nimbark was born on Vaishakh *sud* 3 – Akhatrij.

Harivyasdev's commentary on Nimbark's *Dashashloki*, cites Nimbark's father's name as Jagannath and mother's as Saraswati. From childhood he was a devotee of Krishna. He later settled with his parents in Vrundavan, near Mount Govardhan. In the Nimbark Sampraday, it is believed that he was an incarnation of either Vishnu's *sudarshan chakra* or Surya.

The *Bhaktamal* text by Nabhadas cites the arrival of a Jain Udasis sadhu at Nimbark's ashram, near Vrundavan. Both entered into a scholarly debate on Brahman. An invitation for food only arrived after twilight. The Jain sadhu declined to eat, saying that his vow did not allow food after sunset. Pained by this, Nimbark sat in meditation and prayed to Paramatma. In response, Paramatma placed His *sudarshan chakra* over the sunset. This created bright sunlight, and the sun appeared as if it was over the neem tree, under which both were seated. Seeing this, the Jain sadhu agreed to have food. The moment he finished, night shrouded the sky. The sadhu attributed this supernatural event to Niyamanand. On departing, he said,

"By the might of your bhakti you showed the sun to me on top of the neem tree. Henceforth, you will be famed as Nimbark and Nimbaditya." *Nimb* in Sanskrit denotes the neem tree. He showed many other miracles and preached the path of bhakti, dharma and darshan. For the first time since Shri Krishna's demise, he introduced *mādhurya* bhakti (melodious devotion) of Shri Krishna with Radha, with the attitude of a female friend – *sakhi–bhav*. In his principle of bhakti, he has shown five factors worth knowing *(gneya)*: (1) *upasya–rup* – the form of Bhagwan; (2) *upasak* – the devotee; (3) *krupa–fal* – the fruit of grace; (4) bhakti–*ras* – devotional sentiment; and (5) *virodhi* – factors hampering devotion.

For the *jiva's* ultimate goal he declared,

Nānyāgatihi Shri Krishna padāravindāt

– there is no other final goal than the lotus–feet of Shri Krishna. One on whose left is Shri Radhikaji with a thousand of her *Gopi* companions, is to be offered *mādhurya* bhakti with the sentiment of *sakhi–bhav*. He advocated this on the Vedic injunction of *ras upasana* i.e. *raso vai saha*. For him Shri Krishna himself is *ras–rup* Paramatma.

In the Nimbark Sampraday, the emphasis is on worship of Radha–Krishna during all the eight *pahors* (divisions) of the day. The relationship between Radha and Shri Krishna is interdependent; one cannot survive without the other. Although they are two by name, by form they are one. While Shri Krishna is *anandswarup* (bliss), Radha's bliss is Shri Krishna:

Ek swarup sadā dwe nām,
Anand ki āhlādini Shyāmā,
Ahlādini ke ānand Shyām. (Mahavani)

According to Shri Harivyasdevacharya, only an aspirant who successfully passes through the following ten steps becomes eligible for *nitya vihār raspān* – joy of the eternal sentiment of loving devotion: (1) service of the devotees, (2) mercy towards all creatures, (3) total faith in the conduct enjoined by the Sampraday, (4) listening tirelessly to Paramatma's *katha*, (5) affection for the lotus–feet of Paramatma and love towards the form to be worshipped, (6) heartfelt love of Paramatma, (7) meditation on Radha–Krishna, (8) singing bhajans about His virtues, (9) firm faith in one's devotional sentiment and (10) being wholly drenched in the supreme sentiment of divine love.

Nimbark's greatest contribution to the Bhakti movement and *upasana* of Bhagwan along with his foremost bhakta, is that he was the first to establish Shri Radhikaji on Shri Krishna's left side (Sharma 2003:45). He cites this in his *Dashashloki*:

Ange tu vāme vrushabhānujām mudrā, virājamānāmarupa – saubhagām…

– Vrushabhanu's daughter Radhaji is joyously presiding on the left...

Dvaita–Advait philosophy

Dvaita–advait means dualistic non–dualism. Like Ramanuj, Nimbark believes in three eternal realities; Brahman (Ishwar), *chit* (*jiva*) and *achit* (*jagat*), a relation of identity–in–difference. Whereas Brahman for Ramanuj and Madhva is Narayan or Vishnu, for Nimbark He is Shri Krishna with Radha. This Brahman is omniscient, omnipotent and the ultimate cause.

Brahman has two aspects: the majestic and the sweet. He is all–powerful yet all–merciful, transcendent yet immanent, all–pervading yet residing in the heart of man. He essentially graces devotees and helps the deserving ones to attain moksha by enabling them to have a direct vision of Himself (*sakshatkar*). He also incarnates Himself on earth for their guidance.

For Nimbark, all five sadhanas lead to moksha, and are to be resorted to either separately or jointly. Not only does he enjoin performance of external rites and rituals, but also the inner cultivation of the supreme attributes of self–control, purity, simplicity and the like. For Nimbark, both the householder and the ascetic can realise Brahman, provided each performs his duties in a disinterested, unselfish spirit. It is the spirit with which one does one's duties that counts.

Foremost, Nimbark extolled *mādhurya–pradhān* bhakti – an intimate relation of love (*prem*) and friendship (*sakhi–bhav*) between bhakta and Paramatma, while Ramanuj emphasised *aishvarya–pradhān* bhakti – a distant relation of awe and reverence. Though Bhagwan Swaminarayan upholds such *rasik* bhakti propounded by great *acharyas*, He points out a potential pitfall in Vachanamrut Gadhada I–26 and Gadhada II–3, which can lead to a bhakta's downfall. This pitfall is *dehabhav*. Therefore, to offer true *rasik* bhakti, without falling, He advocates and upholds Nimbark's (Madhva's and Vallabh's, too) principle of *brahmaswarup priti* in Vachanamrut Gadhada II–43 (*Siddhantpradeep Tika* 11/18/46, 11/25/35). This means to offer bhakti by believing oneself as *brahmarup* or *gunatit* – above the three bodies and three states (Shikshapatri 116). Without this, the bhakta unequivocally succumbs to *dehabhav* and is bound to fall from the path of moksha.

Nimbark's texts

Nimbark's commentary on the *Brahma Sutras* is known as *Vedant Parijat Saurabh*. His disciple, Shrinivas, wrote a commentary on this called *Vedantkaustabh*. Nimbark's other works include *Dashashloki*, *Shri Krishna Stavraj*, *Guruparampara*, *Madhwamukh Mardan*, *Vedant Tattvabodh*, *Vedant Siddhant Pradeep*, *Swadharmadhva Bodh* and *Shri Krishnastava*.

Means to Moksha

According to Nimbark, there are five sadhanas – means to moksha: karma, *jnan, upasana, prapatti* and *gurupasatti.*

1. Karma	performed with *nishkam bhav* (selfless spirit), in accordance with the injunctions of the shastras they purify the mind, which leads to rise of knowledge.
2. *Jnan*	knowledge of Brahman and the self.
3. *Upasana*	meditation of three types: on Brahman as one's self – as the *antaryami* (inner controller) of the sentient; on Brahman as the *antaryami* of the non–sentient; and on Brahman as different from the sentient and the non–sentient. For Nimbark, *upasana* is not a synonym for bhakti as it is for Ramanuj, but a special kind of deep love for Paramatma.
4. *Prapatti*	total self–surrender to Paramatma, to be dependent on Him alone in every way. This does not mean total inaction (*nivrutti*) on the devotee's part. He has to endeavour to do what is liked by Paramatma and avoid what is disliked by Him. This then earns His grace.
5. *Gurupasatti*	self–surrender to the spiritual preceptor and not directly to Paramatma. The guru leads the devotee to Paramatma and does whatever is necessary for the devotee, just as the mother of a suckling child who is ill herself takes medicine to cure her child.

18. Madhvacharya

(Dvait)

Madhvacharya, the founder of the Dvait school of philosophy, was born on Aso *sud* 10 (Vijaya Dashmi), Samvat 1294 (1238 CE). He lived for 79 years and passed away in 1317 CE. The youngest son of one of his foremost disciples wrote his biography a few years after his demise, which provide details of his life.

Madhva was born in Pajak, a village eight miles south–east of modern Udipi in Mysore state. His father, Narayan, was a Nakuntillay Brahmin. Madhva's original name was Vasudev. At the age of seven he underwent *upanayan* samskar. He then studied the Vedas and other shastras from Totacharya. At about sixteen, he accepted *diksha* from guru Achyutpreksh and was named Purnapragna. He then studied *Ishtasiddhi* of Vimuktaman. His guru then appointed him as head of the *math* and re–named him Anandtirth. He also adopted the name 'Madhva' as being synonymous in meaning to Anandtirth. He is believed to be Vayu Dev's third incarnation; the two previous being Hanuman and Bhim.

U – Udipi
P – Pajak
M – Mysore

Madhva then spent time in teaching his disciples, as well as debating with and defeating scholars of Advait, Jain and Buddha *sampradays*. In a span of about three years he defeated scholars throughout south India. He cogently refuted Shankar's Advait beliefs and preferred the Dvait of Bhakti tradition. In Shrirangam he exchanged views with Ramanuj's scholars.

He then visited Badrinath. Here he spent 48 days in fasting, prayer and contemplation. He then felt an inner voice directing him to visit Vyasashram, further north of Badrinath. He visited this mystical place alone. Some months later he returned with greater inspiration from Vyas. This led him to write his *bhashya* on the *Brahma Sutras*.

After returning to Udipi, he debated with and defeated Swami Shastri and Shobhan Bhatt. The two then accepted *diksha* from Madhva. The former was named Narhari Tirth and the latter, Padmanabh Tirth. Soon after, even Achyutpreksh, the former guru became Madhva's disciple, in a similar manner to Yadavprakash who became Ramanuj's disciple. To keep these disciples united, he consecrated Shri Krishna's *murti* in his *math* in Udipi. He advocated offering a ball of rice flour shaped like a sheep in *yagnas* in place of actual animal sacrifice. Brahmins of several *gotras* strongly objected to this. However, Madhva remained firm in his belief. A similar stance against animal sacrifice in *yagnas* occurred some eight centuries later. Bhagwan Swaminarayan established *ahimsac yagnas* by advocating the offering of barley and sesame seeds in *hom,* in early 19th century Gujarat. Madhva also established a strict observance of Ekadashi.

He then performed a second *yatra* of north India. He spent his subsequent years in south India, acquiring new disciples and composing Sanskrit works and commentaries on the ten major Upanishads, the Mahabharat and Bhagvatam. His fame created jealousy among rivals, who instigated stealing his library of valuable reference texts. However he recovered some of these with the help of King Jayasinh of Kumbla. This led to a major debate with the court's Advait Vedant pundit, Trivikram. The debate spanned fifteen days, culminating in Madhva's victory. Trivikram then became his disciple. Madhva consigned him to write a commentary on the *Brahma Sutra Bhashya*. This he did, named *Tattvapradip*. It was his son, Narayan Panditacharya who wrote *Madhvavijay,* Madhva's biography. Madhva then founded eight *maths* in Udipi. On Magh *sud* 9, Samvat 1373 (1317 CE) he left for Vaikunth.

A prolific writer in Sanskrit, Madhva composed 37 works, collectively known as *Sarvamul.*

Madhva's Dvait

Madhva propounded the Dvait school of Vedant. Dvait means dual. This was an antithesis to the Advait of Shankar. While Advait regarded only Brahman as truth and the external world of matter as *mithya* – unreal – Dvait upheld the difference between Brahman and the individual *jiva* and matter. The latter two are completely different between themselves and individual *jivas* also differ from one another fundamentally.

Madhva regards Brahman as the Supreme Reality and advocates its adoration. Hence, his is a school of bhakti, identifying Brahman with Vishnu. He bases this on the Vedic glorification of Vishnu and on the religious tenets of the *Itihasas, Purans* such as the Bhagvatam, and the *Panchratra Agam*. Therefore, Madhva's Dvait is a Vaishnav system of Vedant in the mould of bhakti.

Vishnu's resides in Vaikunthdham with his supreme bhakta, Lakshmi. Madhva propounds *upasana* of Narayan with Lakshmi.

Concept of Moksha

Madhva accepts both *jivan* mukti and *videha* mukti. When the *jiva* observes vows of dharma, develops staunch faith, offers *param* bhakti as *das* and accepts Paramatma's *sharanagati* to please Him, then Paramatma graces the *jiva* with *aparoksh jnan* – direct vision. However, this effort by the jiva undergoes three stages: *shravan* (listening to and learning the shastras), *manan* (critical reflection upon what has been learnt) and *nididhyasan* (meditation on what is intellectually established as true). When *nididhyasan* matures, direct vision results by Paramatma's *krupa*.

For this entire process to be possible, there are two pre-requisites: total *vairagya* – renunciation from all other worldly interests - and karma–Yog – devout performance of actions, ordinary and religious, as inculcated in the Gita. In short, bhakti is based on knowledge, which is facilitated by *vairagya* and karma–Yog.

After attaining mukti, the *mukta* transcends to Vaikunth where he offers *seva* with *dasbhav* to Narayan. Attaining Vaikunth is itself mukti.

Madhva advocates *seva* (serving) Narayan in three ways:

(1) to accept the imprints (*chhap*) of Narayan's weapons on one's body, known as *taptamudra*, (2) to name one's offspring with names of Narayan and (3) ten forms of devotion (bhajan), which can be done physically, mentally and by speech. The four forms of speech are to speak the truth, to speak benevolently (*hitvachan*), to speak soothingly (*priyabhashan*) and to study (*swadhyay*). The three forms of physical bhajan are donating to deserving persons, uplifting the needy and protecting the devout helpless. The three forms of mental bhajan are mercy – on the helpless, *spruha* – to entertain only one wish, that is to become the servant of Narayan, and faith (*shraddha*) in the guru's commands and shastras.

All the foregoing are considered as instrumental bhakti (*sadhanrup*). However the foremost endeavour for moksha is bhakti with intense love with the understanding of the glory and greatness of Narayan devoid of *mayic* attributes (*mahatmyagnanyukta, malrahit, atishay snehyukta pritibhakti*). Hence the sequence for moksha is *sadhanrup* bhakti, followed by *ishwarsakshatkar* after which manifests *param*–bhakti. In this an incessant stream of intense love for Narayan springs forth from the knowledge of His infinite redemptive attributes. Such *premlakshana* bhakti of the *jiva* pleases Narayan immensely. He then showers His grace on the *jiva*, who is then released from *avidya*–maya and attains moksha.

In Vachanamrut Gadhada II–43, Bhagwan Swaminarayan cites Madhva's principle of offering love to Bhagwan by believing oneself as atmarup, as brahmarup. This love is known as brahmaswarup priti (Bhāgvatatāttparyanirnay 2/1/7–9).

After release from their *parabdha* karmas, *jivas* exit their physical bodies and migrate step by step to Vaikunth. During the transcending journey, Brahmā gives a sermon in Satyalok, followed by Vasudev's darshan in Shvetdwip. Finally in, Vaikunth, the *muktas* enjoy four types of *bhog*: *sālokya, sāmipya, sarupya* and *sāyujya*. The *muktas* are without jealousy and other *mayic doshas* and endowed with bliss. Some sing the glory of Narayan.

Madhva's final message to his disciples was from his favourite Aitareya Upanishad: "Do not sit idly, but keep moving. Continue to give sermons to aspirants and propagate true knowledge." To his disciple, Padmanabh Tirth, he entrusted Shri Ramji's *murti* and the *shaligram* given by Vyasdev and instructed him to propagate the Dvait philosophy.

Madhva Sampraday's unique contribution to the religious firmament of India includes the inspiring of the Chaitanya movement of Bengal. Paramhansa Chaitanya came in contact with Advaitanand and Ishwar Puri, both Madhva devotees who acquainted him with the Vaishnav tradition. In 1510, at the age of 24, Chaitanya received *diksha* from Madhva Sampraday's Keshav Bharati, who named him Shri Krishna Chaitanya. During his tour in south India, Chaitanya Mahaprabhu propagated Madhva's principles through sermons and bhajans. It is believed that *nagarkirtan* and *sankirtan* in the Madhva Sampraday were initiated by Chaitanya.

The ascetics of Madhva Sampraday have names ending with Tirth, Bharati and Puri. Madhva founded eight *maths* for his disciples in Udipi. In these he consecrated: Ram–Sita, Lakshman–Sita, Dwibhuj Kaliyadaman, Chaturbhuj Kaliyadaman, Vitthal (Shri Krishna) and others. The main Shri Krishna mandir in Udipi has puja performed by each *math* in rota every year. All eight *maths* are built around the Shri Krishna mandir. In this manner, Udipi is the focal point of the Vaishnav Bhakti sampraday.

During his second pilgrimage of Bharat, he is said to have walked on water without getting wet and, by just looking at the ocean, calmed its thundering rollers. Along with his spiritual powers, he was tall, well built and sturdy, with noble eyes and nose. He was endowed with other virtues: profficiency in several languages, expert in dance, music, poetry, architecture, sports, an expert in wrestling, unbeatable in scriptural debate and propounder of the *upasana* of Lakshmi Narayan.

Madhva's Contributions

Madhvacharya had a predilection for Vaishnav theism. Sharma (1970: 24) posits that, unlike Shankar or Ramanuj before him, "Vishnu had struck deep roots in the Indian spiritual soil and was the link that connected the Vedic with the Upanishadic and the Upanishadic with the Epic and Puranic phases of Hindu throught."

Vede Rāmayane chaiva Purānu Bhārate tathā,
Ādāvante cha madhye cha Vishnehe sarvatva geeyate.

– Harivamsha.

– in the Vedas, Ramayan, Purans and Mahabharat, Vishnu is praised everywhere, in the beginning, in the middle and in the end. He is therefore their central theme.

Even in the Gita (7/19), Vishnu is the Supreme Being: *Vasudevaha sarvam.* Such a legacy in the shastras endeared Vaishnavism to the people which Shaivism, despite its equally pronounced form of theism could not successfully compete with.

Hence, Madhva was inclined towards Vaishnav theism because of its strong historical and philosophical link with Hindu scriptural tradition. With this he consolidated Vedic Sanatan Dharma from within, when its life and solidarity was threatened from an advancing militant horde.

Additionally, "he was the only Vaishnav Acharya who gave full canonical recognition to the worship of Shiva in a spirit of genuine devotion arising from the basic principles of his own philosophy" (Sharma 1970 : 26).

19. Vallabhacharya

(Shuddhadvait)

The founder of the Pushti Sampraday of the Vaishnav tradition, Vallabh, was born at midnight on Chaitra *vad* 11 Samvat 1535 (4 April 1479 CE) in the Champaranya forest near Raipur, in Madhya Pradesh. His Telugu Brahmin parents, Lakshman Bhatt and Illammagaru, were fleeing from an imminent Muslim invasion in Kashi, to their village Kankaravad, on the banks of the Godavari in Andhra Pradesh. Stillborn at eight months, they wrapped him in a cloth and placed him in the hollow of a *shami* tree and left. At night, Shri Krishna appeared to them and told them that he had incarnated as the baby they left behind. He instructed them to fetch the boy who was now alive. They returned and found the boy. They took him and spent some time in nearby Chaudanagar. By this time peace reigned in Kashi. Therefore, Lakshman Bhatt returned to Kashi. At the age of eight, Vallabh received the *upnayan* samskar. He then studied the Vedas, six *darshans,* all the other *astik* and *nastik darshans,* and the Shaiv and Vaishnav Agamas. Among all the Purans, his favourite was the Shrimad Bhagvatam. He later wrote a commentary on it called *Subodhini.* By the age of eleven, he completed studying the above shastras. The family then embarked on a pilgrimage.

In Jagannath Puri, the local king was holding a debate in the mandir. Vallabh entered the debate and defeated Shankaracharya's *mayavadi* (Advait Vedant) pundits.

At the Shri Venkateshwar mandir (Tirupati Balaji), Lakshman Bhatt died. Vallabh then accompanied his mother to his maternal uncle's home in Vijaynagar.

In the following two decades of his life, Vallabh performed three pilgrimages of India. During this period, he perfected his philosophical system called Shuddhadvait Brahmavad (pure non–dualism undefiled by maya) and wrote Sanskrit texts. The

R – Raipur
B – Bhopal

115

most prominent was the *Anubhashya* – a commentary on the *Brahma Sutras*. Wherever an important event occurred during the pilgrimages, there his followers later established seats known as *mahaprabhuni bethak*. In all, eighty–four such *bethaks* exist all over India.

He once reached Jagannath Puri on Ekadashi. A *pujari* offered him *prasad* of *sukhdi,* which he could not refuse. However, as he was fasting, he held it in his palm and sang bhajans all night. In the morning he ate the *sukhdi*. Thus he honoured both the *prasad* and his fast.

Around 1509, towards the end of his third pilgrimage, the Vaishnav ruler of Vijaynagar, King Krishnadevray, was holding a *shastrarth* – scriptural debate. When Vallabh entered the city, a dispute had arisen between Madhva's Dvait pundit, Vyastirth, and Shankar's *mayavadis*. Vallabh presented his interpretations supporting the Bhakti *marg* and defeated the *mayavadis*. The king and all Vaishnav pundits then conferred upon him the title Acharya. Krishnadevray performed his *kanakabhishek* – showering with gold. With some of the gold, Vallabh had a golden ornament made for Shri Vitthalnathji in Vijaynagar.

After the victory, Vyastirth offered Vallabh the *acharyaship* of the Madhva Sampraday, which the latter declined. A second *acharyaship* was offered by Bilvamangal, the *acharya* of Vishnu Swami's Sampraday, which Vallabhacharya accepted. In the Vallabh Sampraday, it is believed that his reason for accepting was that this would help propound his doctrine, since he had no guru nor affiliation to any established sect or school of philosophy.

In many places during his travels, he expounded on the *Bhagvatam*, which also attracted many followers. In the latter part of 1493, Shri Krishna appeared to him in a dream, commanding him to go to Vraj to establish his true *swarup* of Shri Govardhannathji – the *murti* which the local people around Mount Govardhan had named Devdaman. He obeyed, instructing the devotees to change their mode of worship. A makeshift shelter was erected over the *murti* and he appointed Ramdas Chauhan to perform its *seva,* and Kumbhandas to compose and sing bhajans. In 1494, still in Gokul, at midnight on Shravan *sud* 11 – Ekadashi – Shri Krishna gave him darshan, commanding him to initiate *jivas* in his service. This ritual was known as *brahmasambandh,* literally, association with Shri Krishna. Vallabh offered a *pavitru* (ball) of *sutar* (thread). Since then, all Vaishnavs celebrate this day as *Pavitrā Ekadashi.* During *brahmasambandh,* the new devotee held tulsi leaves in his hand. He then repeated the mantra, '*Shri Krishna sharanam mama*', uttered by Vallabhacharya. The person then became eligible (*adhikari*) to offer *seva* to Shri Krishna. Hence, 1494 was the year in which Vallabh founded his Pushti Sampraday.

From the Shrimad Bhagvatam's (2/10/4) shlok – *poshanam tadanugrahah* – he advocated divine grace as his mode of worship. Construction of a proper mandir began in 1500 and was completed in 1520. Vallabhacharya then consecrated the mandir, the only one in his life and Sampraday. The buildings of worship which appeared during and after his son, Vitthalnathji's, time, came to be known as *havelis* – mansions. During Aurangzeb's reign of destroying mandirs, the *murti* of Shri Govardhannathji was shifted to Nathdwara in modern Rajasthan. Since then it is popularly known as Shrinathji.

Around 1501, Vallabhacharya married Mahalakshmi. They bore two sons, Gopinath and Vitthaleshwar (Vitthalnath). Vitthalnath expanded the Sampraday, completed the unfinished *Anubhashya* and laid down details of *seva* and puja and celebration of *utsavs* throughout the year.

As Vallabhacharya's fame spread, people from all over entered the fold. He accepted people from all *varnas,* including Muslims. He came into contact with Keshav Kashmiri, the famous Nimbark scholar, who presented him his disciple, Madhav Bhatt Kashmiri. Madhav Bhatt acted as Vallabh's scribe throughout life. Vallabh also met Shri Krishna Chaitanya (1485–1533) the eminent Shri Krishna bhakta of

Bengal, founder of a sect which flourished in Vrundavan.

Seva

Vallabh's *bhaktimarg* negated asceticism. In fact, in his *Samnyasnirnayah* he reasoned that renunciation only fostered pride and arrogance, which acted as obstacles between the aspirant and Paramatma. In verse 7, he grants an exception, that a bhakta may renounce his family only if the *samsaric* life hindered bhakti. Hence he advocated *seva–marg* – constant *seva* of Shri Krishna.

He established two types of *seva*. The first follows Shri Krishna's daily activity as Shri Krishna Gopal. The second follows Shri Krishna through the six seasons of the year. In the first type, *seva* is of eight periods, from early morning until evening: *mangala, shrungar, gval, rajbhog, utthapan, bhog, sandhya* and *shayan*. The *seva* during each period lasts about fifteen minutes, in which the bhaktas gather for the *swarup's* darshan. He initiated singing bhajans as part of darshan *seva*. From this arose his famous group of eight poets and singers known as *ashtachhap* or *ashtasakhas*. He initiated four: Kumbhandas, Surdas, Parmananddas and Krishnadas. Vitthalnath, his son, initiated the other younger four: Govindswami, Chhitswami, Chaturbhujdas and Nanddas.

Vallabh accepted the four types of *bhaktibhav* common in Bhakti traditions – *das bhav, sakhā bhav, vātsalya bhav* and *madhur bhav*. Of these, *vātsalya bhav* is predominant in Pushti Marg. In this, the bhakta regards himself as a parent of *balswarup* Shri Krishna, similar to Yashoda and Nand, Shri Krishna's foster parents. The bhakta is able to shower his devotional love in caring for the child Shri Krishna. In Vraj today, there are many mandirs with Shri Krishna's *balswarup* (Lalji) placed in cradles, which bhaktas swing. Surdas, one of Vallabh's *ashtachhap* poets composed many bhajans of *vātsalya bhav*. Later Vitthalnathji encouraged and increased the importance of *madhur* bhakti, influenced by the Chaitanya Sampraday, in which *madhur bhav* was dominant.

Vallabh spent the final years of his life in Adel, on the opposite bank of the Ganga, away from Kashi. In 1532 CE, at the age of 52, he left his home and family, adopted *samnyas* and returned to Kashi. He observed a month–long fast, followed by eight days of *maun–vrat* (vow of silence). On midday of Ashadh *sud* 7, Samvat 1587, he entered the Ganga at Hanuman Ghat. In the Sampraday, it is believed that he was shrouded in brilliant light, which gradually ascended into the sky.

Vallabh himself wrote that Paramatma had twice commanded him to leave the world, but he failed to obey promptly. This confession reflects his great humility. He considered himself as a servant of Paramatma, aiming to become like one of the *Gopis*.

Concept of Realisation

Pushti means *poshan* – to nourish, to support. Vallabh considered *anugrah* (ref. *poshanam tadanugrahah* cited earlier) – grace and *pushti* – to be synonymous. Divine grace is the only support and *sadhan* means, for the *jiva* to reach the final goal. This is Shri Krishna's eternal association in his eternal *lila*, which for Vallabh is higher than moksha. No personal endeavour can invite his grace. The *jiva* can only immerse himself in Shri Krishna's *seva* by eradicating *ahamta* (I–ness) and *mamta* (mine–ness). How does a bhakta know that he has received grace? When he is able to perform *seva* wholeheartedly, as the *das* or *sevak* of Shri Krishna. This is because only by his grace does one acquire the ability to perform *seva*. The means and the *phal* (fruits) are the same – Shri Krishna. *Avirbhav* – manifestation of Shri Krishna in the *sadhak* is his *phal,* not moksha.

Pushti Marg & Swaminarayan Sampraday

While comparing the beliefs of Shankar and Ramanuj in Vachanamrut Loya–14, Bhagwan Swaminarayan says, "Vallabhacharya has intense faith in only bhakti." In Gadhada II–43, He observes that great *acharyas*, such as, Madhva, Nimbark and Vallabh have advocated the principle of love for Paramatma by believing oneself as *atmarup*, as *gunatit*, which is known as *brahmaswarup priti*. (Gita, *Tattvadipika Tika* 18/54). Bhagwan Swaminarayan has also enjoined this principle in the Shikshapatri (116). He has also accepted and advocated the rites, rituals and *utsavs* prescribed by Vitthalnathji (Shikshapatri 81–82).

Bhagwan Swaminarayan third spiritual successor, Shastriji Maharaj often compared and praised Yogiji Maharaj's intense bhakti for Thakorji with that of Vallabhacharya's.

Principles of Vallabhacharya's Shuddhadvait

1. Brahman is the independent reality and is identified with Shri Krishna.

2. His essence is Existence *(sat)*, Knowledge *(chit)* and Bliss *(anand)*.

3. *Atmas* and matter are His real manifestations. They are His parts.

4. He is the abode of all qualities – good and seemingly bad.

5. He is one as well as many.

6. He is smaller than the smallest and greater than the greatest.

7. Maya or *avidya* is His power through which He manifests Himself as many.

8. Creation of the universe means real manifestation of Paramatma and not an unreal appearance.

9. From His nature as Existence springs forth life (pran) senses and bodies.

10. From His nature as Knowledge springs forth the *jivas* or atomic *atmas*.

11. From His nature as Bliss springs forth the *antaryamins* or the presiding deities of the *atmas* or *jivas*.

12. Shri Krishna is the one supreme *Antaryamin* – the inner ruler of all.

13. Bhakti is firm and all–surpassing affection *(sneh)* for Paramatma with a full sense of His greatness. It is the only means of moksha.

14. It is 'loving service' and 'attachment to Paramatma', it is neither worship nor knowledge.

15. It is gained through His grace, which destroys sins.

16. Pushti Marg bhakti is attained without any individual effort, simply by the grace of Paramatma, unlike *maryada marg*, in which bhakti is attained by karma and *jnan* of individuals.

20. Vitthalnath

(Vaishnavism)

He was born in Chunar, near Kashi, in Samvat 1572 (1516 CE). When his father, Vallabhacharya died, his elder brother, Gopinath, became head of the sect. However, he too passed away soon after, leaving a son, who was only a child. The mother insisted that her little son be appointed as head of the sect. Some of Vallabh's disciples supported her. Others supported Vitthalnath who was around fifteen years old. Finally the leaders considered it prudent that Vitthalnath lead the sect just when it was in its infancy. Gopinath's wife left with her son. Some time later he died, leaving Vitthalnath as undisputed leader of the Sampraday.

After appointment as Acharya, he lived alternatively in Gokul and Mathura. In Samvat 1600 (1544 CE) he embarked on a pilgrimage to Gujarat, Madhya Pradesh and south India. In Gujarat, he focused his activities in Amdavad, the capital. He returned here in 1557. During his life he visited Gujarat six times, which reflected the enthusiastic acceptance of the Sampraday by the Gujaratis. A mute disciple named Gopaldas of Amdavad was cured by Vitthalnath. Henceforth Gopaldas composed many *padas*. The most important was the *Navakhyan*, which described the growth of the Sampraday. His *padas* were the first Gujarati compositions and considered classics in the *sampradayic* literature. They are recited even today by Vaishnavs in Gujarat and other Hindi–speaking parts of India.

Hitherto, Jainism predominated in Gujarat. However, Vitthalnath attracted influential Jain Banias such as Bhail Kothari of Amdavad and Jiva Parekh of Khambhat. With their help, Vitthalnath attracted others from Jain society. Thus the sect spread in Gujarat.

In *Sri Vallabhacharya* M.C. Parekh, notes that Vitthalnath was a man with versatile talents, "a genius of a high order" (1969:158). He was a poet, a musician, a composer and a creative artist. Contemporary rulers and ministers of the time

K – Kashi
C – Chunar

such as Akbar, Mansinh, Birbal and Rani Durgavati admired him. The latter was a widowed queen, and Rajput ruler of Gadh, a small state in Central India. She was famed and immortalised in the annals of Rajput history by her sagacity and valour on the battlefield against the Moguls. By her strong stance and heroic victories, the state remained Hindu. Such a combination attracted Vitthalnath to Gadh during the few years after Humayun's defeat and Akbar's accession, when the country around Delhi was in constant turmoil.

Rani Durgavati venerated Vitthalnath, impressed by his piety and bhakti. She helped him in every way possible, including a gift of 108 villages for religious work. While residing in Gadh, Vitthalnath's wife Rukmini passed away. Vitthalnath was then 48. At Rani Durgavati's insistence, he re–married a girl from the Telugu Brahmin community who had settled here. After three years, Vitthalnath considered Gadh unsafe due to Muslim depredations. By this time, Akbar's rule was well–established, with peace prevailing around Delhi. Therefore, Vittalnath returned to Mathura. Here Rani Durgavati provided funds for building Seven Houses, known as *Sat–Ghara*, because he later lived here with his seven sons. Antagonism of local Brahmins later forced him to migrate to Gokul, his final place of residence, till he passed away in Samvat 1642 (1586 CE), at the age of about seventy.

Contribution to Vaishnavism

Settled in Gokul, Vitthalnath then embarked on his most important contribution to Vaishnavism. He laid forth the precise rituals of *seva* of the deity, as contrasted with puja – worship. This *seva* was a re–structuring to re–create the conditions described in the tenth *skandh* of the Bhagvatam. An important event boosted this venture. Some time after residing in Gokul, the *murti* of Shri Govardhannathji was brought to his house from the mandir on the hill. The *murti* which had appeared miraculously on Govardhan, was believed to have been worshipped centuries previously by Vraja, king of the Yadavs, after Arjun brought it from Dwarka. It was also worshipped by his father, Vallabhacharya. The *murti's* constant presence at home inspired Vitthalnath and his family to offer *seva* even more profoundly. This again helped him in laying down the finer details of the *seva* rituals. In the Swaminarayan Sampraday, Bhagwan Swaminarayan has accepted and advocated the rites, rituals and *utsavs* prescribed by Vitthalnathji (Shikshapatri 81–82).

He advocated offering every mudane *(laukik)* object to Shri Krishna which rendered it *alaukik*. The 'a' preceding *'laukik'* symbolised Shri Krishna. Similarly, a life totally surrendered to Him became *alaukik* – true *atmanivedanam*.

Being a poet and musician, he composed a number of bhajans and *stotras*, some of which are sung daily in almost every haveli. A famous *stotra* begins with *'Mangal mangalam...'*, which is sung every morning to awaken Thakorji.

Added to this, Vitthalnath organised bards of amateur dramatists, whom he sent to different areas of India to give public performance of some of Shri Krishna's life. According to Parekh, this was to make up the serious deficiency of the lack of sadhus in the Sampraday, and by which it has suffered through its entire history. In Gujarat, such devotional dramas proved successful, which induced whole communities to join the sect. Parched dry of devotion by the negative influence of Jainism and Shankar Vedant, people thirsted for something to revive their innermost yearnings for Paramatma. Vitthalnath's *premlakshana* bhakti, enacted through the dramas, immeasurably quenched this thirst. Little wonder that oases of bhakti sprung and began to flourish in Gujarat.

Vitthalnathji's personal and greatest contribution to Pushti Marg Vaishnavism was the introduction of dual worship – the *upasana* of eternal consort Radha with Shri Krishna. Parekh contends that this may have been due to the direct or indirect influence of Chaitanya's sadhus. Hitherto there was no *stotra* or writing by Vallabh extolling Radha (1969:169). Vitthalnath venerated Radha as supreme – *param ārādhya*. For him Radha was the manifest form of *premlakshana* bhakti. Therefore, he earnestly prayed to Shri Krishna, "Let Raseshwari Shri Radhikaji become my venerable devi for countless births." In the Sampraday, she is known as *Shri Swaminiji* and *stotras* named *Swaminiyashtak* and *Swaministotra* extol her glory.

Bhajans for eight artis by Vallabh's eight poets

He also appointed the *ashtachhap* poets to compose bhajans for each *arti*. These *padas* glorified devotion to the *balswarup* of Shri Krishna.

1	Parmananddas —	*mangala arti,* to induce affection — *anurag* and *khanditabhav* — (sentiments which arise with the yearning to be liked by Shri Krishna especially after being avoided) and also *padas* of yogurt churning *(dadhimanthan).*
2	Nanddas	— *shrungar arti* — to sing child *lila* and *padas* evoking love for the infant form of Shri Krishna.
3	Govinddas	— *gval arti,* and to sing *padas* of *sakhyabhav* (as friend), play *(krida),* cow–grazing *(gochaaran),* milking cows, stealing butter and *hindola* (swing).
4	Kumbhandas	— *rajbhog arti.*
5	Surdas	— *utthapan arti* and *padas* of *gochaaran* and forest *lila.*
6	Chaturbhujdas	— *bhog arti* and *padas* of *annakut,* the *Gopis,* Shri Krishna as *Murlidhar* (with flute) and *maadhuri* with cow.
7	Chhit Swami	— *sandhya arti,* arrival of the cowherds, milking cows, mother Yashoda's love for the infant Shri Krishna.
8	Krishnadas	— *shayan arti* and *padas* of *anurag, Gopibhav, nikunjlila* (divine sport in the gardens of Gokul) and *raas.*

Additionally, Vitthalnath revived the celebrations of sacred festivals such as Vasantotsav, Hindola, Sharad Punam and the Rāsotsav. One important festival that warmed Vitthalnath's devotional heart, was the Rath Yatra in Jagannath Puri. When he visited Puri in 1560 CE, he took a carpenter with him, who observed Jagannathji's magnificent *rath* in detail. On returning to Adel, the carpenter constructed a similar *rath*. Vitthalnath then joyfully took his deity around Adel in a grand procession. While living in Gadh, he similarly celebrated the Rathotsav. He infused new vitality into people by introducing the concept of unalloyed love for Paramatma and by re–establishing ideals of dharma.

Thus, Vitthalnathji became a stalwart propounder of *premlakshana* bhakti and *madhurya* bhakti, as well as bhakti *sangit* in medieval Bharat.

Introduction

A mystic is a person who, by endeavours such as meditation, austerities, association with true sadhus and/or other means, has realised *(sakshatkar)* Paramatma. In the following chapters we witness how the greatest mystics in the world endeavoured and offered devotion to Paramatma. For many of these, their devotion manifested through sublime poetry. Others, such as the *Gopis*, simply lived lives suffused with intense devotion, such that they experienced constant *sakshatkar* of their beloved Shri Krishna.

Such direct experience warrants unstinted *vairagya* – detachment from all that is mundane. Simultaneously, it demands unalloyed affection for and *sharanagati* (surrender) to the Divine. To achieve this, the majority had to bear harassment, ridicule and society's calumny. Yet this did not deter them the slightest. Their lives or devotional literature reflect this.

The lives of these mystics and bhaktas, and the voluminous bhakti literature they bequeathed to posterity, similarly inspire us to inculcate tolerance, offer exuberant devotion and with immeasurable faith continue to strive to realise Paramatma.

21. Gopis

Through intense devotion, the Gopis (*circa* 3000 BCE) achieved constant rapport with Shri Krishna. The *Narad Bhakti Sutra* (21) asserts:

"*Parabhakti*, the highest form of devotion to Paramatma, is seen manifest in the lives of the Gopis of Vraj."

In the Vachanamrut (Gadhada I–1), Bhagwan Swaminarayan declares that the greatest sadhana – endeavour – in life is to attain constant rapport with Paramatma. The Gopis achieved this by their *premlakshana* bhakti. This bhakti is of the purest form – *nirgun*, devoid of any *mayic* attributes. To remove misconceptions about the Gopis projected by poets and writers with *dehadrushti* (body consciousness) a few points need to be borne in mind.

First of all, when an avatar descends on earth as a human being it is not because of his karmas. He does so solely by the Supreme Reality's wish for some specific purpose. Shri Krishna's primary purpose focused on vanquishing evil elements. Simultaneously, he also fulfilled the devotional aspirations of bhaktas, such as the Gopis. Hence, one of Paramatma's names is Bhaktavatsal.

Secondly, whatever actions he performs as a human being are divine (Gita 4–9) and *nirgun* – devoid of *mayic* attributes.

Thirdly, when an avatar incarnates, his divinity innately attracts people to himself. Moreso if they are noble and pious *atmas*, and especially so during his childhood. Shri Krishna was only about ten or eleven years old when he played the *Maha Raas* with the Gopis. We glean this from the Devi *Bhagvatam* (4/24) which cites that when Shri Krishna vanquised Kamsa in Mathura, he was twelve years old. And the *Raas Lila* occured before he left for Mathura. This means thatm at the time of the *Raas Lila* Shri Krishna was only a child of about ten. Thus, the question of amorous sport for a child does not arise.

As for the Gopis, one meaning of the Sanskrit root *go*,

M – Mathura
V – Vrundavan
D – Delhi

from which the word *Gopi* is derived, is 'one who has control over the *indriyas*'. Therefore, the *Raas Lila* was a form of exuberant bhakti, transcending the three bodies, towards the divine Shri Krishna. *Raas* itself means the divine *lila* of the *chaitanya, alaukik, sat–chit–anand* form of Shri Krishna. Only then, hearing the *Brahma Naad* – divine sound – of his flute, could the Gopis instantly fly to him, leaving everything – whether milking cows, cooking food, tending to children, or fetching water. Those whose husbands prevented them, forsook their bodies, to join Shri Krishna as jiva – in spirit (Bhagvatam: 10–29). This is one of the sublime examples of *premlakshana* bhakti in Bhakti literature.

To fully appreciate the import of this phenomenon, a deeper reflection is neccesary. The Gopis who forsook their bodies experienced a state equivalent to that of Ashtang Yog, in which an adept yogi can voluntarily leave and re–enter the body. This is known as samadhi. However, the Gopis' intense love for Shri Krishna resulted in their constant rapport with him. Bhagwan Swaminarayan endorses this in Vachanamrut Gadhada I–25, saying that one whose *chitt* has become devoid of *vasana* and then attaches it to Bhagwan, that bhakta has mastered Ashtang Yog, without having strived for it. Therefore attaining constant rapport with Bhagwan, some of the Gopis shed their bodies (died) and attained moksha.

However, while the Sage Shukdevji narrated this episode to King Parikshit, doubts arose in the king's mind; if the Gopis regarded Shri Krishna amorously, how could such mundane love, based on *dehabhav*, from *rajogun*, redeem them? In Vachanamrut Gadhada I–42, Bhagwan Swaminarayan gives an answer similar to Shukdevji's. The reason, He says, is, "Shri Krishna himself was divine. Therefore, even if the Gopis knowingly or unknowingly loved him, they too, transcended maya. Just as Bharatji, who, out of mercy, became attached to a fawn, fell from his path of moksha and was born as a deer... No matter how sinful a *jiva*, if he associates with the truly Divine, he becomes supremely pure and attains moksha."

Shukdevji's answer is similar, but also gives the evil Shishupal's example, which he cited earlier in the 7th *skandh*. Though Shishupal incessantly thought of killing Shri Krishna, the latter redeemed him too, just as a person who unknowingly drinks *amrut* will attain immortality.

The Gopis' inner *bhavnas* (sentiments) and spiritual status can only be truly known by either Shri Krishna or Bhagwan Swaminarayan. Astonishing as it may seem, 5000 years after Shri Krishna's *lila*, Bhagwan Swaminarayan revealed, "The Gopis possessed great *vivek* in their understanding (of Paramatma's glory). Therefore, it cannot be said that their love stemmed from 'false' understanding (i.e. from body – consciousness – *rajogun*). And the Gopis knew Paramatma's glory fully. By the strength stemming from this glory, they easily imbibed *atmanishtha* and *vairagya* in their hearts" (Vachanamrut Sarangpur 15).

The sentence He then utters is profound and a new revelation, which acts as 'the final nail in the coffin' endorsing the Gopis' exalted spiritual status. Reiterating, He asserts, "Therefore these Gopis possessed *atmanishtha* and *vairagya* and other countless redemptive *(kalyankari)* attributes, which fully manifested in them by the strength arising from Shri Krishna's *mahatmya* (greatness and glory)."

Therefore, to Bhagwan Swaminarayan, the Gopis' love for Shri Krishna was of the purest form *(nirgun)*, devoid of *mayic* attributes.

Devotion and pride

During the *Raas Lila* on the night of Sharad Punam (full moon), Shri Krishna fulfilled their devotional yearning by dancing with them individually, assuming as many forms as the Gopis. However after a while, each Gopi in her intense devotional fervour entertained a thought, "Nobody is so fortunate as me in being granted such divine bliss." Amidst the pure and divine atmosphere, how could the entry of maya, as pride, be tolerated? Hence, Shri Krishna decided to teach them a lesson by disappearing from their midst.

As if struck by lightning, the Gopis became senseless. Unable to bear his slightest estrangement, they wandered around searching in a grief–stricken daze. Finally, they came across his fresh footprints. However, next to these, they noted a woman's footprints too. Burning with jealousy, they followed the prints. Suddenly the woman's footprints disappeared. The Gopis surmised with awe and jealousy that Shri Krishna had lifted her, for his prints were now even deeper! They wondered about this fortunate Gopi's identity.

Meanwhile, the Gopi accompanying Shri Krishna, too, felt thrilled, priding herself to be more fortunate than the others. Again, the entry of such a *mayic* thought induced Shri Krishna to teach her a lesson too. Vanishing into thin air, he left her distraught. When the others met her she related her bittersweet experience. Although this fortunate Gopi's name is not cited anywhere in the Bhagvatam, she was Radha, Shri Krishna's foremost bhakta.

Grieving and sobbing, the Gopis returned to the banks of Yamuna. Realising their folly in priding themselves, they repented and sincerely prayed to Shri Krishna to present himself. Their sentiments of estrangement and lament are known as *virahbhakti* and versified in nineteen shloks as the *Gopikageet* in the Bhagvatam 10/31/1–19).

Jayati te–dhikam janmanā vrajaha shrayata indirā shashchadatra hi,
Dayita drushyatām dikshu tāvakāstvayi drutāsavastvām vichinvate.

– Bhagvatam 10/31/1.

– Vraj is victorious because you reside in it. Lakshmi also eternally resides here

O Beloved! Cast your eyes in all directions, those who verily dwell in you, are searching for you."

Each shlok of *Gopikageet* was suffused with bhakti. Shri Krishna gleaned that their ego had dissolved in the flow of bhakti. Pleased by their exuberant love, he once again appeared in their midst!

Exalted status

The Gopis' exuberant devotion induced in them a

constant rapport with Shri Krishna. It is said that they cursed Brahmā – the Creator - for having created the human eyelids. For while blinking, these created a fractional gap in Shri Krishna's constant darshan. This, too, was unbearable.

When Shri Krishna sent Uddhavji to the Gopis, supposedly to solace them, to assuage their pangs of estrangement from him, their reply humbled him. Far from being despondent, they jubilantly revealed that their bhakti for Shri Krishna was ever intense and vibrant. And if he, Uddhav, were to pick a bone from their bodies (after death), and blow through it like a flute, the only sound to emanate would be 'Shri Krishna! Shri Krishna! Shri Krishna!' Realising their glory, he then wished to be born as one of the vines and shrubs of Vrundavan in his next birth (Shrimad Bhagvatam 10/47/61). This would ensure that when the Gopis passed by, the dust swirling from their feet would sprinkle on him and he would be thus hallowed.

In Vachanamrut Sarangpur 5, Bhagwan Swaminarayan makes an important observation about the Gopis' spiritual edification after associating with Shri Krishna. From the Bhagvatam He quotes the Gopis, "O Bhagwan! Since the day we touched your lotus feet, all the pleasures of samsara are like poison to us."

Bhakti's true form

The highest level of *premlakshana* bhakti demands *ananya sharnagati* – total surrenderance. This means that the bhakta's *chitt* (consciousness) should be so engrossed in Paramatma, that he loses all *dehabhav* (body consciousness). This also includes the mind and *atma*. Hence, this state is totally bereft of personal will and thought. In Vachanamrut Kariyani 11, Bhagwan Swaminarayan defines true love for Paramatma. He says, "One who has love for his beloved Bhagwan will never disobey His wishes." Illustrating this with the Gopis' example, He says, "The Gopis loved Shri Krishna. When he decided to go to Mathura they gathered together and decided to prevent him forcibly, even if this meant lying down in front of his chariot." However, prior to his departure, when they looked at his eyes, they gleaned that he did not wish to stay. Frightened by this, they kept their distance and thought "If we do not abide by Bhagwan's wishes then his love for us will wane.' With this thought they could not utter a word (to him). After Shri Krishna arrived in Mathura, which was only three *gaun* (about 7.5 km) away, the Gopis never entertained a thought to disobey his wish and visit him for darshan. The Gopis thought, Without Bhagwan's wish if we go to Mathura, then his love for us will disappear."

Therefore, Bhagwan Swaminarayan lucidly reiterates, "True love is to live according to the loved one's wishes. This means that if it pleases the loved one for you to live near him, then you do so. If it pleases him for you to live afar, you do so. But on no account should one disobey the commands of the loved one. This is the attribute of true love."

Bhagwan Swaminarayan further adds, "Only when (about sixty years later!) Shri Krishna sent for them from Kurukshetra, did they have his darshan. But on no account did they disobey his wish."

In retrospect, these pastoral peasants performed no harsh sadhana to attain Paramatma. Neither did they compose any sacred texts nor write magnificent commentaries. Their only sadhana was their exalted *premlakshana* bhakti towards Shri Krishna. That is why bhaktas have remembered them over the ages and sung their glory:

Kānudā   kede   faravu   re   koithi   na   darvu,
durijan lok dukkhambhar bole, te haide nava dharvu re...

– one should follow Shri Krishna without fearing anyone, one should not allow painful words from evil people to enter one's heart.

Brahmanand Swami, Muktanand Swami, Premanand Swami and other poet *paramhansas* of Bhagwan Swaminarayan have composed many such bhajans glorifying the Gopis and exhorting devotees to emulate their exemplary devotion and *bhav* for Paramatma.

Hence the word 'Gopi' has attained synonymity with *Gopibhav* and the acme of *premlakshana* bhakti. Not surprisingly, Bhagwan Swaminarayan has repeatedly lauded this exuberance in at least fourteen Vachanamruts: Gadhada I 42, Sarangpur 5, 15; Kariyani 9. 11; Loya 14, 15, 16; Gadhada II 10, 17, 19; Vartal 3 and Gadhada III 1, 28.

22. Alwars

Alwars is the collective name for twelve Vaishnav poets of Tamil Nadu. In Tamil 'Alwar' means 'immersed in Paramatma's love'. The term 'Alwar' is added after the poet's name, as in Pey Alwar, Poigai Alwar. Some, whose true birthnames are not known, are named after the place in which they were born, e.g. Tirumazhisai Alwar the Alwar born in the village Tirumazhisai. Some of the others have been named by their characteristics or given names which indicate the devotion of their followers. For example, Vishnuchitta is called Periya (the great) Alwar; Vipra Alwar is named Tondavadippodi – the dust of the feet of those who serve Paramatma; Godai, the poetess, is named Andal – she who rules over us, accepts us and is our refuge; and Tirupan is so called because he was a singer.

The twelve Alwars of the Tamil Vaishnav tradition are Poigai, Bhutattalwar, Pey, Tirumazhisai, Kulasekhara, Periyalwar, Andal, Tondavadippodi, Tiruppan, Tirumangai, Nammalwar and Madhurakavi.

The Alwars came from different sections of society – from Brahmins to harijans – and some are ascribed miraculous births. Scholars say that the period of the Alwars was from the sixth century to the early tenth century. Inscriptions, references within their poetry and the nature of the Tamil language used by them form the evidence that has led to this conclusion.

Vaishnav traditions consider each Alwar as the avatar of an article connected with Vishnu. Thus, Poigai, Bhutam (Bhutattalwar) and Pey are the conch, staff and sword of Vishnu respectively. Tirumazhisai is the discus. Periyalwar is Vishnu's vehicle, Garuda, and Andal is Bhumidevi. The other Alwars are considered avatars of Vaijayanti – Vishnu's garland, Kaustubha – the jewel worn by Vishnu, Srivatsa – the mark on Vishnu's chest and Vishnu's bow.

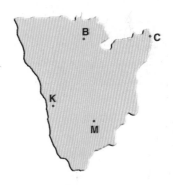

B – Bangalore
C – Chennai
M – Madurai
K – Kerala

The poetical works of the Alwars is known as the *Nalayira Divya Prabandham* – The Divine Four Thousand. All the poems are chanted once a year during the *Adhyayan festival* in South India's Vaishnav mandirs. For the Alwars, Paramatma is omniscient and beyond the comprehension of the mind and senses. He can be realised only through the consciousness. The salient feature of the Alwars was that they substituted experience for speculation. This experience was bhakti, fulfilled through surrender, *sharnagati*. Scholars believe that this principle of *sharnagati* influenced Sri Ramanuj when he founded his philosophy of *sharnagati* – the doctrine of complete surrender. Poigai Alwar's view of *sharnagati* was:

Think of Him, my heart.

Only think of Him.

You may praise Him, you may speak of Him,

'As low as you please', only think of Him.

The poems of the Alwars are not philosophical or theological utterances, though these do occur in them. In their works, the Alwars describe the initial stages of the journey towards the Divine and of the restlessness of the *jiva*. They admit that the senses are difficult to tame and they chide and coax the mind away from the material objects. Kulasekhara, a king, sang with great *vairagya* (detachment) from the mundane pleasures:

No, no, I do not care for any of these.

To be the ruler of untold wealth,

Of the wide earth,

To ride on the swaying elephant strong,

To taste kingship, To revel in the songs and dances Of Urvashi and Menka... No, no I care not for any of these.

— Perumal Tirumozhi: 4–2,5,6

The Alwars prescribe conquering the senses, not by starving them, but by changing their direction towards Paramatma. The senses and the mind rather than being uprooted, are nurtured towards Paramatma. Therefore, instead of being obstacles, they become instruments of spiritual progress. The Alwars believed that the various shrines dedicated to Paramatma were abodes in which He dwelt. The earth, sky and the whole universe was the *viratswarup* of Paramatma. Collectively, these satisfied the mind and the senses and drew them away from mundane objects.

The Alwars also believed in *avatarvad* – that Paramatma has incarnated on earth many times. Periyalwar conceives of Paramatma as a child and his lyrics are primarily of *vatsalyabhav* – akin to the love of a mother for her child. Another Alwar, Kulasekhara, identified himself with Devaki, the mother of Shri Krishna and speaks of Paramatma as King. Odd as it may seem, to him this Paramatma is Shri Ram, King of Ayodhya, and not Shri Krishna as one would expect.

There are other works of the Alwars in the *madhur–bhav* or the *nayak–nayika bhav* – the path of bridal mysticism. Andal, the only female among the Alwars, uses this *madhur–bhav* in her poems. Nammalwar also resorts to this *bhav* in some of his poems. Of Bhagwan Swaminarayan's poet *paramhansas*, Premanand Swami's bhajans reflect this *bhav*, also known as *Gopibhav*.

When an Alwar is describing his relationship with Paramatma in terms of one avatar, he may refer to other avatars too, or other incidents of the same avatar. Andal does just this in Tiruppavai when she speaks of the nearness of Paramatma with an analogy of how Shri Krishna appeared before the *Gopis*. The *Gopis* marvel at Shri Krishna's lotus feet, as he walks before them, uttering:

Blessed be Thou,

Who measured of yore this earth with Thy feet.

Blessed be Thou,

Who went all the way on foot,

To Lanka to destroy it.

Andal first refers to Vishnu's Trivikram avatar, or Vaman avatar, when he took the *triloks* – three worlds in three strides. Her second reference is obviously to Shri Ram. The Gopis, continues Andal, are awed:

The feet that measured the whole earth, the warrior feet that walked the long, long way to Lanka are now moving before us as those of an ordinary mortal.

Later, after singing many intimate songs, Andal feels that she may have overstepped her close intimacy in cajoling Paramatma. After all, despite her *nayak–nayika bhav*, she is mortal and He is divine. So she asks for forgiveness while still in her mystical fervour as a Gopi:

We follow our cows to the woods
And take our dinner there.
Though born of an illiterate shepherd community
We had the good fortune to have you with us.
O Govind! Perfection incarnate!
Our relationship will never sever.
Maybe, often out of ignorance and affection
We have called you by common names.
Take them not to your heart, my Lord,
But bless us with thy boons.

In another verse, she clarifies what these boons are:

Here then is the meaning and purpose
Of our early morning approach to you,
For worshipping at thy golden lotus feet.
Though we belong to a clan of cattle–grazers
Never must you shun our services as mean.
Not for today's worship only have we approached you Govind,
But always, for seven generations to come, forever,
Will we feel related to you, we will be at your service.
Let all our other desires be destroyed.

Therefore, the boons she requested were the destruction of mundane desires and the wish to remain, as a true devotee would, in His eternal service. And perhaps because of her fierce intensity of bhakti compared to the other Alwars, she is probably the favourite Alwar of Tamil devotees today.

The Alwars advocated bhakti to realise Paramatma. The symbolism in their poetry consists of anecdotes in which

Paramatma, in His various avatars, has played a visible role. They have also used the *Sangam* technique of oblique suggestion. Their works, springing forth from personal experience, rather than intellect, have thus enriched Tamil Vaishnavism.

23. Jnaneshwar

Jnaneshwar is considered as one of the stalwarts among sadhus of the Bhakti tradition in India. He was born in Alindi, in the district of Pune in Maharashtra, at his maternal grandfather's home. His family came from Apegaon, eight miles north from Paithan. Jnaneshwar's father, Vitthalpant, was a learned and humble Brahmin. Therefore he spent more time in devotion and service than domestic affairs.

Some time later, noting his intelligence and handsome features, Siddheshwar Pant had his daughter, Rukmini, married to Vitthalpant. But the latter wished to renounce samsara (material living) and repeatedly requested her permission to become a *samnyasi*. Once, for some reason she blurted out, "Begone!" Vitthalpant left home to become Swami Ramanand's disciple. Saying that he was unmarried, he attained *samnyas diksha*. He was named Swami Chaitanyashram.

Later Swami Ramanand came to know that Chaitanyashram was married. The guru therefore commanded the disciple to resume domestic life. He returned home. Since he became a householder from a *samnyasi* his clan ostracized him. Both husband and wife spent their days in misery. They had four children: Nivruttinath, Jnandev, Sopandev and Muktabai.

Of the four, Jnandev was born on Bhadarva *vad* 8, Samvat 1385 (1329 CE). He was extremely intelligent and inclined towards bhakti. When he was five, his parents voluntarily entered the waters of Triveni Sangam at Prayag and died. The reason was that children of a samnyasi would only be considered pure and accepted by the Brahmin community if the parents atoned by commiting suicide.

The four orphaned children now lived by begging alms. Observing their pious character, society began to venerate them. But when the time arrived to receive *yagnopavit* (sacred

A – Aurangabad
P – Paithan
A – Apegaon
M – Mumbai

thread), nobody would perform this ceremony, simply because they were children of a *samnyasi*. Some pious Brahmins requested them to obtain a letter attesting to their purity from the Brahmin pundits of Paithan. They would then perform the ceremony.

So from Alindi the four walked to Paithan. Here people noted their detached attitude from samsara. Of the four, Jnandev, also called Jnaneshwar, was an adept yogi from birth. In scriptural knowledge he was also an erudite pundit. After listening to their plight, the Brahmins of Paithan held a meeting. In accordance with the atonement prescribed in the Shrimad Bhagvatam, the Brahmins asked the children to atone by offering prostrations to those who jeered at them, the low *varna* and dogs. Pleased by this, they implemented the ruling. Just then an impudent Brahmin asked Jnaneshwar,

"What's your name?"

"Jnandev."

Laughing sarcastically, the Brahmin said, "This buffalo's also called Jnandev".

Calmly, Jnandev replied, "Yes, it is. A buffalo is also an *atma*. We are all *atma*. Names are ephemeral and insignificant".

"Is that so?" sneered the Brahmin. Infuriated, he started hitting the buffalo with a stick. Instead of the buffalo, weals swelled up on Jnaneshwar's back!

On seeing this, the Brahmin was horrified. He begged Jnaneshwar's forgiveness. Jnaneshwar replied, "O Bhudev! Who will forgive whom? You are also Jnandev. Bhagwan Pandharinath resides in all".

Having attained *atma*–realisation at such a young age, his fame spread afar. Once a Brahmin tested him in a taunting manner saying, If a buffalo and you are similar, then the buffalo should also be able to recite Vedic mantras. Jnaneshwar then stroked the buffalo's head. Uttering the Om sound, it began chanting Vedic mantras! Having witnessed many such miracles by Jnaneshwar, people flocked to him to chant Bhagwan's name, listen to his discourses and bhajans.

For a while Jnaneshwar resided in the village Nevase. Here he gave discourses on the Gita, which his disciple, Sacchidanandji, noted down. It became known as *Bhavarthdipika Tika* or *Jnaneshwari Tika*. Later in Alindi, from personal experience, he recited another commentary on the Gita to his elder brother, Nivruttinath. Jnaneshwar was only fifteen years old. At this young age he composed, along with the above two texts, such invaluable texts as *Amrutanubhav*, *Haripath ke Abhang* and *Changdev Paisathi*.

After completing the *Jnaneshwari Tika*, he embarked on a pilgrimage through India with his three siblings. Other famous bhaktas of his time, such as Visoba Khechar, Gora Kumbhar, Chokha Mela and Narhari Sunar also accompanied him. According to one account they became his disciples.

From Pandharpur, another renowned sadhu, Namdev also joined him. They visited Ujjain, Prayag, Kashi, Ayodhya, Gokul, Vrundavan, Dwarika and Girnar. From here they returned to Pandharpur. By this time his fame had spread as a lofty sadhu, a wise pundit and an adept yogi.

When another great yogi named Changdev came to know this, his ego was hurt. It was said that he had attained victory over death. Being extremely egoistic, he arrived to challenge Jnaneshwar, majestically riding a wild lion and using a snake as a whip! At this time, Jnaneshwar, Sopandev and Muktabai were discussing the shastras. When Jnaneshwar saw Changdev approaching, instead of moving forward to welcome him, he caused the whole rock slab they were sitting on, to move. Changdev's ego disintegrated. Until then he had considered himself as invincible for being able to control a lion and a snake. But at least these were living things, whereas the slab was itself non–sentient, inert, which Jnaneshwar had been able to put in motion. He then became Jnaneshwar's disciple.

On Magshar *vad* 13, Samvat 1407 (1351 CE), at the age of only 21, this unique sadhu left his body. Though a yogi of a high calibre, he practised and preached the easier path of Bhakti. He was the first propounder of the Vaarkari sampraday, a bhakti movement in Maharashtra. Followers fast on Ashadh *sud* Ekadashi and Kartik *sud* Ekadashi and go to Pandharpur to have darshan of Vithoba. Singing bhajans is one form of sadhana in the sect.

Jnaneshwari Gita

Jnaneshwar greatly exhorted a perfectly celibate and ethical life. Though he regarded austerities highly, he repeatedly emphasised "Bhakti and service to the enlightened Guru", on the path of realising Paramatma.

Of the three endeavours of sadhana; Guru worship, association with sadhus and *nam japa* – repetitive chanting, Jnaneshwar laid the greatest emphasis on Guru worship. He firmly believed that Paramatma's grace comes by meditation on the Guru. In his commentary (8/7) on the Gita he acknowledges his deep heartfelt sentiments:

"The service of the Guru is the gateway to Realisation – separation for a moment from him for me is like the length of an age – a difficult time to pass. I meditate on my Guru with love and yearn to serve him bodily with all my heart and soul... I yearn to become the very air of the fan he uses; I wish to become the clod of earth on which fall his feet as he goes for his devotion to the mandir... I long with my atma to perform his *arti*... In life and after death with the very elements of my body, I desire to serve him. O my Guru, grant my wish."

●

Finally, according to Jnaneshwar, the Gita's (4/15) central theme is that Karma Yog which has for its goal realisation of Paramatma and cessation of the pain of rebirth. All other works of the world for political or social uplift, no matter how *sattvic*, are to be abandoned by the advanced seeker. They are golden fetters to bind man to the world (Gita 10/28).

24. Kabir

Near Kashi, there is a lake named Lahartara. While passing by, a Muslim cloth weaver named Niru noticed a newborn baby boy floating on a lotus leaf in the water. Considering it an exceptional phenomenon for a baby to float on such a flimsy leaf, he took the boy home to his wife Nima, and named him Kabir. 'Kabir' means 'great'. Scholars differ in assigning his date of birth. The usually accepted date is Jeth *sud* 15 (Punam), Samvat 1455 (1399 CE). The *Bijak* text of the Kabir Panthis cites Kabir as being *ajanma* – not born as usual, but appearing from a divine flash of light on a lotus leaf.

From childhood, Kabir was spiritually inclined, and associated with sadhus and mystics. By the age of eleven he began to preach to people and take part in *satsang*.

Once while sleeping on the bank of the river Ganga at Kashi, Swami Ramanand (of south India, 1268–1359), on his way to bathe in the river, accidentally stepped on Kabir's leg. In an apologetic tone, Ramanand uttered 'Ram, Ram'. Kabir heard these words and accepted them as a guru mantra and Swami as his guru. In turn, Swami willingly accepted him as his disciple.

V – Varanasi (Kashi)

After some time, by the guru's grace, he had the darshan of Shri Ram. He then uttered a verse which is well known even today.

> *Guru Govind dono khade, kisko lāgu pāya,*
> *balihāri gurudevki, jine Govind diyo batāya.*

– when guru and Govind (Paramatma) are both present together, to whom should I bow first? Glory to the guru, for it is he who showed (me) Paramatma.

Though Kabir had no formal education he composed poetic verses of devotion from childhood. His poems revealed deep spiritual insights. The Brahmins of Kashi objected to Kabir's chanting Ram's name, for he was raised as a Muslim. Some Muslims slurred that by associating with sadhus and *fakirs* (ascetics), he had turned bad. To this he smugly replied,

Sādhuke   sangme   Kabir   jo   bigadā
bigad, bigad wo to sant banāyo re, Kabirā bigad gayā.

– if by associating with sadhus I have become bad, then by becoming 'bad' I turned into a sadhu.

The dissenters were confounded by his reply. Another Muslim taunted him that he was not a Muslim but a *kafar* – a derogatory term for a non-believer. Kabir replied,

Galā kāt bismil kare, voh kāfar bebuz!

– it is you who are *kafar*, since it is you who slash goats and then offer *namaz* (prayers).

· Once dissenters even hired assassins to kill him. When they entered his house at night, they overheard him saying to his son, "I have given you a *parasmani* (a mythical stone which turns iron into gold), with which you will be able to remove the pain and misery of the people." Kabir had used the word *parasmani* symbolically to mean 'offering devotion to Paramatma and giving food to the poor.' The poor assassins only heard the word 'parasmani' and so decided to steal it rather than kill Kabir and his family, for which they would get punished if caught. Hence they demanded the gem from Kabir. Readily, he replied for them to go ahead and take not one but five:

'Kabir! Ya samsār me pānch ratan he sār,
Sādhu milan, Haribhajan, denyā, din, upkār.'

– Kabir says there are five gems in this world: associating with sadhus, devotion to Paramatma, mercy, humility and altruism.

Finally, the Muslim community complained to Sikander Lodi, the Muslim sultan in Delhi, and falsely alleged that Kabir was insulting Islam by misguiding people. Lodi ordered Kabir to be trampled by an elephant. When the animal arrived, it became calm, raising its trunk as if offering a salute to Kabir. Lodi realised his error and asked to be forgiven.

Being a noble bhakta, he had immense faith in Paramatma. Once a group of people came to his house for guidance for a vexing problem. Kabir had gone to the river Ganga for a bath. In his absence, his wife advised them to daily chant 'Ram' three times for delivery from their misery. The group then departed. When Kabir returned his wife related the incident. Disheartened, he said, "You were wrong to ask them to chant Ram's name three times."

"Why?" she asked.

"By uttering Ram's name only once, their mundane problem would have been solved. Chanting Ram's name three times leads to moksha!'

Such was his singular faith and belief in the power of Paramatma's name.

With his life totally devoted to spiritual pursuits, he shunned material cravings. Once a sadhu arrived, converted an earthen bowl into one of gold and gave it to him. Kabir replied that all the riches that he wished for were at Ram's lotus feet. He then touched the gold bowl and it reverted to its original earthen form!

Towards the end of his life he wandered with his family in Uttar Pradesh. He left Kashi and passed away in Maghar, near Gorakhpur on Magshar *sud* 11, Samvat 1571 (1515 CE), at the age of 116.

The Muslim community wished to bury his body, whilst Hindus preferred cremation. While the two groups haggled, he appeared to devotees and told them to lift the shroud covering the body. When they lifted it they discovered a heapful of flowers! Each group took half of the flowers to bury and cremate, respectively.

His poetic verses are compiled in *Adigranth*, *Kabir Granthavali*, and *Kabir Bij*. The verses have traces of several languages and dialects: Rajasthani, Punjabi, Khadiboli, Vraj, Awadhi and Purbi. Being a mystic, his verses reflected his personal experiences. The poems discussed a wide array of topics, such as, karma, rebirth, *ahimsa*, bhakti, *jnan*, *vairagya* and faith. For Kabir, 'Ram' signified *nirakar* – Brahman. During his wanderings he arrived in Gujarat at Shukla Tirth, near Bharuch. The famous Kabir Vad (banyan tree) is named after him.

Incidentally, the famous bhajan of Kabir which Bhagwan Swaminarayan sang during the Fuldol in Sarangpur, while pointing a stick to Aksharbrahma Gunatitanand Swami as being the Sadguru mentioned in the bhajan, is attributed to a later Kabir who believed Bhagwan to be *sākār* – with a form:

> *'Koti Krishna jode hāth, koti Vishnu name māth,*
> *Koti Shankar dhare dhyān... Sadguru khele vasant.'*

A few of Kabir's bhajans sung today in the Swaminarayan Sampraday include *'Ram ras eso hai mere bhai...'* and *'Kuchha lenā na denā, magan rahenā....'*

During his period Kabir instilled true faith against blind faith. He believed in unity in diversity. To establish such unity in society, he advocated piety, generosity, humility and tolerance. He was a firm proponent of harmony between Hindus and Muslims.

Kabir's Sakhis

"Difficult is the path leading to the Beloved. It is like the edge of the sword. When ye have started to woo Him let not the decorum of society stand in your way."

•

"Do thou want to drink the draughts of love, and (simultaneously) to maintain thy pride? Two swords have never been seen nor heard of in one sheath."

•

"Let thy love be the chakor's love for the moon: Even if the head severed from the body falls to the ground, its gaze is still fixed on the moon."

•

"So long as "I" existed in me the Teacher was not met Now the Teacher exists, "I" has gone,
Narrow is the lane of love, it cannot contain both the ego and my Lord."

•

"Be not vain : death is holding thee by the hair,
There is no knowing, when it shall kill thee whilst dwelling in home or when ye are abroad."

•

"Happy is the whole world that eats and sleeps.
Unhappy is Kabir das who keeps awake and weeps."

25. Raidas

Born in Mandur near Kashi, bhakta–poet Raidas was the son of a cobbler. It is a general consensus that he was born in Samvat 1455 (1399 CE), on Magh *sud* 15 (Purnima). Since the day was a Sunday, he was named Ravidas, which later became Raidas in Hindi and Rohidas in Gujarati.

It is said that during his previous birth Raidas was a Brahmin pundit, the disciple of Swami Ramanand. The disciple begged alms from which he cooked for the guru. Swami had instructed him not to beg alms from an unscrupulous man in town. Once during the monsoon, the disciple had no choice but to obtain alms from this man. After having the food cooked from these alms, the guru lay down for his usual nap. But he could not sleep; his mind in turmoil. Swami then questioned the disciple, who admitted to begging alms from the evil man. For this error, he had to take another birth. In this birth Swami Ramanand was still alive. Later, once again, Raidas adopted him as his guru. Along with Kabir and ten others, Raidas was among the twelve senior disciples of Ramanand.

V – *Varanasi*
P – *Prayag (Allahabad)*

From birth he enjoyed the company of sadhus which angered his father. Once in a fit of anger he kicked Raidas out of the house.

Raidas built a hut outside the town, spending his time in singing bhajans and sewing shoes. He possessed a beautiful *murti* with four arms – the *chaturbhuj* form of Paramatma. Everyday he sang devotional bhajans in front of this *murti* such as,

> *'Prabhuji tum chandan ham pāni,*
> *jāki ang ang bāt samāni....'*

– O Prabhu, You are the sandalwood paste and I am mere water, your fragrance is pervading this *chandan*.

Unable to tolerate Raidas's worship of the *murti*, a jealous Brahmin once complained to the local king, that this practice would wreak havoc in the kingdom. The king summoned Raidas with the *murti*. In the palace, Raidas listened to the complaint and then placed the *murti* on a *bajoth*. He then challenged the Brahmins:

'O Brahmins! You are the beloved bhaktas of Bhagwan. Chant your mantras so that the *murti* jumps onto your lap.' The Brahmins began their recitation but the *murti* did not budge an inch. Then Raidas began to sing:

'Narhari chanchal hai mati meri, kaise bhakti *karu me teri?'*

– O Hari, my intellect is unstable, with what shall I offer you devotion?

When the bhajan ended the *murti* literally flew into Raidas's lap! Shamed, the Brahmins scrambled out. The king then honoured Raidas.

On one occasion a thirsty merchant passing by asked Raidas for some water. Raidas poured some into his cupped palms from a leather container. Water in a leather container is considered impure. Therefore, instead of drinking it, the merchant let it drip down his elbows onto his upper garment, causing a stain. The next morning when his washerwoman noticed the stain, she chewed the patch in the hope of dissolving it. By the intake of even a minuscule remnant of Raidas's water, the woman attained *trikal jnan* – the power of knowing the past, present and future! Later a friend of the merchant paying him a visit, questioned her whether her master was at home. She replied, 'No, he has gone to the leather market.' In reality the merchant was indoors performing puja. Hearing the woman's apparently false reply he stormed out.

'Why did you lie? You knew I was inside.'

'Master, though you were inside, physically doing puja, your mind was at the leather market!'

The merchant was astonished and inquired how she had attained such power. She recounted the previous day's chewing of the stained patch. The merchant then realised his error and Raidas's exalted status and returned to venerate him.

Once, a sadhu pained on seeing Raidas's poverty, gave him a *parasmani*. In his presence the sadhu took the cobbler's needle and touched the gem. The iron needle turned into gold. Raidas was not the least bit enticed and replied, "I do not want this maya." But the sadhu placed the *parasmani* on a shelf in the house and left. Thirteen months later he returned. Raidas told him, Collect it from where you left it. I have not touched it. Thus he remained detached from worldly enticements.

Once Queen Zali Ratnakunvarba, wife of Maharana Kumbh of Chitor visited Kashi on a pilgrimage. Along with the Brahmins, she invited Raidas to have a meal. The Brahmins refused to sit with him. Therefore, he sat separately. When everyone started eating, to their horror, they saw one Raidas sitting between every two Brahmins! When the Brahmins stood up, they saw only Brahmins. As they sat down to eat, they again saw images of Raidas sitting between them! The Brahmins then realised that whatever *varna* a bhakta is, he may still have attained an exalted status. The *rani* then accepted Raidas as guru. Another Rajput queen, Mirabai, also became his disciple (see Ch. 32). Describing himself, Raidas said,

Jātibhi ochhi, karambhi ochhā, ochhā kisab hamārā,
niche se Prabhu unch kiyo hai, kahā Raidas chamārā.

– my *varna* is low, my deeds are low, my talent is low, yet Prabhu has uplifted me from such a lowly state.

Raidas lived till the age of 120 (105 according to another source) and died in 1519 in Chitor. Here, in the compound of Mirabai's Krishna mandir where he was cremated, there is a shrine named Sant Raidaski Chhatri. Today his following is known as Raidasi.

26. Narsinh Mehta

Narsinh Mehta is well known all over India as a bhakta–poet. His devotional bhajans are sung to this day – mostly in Gujarat and Saurashtra – since he wrote them in Gujarati. He was born in a Nagar Brahmin family, in Talaja, a village near Junagadh in 1414. Scholars give slightly varying versions of certain episodes, dates and names regarding his life. He was either born dumb, or had a speech disorder.

By the age of five his parents expired. So his grandmother, Jayakunvar, raised him. His brother Bansidhar, seventeen years older than Narsinh, had a wife named Gauri.

Narsinh often used to accompany his grandmother to the Hatkeshwar Mahadev mandir for darshan and to listen to bhajans. Once when he was eight–years–old, Jayakunvar approached an ascetic at the mandir. The ascetic glanced at little Narsinh and prophesied that he would become a great bhakta. But Jayakunvar informed him of the boy's handicap. The ascetic then gave him a herb and asked him to chant, *Radhe Krishna*. Miraculously, Narsinh started chanting *Radhe Krishna*.

A – Amdavad
J – Junagadh

He was then sent to a Sanskrit school to study. Everyday after school, Narsinh visited Hatkeshwar Mahadev, joining bhaktas in singing bhajans. Afraid that he might become a sadhu, Jayakunvar arranged his marriage with a seven–year–old girl named Manek.

At the age of sixteen, a daughter named Kunvarbai and at eighteen, a son named Shamal, were born to Manek. The extra mouths to feed became intolerable to Gauri, who often poisoned Bansidhar's ears, bitterly maligning Narsinh. Being a henpecked husband, Bansidhar couldn't argue. However grandma, now quite aged, arranged Kunvarbai's marriage with Vasantrai, the son of Shrirangdhar Mehta, a rich man of Una. Soon after, at the age of 95, grandma died.

Grandma's absence now gave Gauri a free reign. She turned into a quarrelsome nuisance to get rid of Narsinh. She insulted him by taunting him and denying him food. She then complained to Bansidhar that Narsinh ate like a pig while not contributing to the home's upkeep. Bansidhar also scolded and insulted him. Narsinh then left home.

He arrived at a dilapidated Shiv mandir about 18 miles from Junagadh. He stayed there without food or water for seven days. Pleased with his austerity, Gopnath Mahadev (Shivji) gave him darshan and granted him a wish. Narsinh requested for the darshan of Shri Krishna's Raas Lila, which Mahadev granted. He then returned to Junagadh singing jubilantly.

Bhagwan to the rescue

Taking Manek and Shamal with him, Narsinh moved to another house. Once, to perform *pitrushraaddha* (offering oblations to forefathers) he invited several Nagar Brahmins to dine at his house. But one devious Brahmin went around town inviting the whole Nagar clan to Narsinh Mehta's house. Meanwhile Narsinh had gone to buy some ghee. On the way a devotee he met took him to sing bhajans. Narsinh completely forgot to buy the ghee and about the food to be prepared at home. One of the bhajans he sang with the devotee was:

Prān thaki mane Vaishnava vahālā...

– the Vaishanav, Bhagwan's devotee, is even more dear to me than my life.

Back home quite a crowd had begun pouring in. But a miracle occurred. Manek could not understand where the cooks and the raw material were coming from. They had begun to cook sumptuous sweets and other items. The Nagars then sat down to eat and hailed, *"Narsinh Bhagatni Jai!"*

When Narsinh's bhajans ended, he realised that he still had to purchase ghee. On reaching home he saw the guests leaving, having satiated themselves! Narsinh realised that his Shri Hari had surely intervened and come to his aid.

The Hundi

Once a group of pilgrims on their way to Dwarka asked to be directed to a person who would write a note of credit – *hundi*. Out of spite, they were directed to Narsinh Mehta. The gullible Narsinh wrote a *hundi* for three hundred rupees on a merchant named Shamal Shah Sheth. Narsinh then composed a prayer:

Māri hundi swikāro Mahārāj re Shāmalā Girdhāri...

– O Bhagwan! Please accept my note of credit...

When the pilgrims searched for Shamal Shah in Dwarka no one had heard that name. But Paramatma himself assumed that form and accepted the *hundi*.

Equality to all

Narsinh Mehta's devotion to his Beloved was so pure that he had no qualms in singing bhajans in the area where the town's lower classes resided. On one such occasion he sang:

Vaishnavjan to tene kahiyere, je peed parāi jāne re...

– he is called a Vaishnav (Hari's beloved) who understands other people's misery...

But this caused quite an uproar in the Nagar community. In the period of rigid orthodoxy, Narsinh Mehta's venturing into a lower *varna's* residential area was utter taboo, and unforgivable. The Nagars threw him out of their community. Yet Narsinh had equanimity in honour and insult. In reply he composed quite a thought provoking bhajan:

Jyān lagi ātmattatva chinyo nahi,
tyān lagi sādhanā sarva juthi...

– unless one realises the *atma*, all endeavours will be futile...

At the age of seventeen his son, Shamal, died. Manek was devastated. Soon, out of grief she also died. It was then that Narsinh composed another well known bhajan, depicting his deep understanding of life's ephemeral nature and his yearning for devotion to his Beloved:

Bhalu thayu bhāngi janjāl,
sukhe bhajashu Shri Gopāl...

– it is well that the web of maya has broken, now I will be able to worship Bhagwan in peace.

The Floating Garland

Lives of sadhus, mystics and bhaktas are generally filled with tests of faith, in the form of either calumny or physical harm by the ignorant and evil elements of society. Narsinh Mehta's was no different. People spitefully envious of his purity of bhakti once falsely complained to King Ra'Mandalik, accusing Narsinh of behaving contrary to scriptural law. Therefore the king decided to test Narsinh's purity. He summoned Narsinh to the palace and informed him of his plan, "I will place a garland around Damodar's neck in the mandir and lock the door from outside. If by next morning that garland is found around your neck, I will consider you innocent."

In times of grief, Narsinh used to sing in the Kedar *rāg* for inner peace. However, for this he needed his *kedaro* (a string instrument), which he had lent to somebody. While in jail, someone brought his *kedaro* and he started singing devotedly. Then a miracle occurred. The mandir doors flew open. The garland drifted through the air and gracefully fell around Narsinh Mehta's neck. Many people witnessed this and hailed his *Jai*.

Narsinh Mehta's bhajans

They include: *Suratsangram, Krishna Janma Vadhai, Ras–sahasra Padi, Saburi Chhatrisi, Chaturi Shodashi, Bal Lila, Dan Lila, Ras Lila, Sudama Charit* and *Nrusinhvilas.* The bhajans number about 740. His poetry greatly enriched the bhakti literature of medieval India. He died at the age of 66 but through his bhajans, he has attained an eternal place in the hearts of bhaktas.

Bhagwan Swaminarayan often requested His poet *paramhansas* to sing Narsinh Mehta's bhajans during His discourses. In Vachanamrut Vartal 11, they sang, "*Mārā harji shun het na dise re..*" Then Bhagwan Swaminarayan commanded all devotees to sing this *pada* everyday and imbibe its sentiments. In Vachanamrut Vartal 12, He requested the *paramhansas* to sing the bhajan lauding Vrundavan's inhabitants: *Dhanya Vrundāvanvāsi vātni chhāyā re jyān Hari bestā.*

27. Nanakdev

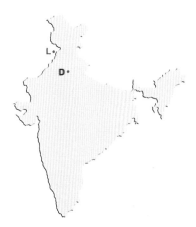

D – Delhi
L – Lahore

Nanak, the founder of Sikhism was born in Talbandi (now Nankana Sahib), a village near Lahore (now in Pakistan), in 1469. His father's name was Kaluchand Mehta and mother's Truptaji (some say Muktaji).

From childhood he seemed to be introspective and disinterested in worldly living. During playtime, he used to teach his childhood friends to 'play a game' by sitting in a lotus posture to meditate and chant 'Satyakartar, Satyakartar.' When Kaluchand sent him to be taught by Gopal Panda, young Nanak's persistence in asking questions so ruffled Panda that he sent him back home. In 1478, his father placed him under pundit Vrajlal to study Sanskrit, and in 1482 under an Islamic teacher named Kutubuddin to study Persian and Hindi.

Young Nanak loved everything about nature. When Kaluchand sent him to look after the fields of a friend named Rai Bhoya, he used to pass his time in meditation instead. In fact, instead of using his slingshot to scare away birds, he used to sing:

Rāmki chidiyā, Rāmkā khet, khā lo chidiyā bharbhar pet

– Ram's birds, Ram's fields, O little birds eat to your heart's content.

Maximum profit

Once his father gave Nanak some money to use and make a profit. Along the way, Nanak met a few sādhus who had not eaten for three days. Taking pity on them, he bought food and gave it to the sadhus. When Kaluchand questioned him about what profit he made, he replied, "There is no greater profit than to do something beneficial to others." This angered Kaluchand, who scolded Nanak. His elder sister could not bear this and took Nanak to live with her in-laws in Sultanpur. Here her husband, Jayramji, got him a job at the

167

court of Dolat Khan Lodi.

Nanakji's honesty soon impressed Dolat Khan, who then appointed him to manage the state's finances. However, this did not interest Nanakji. When weighing out grain, he would give extra and utter, "Your's your's...all this is your's...." When the losses mounted, he was dismissed.

In 1487, at the age of 18, he married Sulakshani.

Divine vision

Once, while bathing in a river he heard an inner voice say, "You have been born to uplift others." He then dived into the river. Three days passed. People thought he had drowned. On the fourth day he surfaced having had a divine experience – *sakshatkar*. He uttered:

Thākur tum sharnai āyā! Dukh nahi sukh sahij samāye,
Ānand ānand guna gāyā!

– O Bhagwan! I have arrived at your lotus feet. There's no misery, only instant grace. I sing your glory jubilantly.

Since then he used to preach *Satnam* (Truthful Name) to Hindus and Muslims alike. He regarded everyone as equal. Hindus regarded him as a guru and Muslims as a *pir*.

Once instigated by a dissenter, Dolat Khan asked Nanakji, "Do you believe in one Bhagwan or many."

"One."

"Then come and pray with me in the mosque!" Accompanied by the *kaji* (Muslim priest), the Suba and Nanakji entered the mosque. When everyone bowed on their knees *(namaz)*, Nanakji remained standing. The Suba questioned him, "Why didn't you offer *namaz?*"

Nanakji laughed, "You did not offer *namaz* either. You were thinking about buying a horse. And the *kaji* was worried that his untied foal would fall into the well."

The two sheepishly remained silent.

True understanding

In 1526, Dolat Khan instigated a Moghul to attack Ibrahim Lodi at Saiyadpur. After a massive encounter, Afghan rule came to an end and Moghul rule commenced. This threw the land into chaos and extreme misery. Nanakji recorded Babar's atrocities and the slaughter of his sons in *Aso Ashtapadi*. He vehemently denounced the attackers and pointed out the duties of rulers. This caused Babar to imprison Nanakji. Later, realising Nanakji to be a saint, Babar released him.

Nanakji then performed four pilgrimages of India's sacred places, including, Haridwar, Assam, Jagannathpuri, South India and Saurashtra. He also visited Mecca and Baghdad and propagated *Sat*–Dharma. In one Muslim holy place, he was invited for prayer. There he gave them a sermon, "How can Khuda (Paramatma) be pleased when you kill those animals to whom He has given life? You should be merciful to all living creatures. Working for the good of others is true sacrifice."

In Baghdad he came to know that the ruler looted even the poor to fill his coffers. He then devised a plan to reform the ruler. Not far from the palace, Nanakji piled a large heap of pebbles. When people asked him what he was doing, he told them, "This is my savings and I want to present it to the king."

When the king heard of this, he decided to meet this 'mad fakir'.

The king arrived and questioned him. Nanak replied, "I want you to look after this saving of mine."

"When will you collect it?" asked the king, mockingly.

"When we both die, I will ask for it in *bahish* (heaven)."

"Fool! Don't you know that people are born empty–handed and die so?"

"O king! Then even you will not be able to take your treasure with you. Therefore, it is as worthless as my pebbles." This enlightened the king. He then gave the treasure away.

Nanak later lived in Kartarpur (now in Pakistan). He had two sons, Shrichand and Lakshmidas. The former founded the Udasi Panth. At the age of 69 in 1538, Nanak left this world.

Guru Nanak's sermons were compiled in the Granth Saheb by Guru Arjundev, the fifth Sikh guru. Their worship place is known as a *gurudwara*, in which there is no *murti*. Only the Granth Saheb is worshipped. The shastra written by Guru Nanak is known as *Japji*, whose beginning starts with *aum*.

In 1916, when Sikh soldiers visited Baghdad, they discovered sixteenth–century stone inscriptions of Nanakji's sermons.

In the Swaminarayan Sampraday devotees frequently sing his famous bhajan,

Sumiran kara le mere manā, teri biti umar Harinām binā...

– O mind! Remember Bhagwan's name, your life has ebbed (wasted) away without Hari's name...

Jaga Swami and Yogiji Maharaj often recited, and today Pramukh Swami Maharaj often recites Guru Nanak's *sakhi* to imbibe humility:

Nānese ho nāne rahiye, jesi nāni dub,
gās fis sub ud gaye, dub khubki khub.

– the plant which stands stiff in the flood will be washed away. Therefore, remain humble like the the small grass stalk which bends with the flow and so will not be washed away.

Sikhism

✦ Belief

Sikhs believe in one immortal Paramatma, who is transcendent and immanent. They believe in the ten gurus and the Guru Granth Saheb. They believe in the law of karma and reincarnation and view human life as the means to attain mukti.

✦ Traditions

Sikhs faithfully prescribe to the five Ks: *Kesh* (long hair, covered by a turban, and uncut beard); *Kangha* (comb); Kirpan (dagger); *Kara* (steel bangle); and *Kaccha* (knee–length trousers usually worn under clothes).

28. Surdas

In a village named Sihi (Sinhin) near Delhi, there lived a Saraswat Brahmin named Ramdas. On Vaishakh *sud* 5, Samvat 1535 (1479 CE) his wife gave birth to their fourth son. He was named Suraj, which means 'the sun'. He was born without eyes.

One night when Suraj was six–years–old, Ramdas placed two gold coins tied in a cloth in a niche in a wall. In the morning they had disappeared. He rummaged through the house but could not find them. Suraj then informed Ramdas that he knew where the coins were, and would tell him provided he granted him a wish. Ramdas agreed.

"Rats dragged the coins to the roof at night," revealed Suraj. Ramdas climbed to the roof and to his delight found the coins.

Ramdas decided to grant Suraj his reward.

"Well, what do you want? An *ektaro* (a string instrument)?" he asked.

"No. Permission to leave home forever."

Ramdas and his wife were stunned. They had not expected such a bold request. With heavy hearts, both relented. Suraj renounced home, thus leaving his native Sihi.

About six miles away he reached a village, where a farmer was searching for a few of his lost cows. From afar, he shouted to Suraj asking whether he had seen any cows. As Suraj came closer the farmer realised that he was blind. Nonetheless to the farmer's astonishment, Suraj told him the location of his cows, for he could see with his heart. The farmer gathered his cows and returned. He realised that this youngster possessed divine sight and so built him a hut to live in.

People began to flock to Suraj to avail of his miraculous ability for their personal gain. In return they offered him grains, vegetables and gold coins. Suraj was not enticed by these mundane objects. Years passed by. Eventually his parents

D – Delhi

heard of his miracles and came to see for themselves. They wished to take him back, but Suraj declined. He then left the hut in search of Bhagwan.

Return my blindness

Once, while travelling he fell into a well. Shri Krishna appeared and rescued him. At that time Bhagwan offered him the gift of sight. After seeing Him, he appealed, "O Bhagwan! Having seen you with my eyes, I do not wish to see anything mundane. Please return my blindness." Bhagwan granted him his wish!

During his wanderings he arrived at Gaughat, on the banks of the holy Yamuna. Here he studied poetry and music. He also spent his time in devotion to Shri Krishna. In 1504 he met Vallabhacharya in Vraj. After hearing a few of Suraj's bhajans, Vallabhacharya requested him to compose bhajans extolling Bhagwan's divine actions. He initiated Suraj into the Vaishnav fold. Suraj then accompanied him to Gokul.

Bhagwan as Scribe

Later, Suraj permanently settled on the banks of Chandra Lake in Parasoli, near Shrinathji in Rajasthan. He visited the mandir of Shrinathji every morning for *mangala arti*, after which he composed and sang bhajans of Shri Krishna's childhood episodes. While he sang, scribes would pen down his bhajans. It is said that whenever the scribes were absent, Shri Krishna, himself would note down the bhajans. Once when Suraj began to compose and sing a bhajan, a scribe completed it before Suraj. The scribe then sang with Suraj. Startled, Suraj caught hold of the scribe's arm, realising that this must be none other than his beloved Bhagwan. But He escaped from Suraj's grasp and vanished. Suraj then wrote:

Bānha chhudāe jat ho, nirbal jānike mohi,
Hirade te jab jāhuge, marad bandāonge tohi!

– knowing me as weak you forced away my hand, but if you are strong, try leaving my heart.

No room in my heart

Suraj's fame as a master–poet and singer reached the ears of the connoisseur of music, King Akbar in Delhi. The king's bard, Tansen, had sung Suraj's praises. Intrigued, Akbar sent for Suraj. In 1567 at the age of 88, Suraj sang devotional bhajans in Akbar's court. Akbar then requested Suraj to compose a verse praising him. Suraj being a staunch devotee replied,

> *Nāhin   rahyo   hiya   manha   thor,*
> *Nandnandan achhat kaise ānie aur?*

– there is nothing in my heart except the son of Nand (Shri Krishna), so how can anything else take its place?

Lost for words, Akbar remained silent. Then he offered Suraj anything he wished. In verse, Suraj replied,

> *Man re, kar Mādhav se priti.*

– O mind, develop love for Bhagwan." Boldly, he said further, "I do not wish for anything else save that do not break my devotion for Bhagwan by summoning me here again!

When Surdas was in Gokul, he was able to have darshan of the *murti*, perceiving the minutest adornments. Once, to verify this unique ability, Girdharlalji, Vitthalnathji's son, decided to test him. He had all the garments of the *murti* in the Priyaji mandir removed. Only the pearl ornaments remained. He then requested Surdas to describe the adornments. Surdas laughed and instantly composed a verse:

> *Dekhari   Hari   nangam   nangā!*
> *Jalasut   bhushan   ang   birājata,*
> *Basan heen chhabi uthata tarangā!*

"I see Hari naked,

Garments of pearls only remain,

Without garments the *murti* sparkles with splendour!"

Surdas was thus a true mystic, devoid of material desires, and a staunch bhakta. He was well versed in Shuddhadvait, the philosophy established by Shri Vallabhacharya. The latter initiated him with the rite of *Brahmasambandh* and told him the eight-syllabled mantra. Vallabh then instructed Surdas to dedicate himself to Shri Krishna. And so he became one of his *ashtasakha* (eight elite friends). Vallabh imparted wisdom of the entire *Subodhini* to Surdas, who could then describe the glory of Shri Krishna's *lila*. *Subodhini* was Vallabh's commentary on the 1st, 2nd, 3rd, 10th and 11th *skandhs* of the Bhagvatam. Surdas then began to compose bhajans in the Vraj dialect about the *lila* extolled in the Bhagvatam. It is said that he composed about one hundred thousand *padas*, collated in *Sursagar*. Today, only about fifteen thousand are available, compiled in: *Sursaravali, Sur pachhisi,* and *Sahitya Lahari.*

Once at the age of 103, illness prevented him from attending the *mangala arti*. Vitthalnathji, Vallabhacharya's son, then went to see him in Parasoli. He saw Surdas facing the Govardhannathji mandir singing bhajans. He blessed Surdas and the poet left his body to join his Beloved in Golok.

In India, the word 'Surdas' is synonymous with being blind. Therefore, a blind man is respectfully addressed as 'Surdas'.

A few of Surdas's famous devotional bhajans often sung in the Swaminarayan Sampraday include:

> *Rākho shyām Hari lajjā meri...*
> *He Govind, he Gopāl, aba to jivan hāre...*
> *Akhiyā Hari darshanki pyāsi...*
> *Sabase unchi prema sagāi...*

Bhagwan Swaminarayan often requested His poet *paramhansas* to sing Surdas's bhajans during His discourses. In Vachanamrut Gadhada II–31, they sang *Halarki lakari, Hari mere halarki lakari...*

29. Tulsidas

The author of the Ramcharitmanas, Tulsidas was born in 1498 CE in Rajpur, near Prayag on the sacred river Yamuna. It is said that at birth he did not cry as normal babies do and he had fully formed teeth! His father, a Brahmin named Atmaram Dube, regarded this as an ill omen and considered disposing of him. Atmaram's wife, Hulsi, realised his hideous intention. And was naturally pained. Therefore, one night she handed the boy to her female servant, Chunia, and gave her some gold ornaments. She instructed her to run away with the boy and raise him using the money from the ornaments.

V – Varanasi
P – Prayag (Allahabad)

When Chunia arrived at her in–laws she revealed the truth to her mother–in–law. They named the little boy Tulsiram. But Chunia died when he was five–years–old. When he asked his grandmother where his mother had gone, she replied, "To Bhagwan." This aroused a yearning in Tulsiram to seek and talk to Bhagwan.

During his wanderings he met a sadhu named Narharyanandji. Perceiving Tulsiram's spiritual potential, he decided to initiate him and keep him as a disciple. Tulsiram was named Rambola.

Rambola stayed with his guru for 15 years, during which he studied the Vedic shastras and the Ramayan. At the end of this period, with his studies completed, Rambola returned to his home town of Rajpur.

Here he discovered that his father had died quite some time back, leaving the house to decay. Out of respect for Rambola's spiritual wisdom, the villagers rebuilt the house for him. Rambola now called himself Tulsidas and began preaching from the Ramayan. People flocked to hear his devotional discourses. Enchanted by his discourses, one of the listeners offered his daughter, Ratnavali, to Tulsidas in marriage. Tulsidas firmly declined. But when the man went on a fast, Tulsidas capitulated.

Unexpected wisdom

However after marriage, Tulsidas's devotional fervour for Shri Ram ebbed markedly. When Ratnavali once visited her parents, he was so distraught by her absence that he followed her. This infatuation induced Ratnavali to taunt him:

Jesi preet harāmse wese Harise hoi,
chalā jāye Vaikunthme palā na pakade koi.

– you have attachment for the perishable things of the world, but if you develop such love for Hari, then you will attain Vaikunth without hindrance.

This verse produced an unexpectedly profound effect; he renounced mundane life! Ratnavali then sent her brother to bring him back. He gave his answer in verse:

Kare ek Raghunāth sang, bandhi jatā seerkesh
ham jo chākhe premras, patni ke updesh.

– associate with Ram with a staunch conviction, just as I experienced his love by my wife's wisdom.

He then wandered as a sadhu for many years in many holy places, delivering discourses about the glory of Shri Ram. He finally settled in Kashi.

Darshan

Every morning after puja, he poured the sanctified water at the foot of a pipal tree. Though a sacred tree, it is also a refuge for condemned *jivas*. Once in this particular tree, such a condemned *jiva* experienced profound peace as a result of receiving the sanctified water. Therefore, it once appeared to Tulsidas and granted him a boon. Tulsidas replied, "I would like to have Shri Ram's darshan."

"That's beyond my capacity. However Hanumanji sits in your discourses daily. He can guide you to Shri Ram," replied the *jiva*. "He will be the first to arrive and the last to leave."

Tulsidas bore this in mind. The next day, after his discourse, he approached and bowed at Hanumanji's feet, who in the form of a Brahmin, was the last person to remain. Tulsidas requested him for Shri Ram's darshan. Hanumanji instructed him to visit Mount Chitrakut, where Shri Ram had performed divine actions.

When Tulsidas arrived at Chitrakut, Shri Ram gave him darshan and blessed him. Shri Ram's divine touch infused such divinity in Tulsidas that he started performing miracles to help the unhappy and the diseased. People from all over flocked to his house. Ultimately this reduced his time for daily puja and study of the Ramayan. Therefore he retreated to a cave and meditated on Shri Ram. But soon, Shri Ram gave him darshan and commanded him to serve for the welfare and moksha of the people.

The Ramcharitmanas

Henceforth, Tulsidas started writing shastras. It is noted that around 1560, Tulsidas met Surdas, the renowned blind bhakta–poet of Shri Krishna. Surdas was 19 years older than Tulsidas. Both discussed their devotional bhajans and other poetic works. In 1575 on the day of Ramnavmi, Tulsidas commenced writing the Ramcharitmanas in the Awadhi dialect. It took him two years to complete. From then on he discoursed in Kashi. People loved his discourses. Soon he became famous. With it arrived trouble. The pundits of Kashi burned with jealously, afraid that no one would now respect them. Therefore, they decided to steal the text and destroy it. For this they sent a few thieves to his house. When they entered, they saw a giant guarding the text. They fled in fear. The exasperated pundits then sent tantrics to kill Tulsidas. Again Shri Ram came to his rescue.

In 1584 plague spread throughout Kashi. Many perished. Others begged Tulsidas to rescue them. He comforted them by instructing them to offer sincere devotion to Shri Ram. Every house in Kashi started chanting the name of Shri Ram. He also joined them. It was then that Tulsidas composed the popular verse:

> *Shri Ramchandra krupālu bhajamana,*
> *harana bhava bhaya dārunam...*

– worship Ram, whose name is the saviour from the intense misery of the cycle of births and deaths.

Miraculously the epidemic subsided.

Tulsidas distilled the essence of the Ramayan in his famous verse:

> *Rām milan ke kārane jo tu bhayo udās,*
> *Tulsi shodhile sangat santki Rām jinho ki pās.*

– if one zealously wishes to realise Ram, then one should seek the association of the sadhu who has realised Ram.

Bhagwan Swaminarayan has referred to Tulsidas's verses in two *Vachanamruts*. In Gadhada II-41 He quotes the verse, *"Kanak tajyo, kāmini tajyo...."* and in Gadhada II-57 He commands devotees to imbibe the message of three of Tulsidas's devotional *padas*: (i) *Jo mein lagan Ram so nāhi...* (ii) *Jāke priya na Ram baidehi...* (iii) *Ehi kahyo sunā! Bed chahun...*

In 1624, Tulsidas died at Asighat in Kashi, at the grand age of 126 years. His works include: *Parvati Mangal, Janki Mangal, Vinay Patrika, Vairagya Sandipani, Shri Krishna Gitavali* and *Ram Salaka*.

For Hindus worldwide, even in places such as Fiji, Surinam and Trinidad, Tulsidas remains endearing for his unalloyed bhakti for Shri Ram in the *Ramcharitmanas*.

In northern India the sacred text is so revered that nearly every home has a copy. It is also synonymously known as the Tulsi Ramayan.

30. Swami Haridas

Swami Haridas was a mystic, musician and poet. He was born in the village Khairwali Sadak, near Aligarh in Uttar Pradesh, in Samvat 1569 (1512 CE). Today, in his memory, the village is known as Haridaspur. His father, Asudhir and mother Ganga Devi were Saraswat Brahmins. When Haridas was 25, Asudhir initiated him into *samnyas*, which in it self is unusual.

Haridas then migrated to Vrundavan, the land of Shri Krishna's divine *lila*. Here he established his ashram, where he composed and sang poems of Radha and Shri Krishna in the Vraj dialect, which is spoken around Vrundavan and Mathura. Life in northern India during this period was politically stable. The Moghul empire was at its height with Akbar on the throne in Delhi. The period produced a brilliance in all walks of life – social, economic, religious and artistic. Haridas was instrumental in spreading devotional music, particularly the style called *dhrupad*, which came into vogue around the 14th century. At that time the *prabandha* style was fading.

D – Delhi
K – Khairwali
A – Aligarh

The *dhrupad* style of music originates from ancient times. *Dhruva* means steadfast. *Pada* means words. The words used in *dhruvpad* compositions were called *dhruvapada*. It is considered the guiding light of music, one by which the musician finds his bearings, and is never omitted. The *dhrupad* had four sections: the *sthayi*, the *antara*, the *sanchari* and *abhoga*. Haridas sang his poems of divine love in this *dhrupad* style.

There were two kinds of *dhrupad*, depending on the text – Vishnupad and Dhrupad. Their musical structures are similar, but different in content. Mimamsas extolled and praised Shri Krishna's divine *lila*. Dhrupads described the seasons, glory of kings and so on. Eventually, Vishnupads gained importance, especially among the devotional poems of the Vaishnavs. Though Haridas's compositions are strictly in the Vishnupad style, musically they were of the *dhrupad* type.

Besides being a fine musician, Swami Haridas was a sadhu–singer of the bhakti tradition, which gained popularity all over India around the 14th century. Bhakti – adoration – is an intensely personal devotion to Paramatma, whom one adores, or worships. The attachment of the devotee to his Adored may take the form of humility *(shant bhav)*, subservience *(dasya bhav)*, friendship *(sakhya bhav)* and the love of the devotee for the Beloved *(madhurya bhav)*. Swami Haridas belonged to the tradition of *madhurya* bhakti.

It is said that Haridas was deeply affected by Nimbark, the famous south Indian *acharya*. Nimbark was a 13th century Telugu philosopher who travelled in the north extolling the bhakti of Radha–Krishna (see Ch.17). He expounded the philosophy of *bhedabhed* – the doctrine of difference-cum-identity between the Supreme Atma and the individual *atma*. Swami Haridas's religious philosophy embraced not only the adoration of Radha–Krishna, but also the love of the human mind – a state of mind known as *rasa*. This aspect of *rasa* was the central theme of all his poems and teachings.

As an ascetic he remained staunchly detached from mundane pleasures. Once, a rich merchant devotee gave him a vial of expensive perfume. Haridas buried it in the soil there and then. The devotee felt hurt that such an expensive gift was treated with such indifference. But the following day when the devotee visited the mandir, he recognised the same fragrance emanating from the sanctum sanctorum and Bhagwan's *murti* appeared scented with it.

This detachment also led him to shun all publicity. He did not allow kings into his ashram, nor did he visit them. When his disciple, Tansen, one of Akbar's nine 'gems', informed the king that his guru was an even better singer and musician than himself, the king wished to hear him. For this Tansen suggested a ruse. Akbar would wear rags and act as his *tambura* bearer to visit Haridas. At the ashram in Vrundavan, Akbar, a connoisseur of music listened with astonishment to Haridas. When they returned, Akbar questioned Tansen, "Being such a maestro yourself, how is it that your music pales compared to Swami's?" Tansen replied, "What else can it be? I sing for the emperor of this land. He sings for the Emperor of the whole creation."

Swami Haridas composed a total of 128 poems, of which eighteen are philosophical, known as *siddhant padas* and 110 are devotional, known as *keli mala*. He also founded the Haridas Sampraday. Some of his more important disciples included Vitthal, Vipul, Viharin Dev and Shri Krishna Das, who further developed and propagated his tradition of devotional music.

The Sampraday's main feature is congregational singing. In the Vraj area, this congregation is called the Samaj and is akin to the *sankirtan* of Bengal and the bhajan *goshti* of South India. Swami Haridas passed away around the age of 80 years.

31. Eknath

A – Aurangabad
P – Paithan
M – Mumbai

Like Tukaram and Jnaneshwar, Eknath was another of Maharashtra's stalwart mystics. Born in 1534 CE in Paithan, to Brahmin parents, not much is known about his childhood. Later, without any care for his own body, he served his guru sincerely. This endowed him with spiritual knowledge.

The Shrimad Bhagvatam was his favourite shastra, on which he gave many sermons. He also composed and sang bhajans. His wife, Girijabai, too, was a devout atma and attended to *atithis* – travellers – passing by who wished for food and shelter.

Food for all

Once some Brahmins were to have food at Eknath's house, on the occasion of *shraaddh* – a ritual offering food to one's ancestors. But before they arrived, some *harijans* (members of the low *varna*) passed by and caught the delicious aroma of the cooking. One of them said, "What *punya* (spiritual merits) must one have, to be able to partake of such food?"

Eknath just happened to hear this and called out to them, "The food is ready. You are welcome to it."

Girijabai added, "Not alone. Come with your families."

Eknath lovingly fed all the *harijan* families. Girijabai then set about cooking again for the Brahmins. When the latter heard of this, they were angered and refused to come. Shrikhand, one of Eknath's disciples then remarked to Eknath, "Prabhu, you have performed such a noble deed today that the ancestors themselves will avail of the food."

Eknath then served food in dishes made of dried leaves and placed them out in the open. Miraculously, the ancestors arrived from heaven to relish the food. On seeing this, the Brahmins repented for having lost a meal and their honour.

It is said that Bhagwan assumed Shrikhand's form to

accept Eknath's loving devotion for twelve years.

Selfless service

Eknath's home was open to guests around the clock. Once some visitors arrived in the middle of the night. While cooking for them, Eknath ran out of firewood. Without thinking twice, he removed some beams supporting the roof, used it as firewood to cook the food and happily fed the guests.

On another occasion, an ill, starving *harijan* arrived. Girijabai fed him warm milk, nursed him and washed his clothes till he recovered. During discourses at his home, Eknath often used to say that people were Bhagwan's forms. No one was of a high or low *varna*. A *harijan* named Ramo heard this and wished to invite Eknath to have food with him. Eknath agreed.

The next day, Eknath arrived at Ramo's house which the latter had cleaned and decorated. Both Ramo and his wife devotedly offered Eknath food. Later, this event became the town's gossip. The Brahmins branded Eknath as a *chandal* (a low *varna*). Eknath calmly replied, "Those who slur me are washing my sins. They are my gurus. I offer them *pranams*."

Epitome of Tolerance

Such trials never angered Eknath. Once his dissenters bribed a Brahmin to infuriate him. The Brahmin arrived at Eknath's house while the latter was performing puja. Without removing his shoes, the Brahmin entered the puja room and thumped down on Eknath's lap! Eknath remained calm. He said, "I am pleased that you have such friendliness with me."

This astonished the Brahmin, who then growled, "I am hungry!" Eknath offered him food. When Girijabai bent down to serve, the Brahmin jumped onto her back like a child. This uncouth act did not disturb Eknath either. He cautioned Girijabai, "Take care that the Brahmin does not fall!"

True to her saintly nature, Girijabai replied, "Do not worry. I am used to carrying children on my back."

Shamed, the Brahmin fell at the couple's feet and begged

for forgiveness. With tears in his eyes he confessed, "To make you angry, I was offered two rupees. And so I committed this sinful act."

Hearing this Eknath replied, "If you had said so in the first place I would have become angry."

A similar event in Eknath's life depicts his saintly disposition.

Every morning Eknath bathed in a nearby river. Along the way he had to pass a Muslim's house. When Eknath returned from the river, the Muslim occasionally spat on him. Eknath would then be forced to bathe again. When he returned, the Muslim would spit again. In this way, Eknath often had to bathe four to five times. Even then he never got angry.

Once, the Muslim decided to really take Eknath to task. He spat on him not five or ten times, but 108 times! After each instance Eknath would return to the river to bathe. Even then he did not lose his peace of mind. Finally, the Muslim relented, fell at his feet and apologised. In fact, Eknath thanked the Muslim for giving him the opportunity to bathe 108 times in the holy river!

Helping thieves

One night some thieves entered Eknath's house. They pilfered what they could from one room and entered the next. In the dim light of a small candlewick, Eknath was chanting Paramatma's name. Seeing the thieves, he removed his ring and held it out, "Take this as well. It'll be useful."

The astonished thieves prostrated at Eknath's feet. He then requested Girijabai to cook food. Having fed them, he packed and gave them extra food and bade them farewell!

Seeing Bhagwan in All

Being of a saintly character, Eknath performed a pilgrimage of India. During his pilgrimage with some sadhus, he carried some sacred water from the river Ganga in Kashi to Rameshwar. The sacred water was to be offered to the deity in Rameshwar. Along the way, the group encountered a donkey dying of thirst. Eknath took heart and poured all the sacred Ganga water down the donkey's throat. This revived the animal. Eknath's fellow travellers admonished him, "What will you now offer to Rameshwar?"

Eknath replied, "I have offered the Ganga water to Rameshwar, for the same Rameshwar resides in this donkey."

Truly wise and devoted

Eknath's son, Hari, was a Sanskrit pundit. Since Eknath gave sermons and composed bhajans in Marathi, this pained Hari. He used to scoff at the Marathi language. Once, a woman from Paithan took a vow to feed one thousand Brahmins for the recovery of her ill husband. But soon, the husband died and she was so steeped in poverty she could not even afford to feed four Brahmins. So she then sought a pundit's advice. He advised her to feed one learned Brahmin, which would be equivalent to feeding a thousand Brahmins.

After thinking deeply, she decided to invite Eknath. Eknath's son, Hari, cooked the food. The woman then offered it to Eknath. After Eknath finished, Hari picked up his father's dish to throw it away. But Hari was dumbstruck, for as he lifted one dish, there was a second dirty one beneath. When he lifted that there was a third beneath. In this way he counted a thousand! This perplexed him. He then realised that though his father was not a Sanskrit pundit, he was a devout *bhakta* and that just by being a Sanskrit pundit did not make him wise and devoted. Hari's arrogance dissolved.

Eknath wrote texts on the Shrimad Bhagvatam, known collectively as *Eknathi Bhagvatam*. He also composed many bhajans. He venerated *Sant* Jnaneshwar. He corrected the discrepancies left by the scribes of the *Jnaneshwari Gita* and rewrote a corrected version.

When he considered that his work had been fulfilled, he sent a message to all his disciples that he would be leaving his body. They all flocked to avail of his last darshan. They accompanied him to the river where he bathed. He then sat in a lotus posture and gave his last sermon, "I am leaving. Follow the Bhagvat Dharma. Live together in harmony. Worship Vithoba and attain the goal of human birth."

He then passed away on Chaitra *vad* 6 Samvat 1656 (1600 CE) at the age of 66.

32. Mirabai

Although the exact dates of Mirabai's life are a matter of debate amongst scholars, she was born in Medata, Rajasthan, sometime between 1499 to 1504 CE (Zaveri 1991:77). The word Mira is not Indian, but a Farsi word, meaning Paramatma's *jyoti* (light/flame). It was probably given by the mystic Raidas, who was influenced by Kabir, his contemporary. She was the daughter of a Rajput noble named Ratnasinh. Her mother introduced her to Krishna bhakti by giving her a *murti* of Shri Krishna. Mira offered such devotion to the *murti* that her mother once jokingly told her that Shri Krishna would become her bridegroom. Her mother died when Mira was young. She then went to live with her grandfather Dudaji. After his death, his son, Vikramdev, arranged Mira's marriage with Prince Bhojraj, son of the famous ruler Rana Sanga of Chitor.

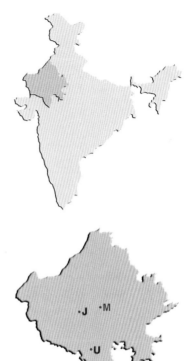

J – Jodhpur
M – Medata
U – Udaipur

By the end of the 15th century, these Rajputs were trying to establish their supremacy against the Muslim sultans. Violence, hatred and internal-feuds among the Rajputs themselves was a prevailing feature. Respect for all life had ebbed. Frequent deaths and strife among her relatives caused young Mira to introspect. She could not understand the hatred, the violence and the loss of peace and love. She felt a stranger amongst her royals and looked around for a loving and peaceful sanctuary. This she found in the Vaishnav tradition. Great Hindu *acharyas* and sadhus like Chaitanya, Vallabh, Ramanand, Kabir, Nanak and Raidas were reviving Sanatan Dharma. They reminded Hindus that the first step towards union with Paramatma was love and respect for all human life. This could be effected through bhakti.

Hence, to quench her spiritual thirst Mirabai resorted to Vaishnav teachings. This led her to adopt Shri Krishna as her Beloved incarnation and called him *Giridhar Nagar* in her bhajans.

After marriage to Bhojraj, Mira's love for Shri Krishna, instead of decreasing, flourished. She immersed herself in Krishna bhakti, composing and singing bhajans, and having religious discourses with sadhus. This infuriated Rana Sanga and other relatives. She was ordered to stop these practices and to live according to the conventions of the royalty. But she remained steadfast. Rana then restricted her movements. She describes this in one of her poems:

"All the dear ones of the house are creating trouble over my association with sadhus and are causing great hindrance to my worship. From childhood Mira made Giridhar Nagar (Shri Krishna) her friend; this attachment shall never be severed, but shall flourish."

When her husband, Bhojraj, died, Rana instructed her to become a sati (to burn on the funeral pyre with her husband), as was the custom amongst the Rajputs. But Mira, wedded to the omnipresent Bhagwan, again defied Rana:

"Mira is dyed in Hari's colour (love), and has set aside all other colours (loves). I will sing of Giridhar, and will not become sati since my heart is overcome by Hari. My relation as the eldest daughter–in–law exists no more, Rana. Now I am a subject, and you are the king."

When her father-in-law, Rana Sanga, died, Prince Ratan Singh became the king. He, too, died soon after. Prince Vikramaditya then ruled Chitor. He also commanded Mira to refrain from singing, dancing and meeting sadhus. Such restrictions in the palace forced her to offer devotion at a public mandir. In her deep devotion she forgot her own self and attained samadhi. People of Mewar began to respect her saintly nature and her fame spread throughout the kingdom. This further angered the king and other relatives. He then subjected her to deadly hardships which she describes in one poem:

"Mira is happy in Bhagwan's worship; Rana presented a basket, containing a snake; Mira performed her ablutions and opening it, found Bhagwan Himself.

Rana sent a cup of poison; after ablutions Mira drank the

contents, which Bhagwan turned into amrut. Rana sent a bed of nails for Mira to sleep on; in the evening when Mira slept on it, it became a bed of flowers.

Mira's Bhagwan removes all her troubles and is ever a beneficent protector. Mira roams about happy in her state of ecstatic devotion. She is a sacrifice to Bhagwan."

Adding fuel to the fire, she accepted the mystic Raidas as her guru. A Rajput royalty venerating a leather worker was outrageous; a disgrace to Rajput nobility. To the infuriated Rana, she boldly replied,

"Ignominy and shame and the scandal of the world I cherish and welcome for Paramatma's love, O Rana,

I care neither for the disgrace nor for the applause of this world - for my spiritual path is different from that of the world. With great difficulty I gained my Guru. If the world condemns me for meeting him, my great preceptor,

Then, says Mira, on such people's heads may hell fires fall."

Unhappy and tired of her long years of harrassment in Chitor and unable to continue her bhakti in peace, she decided to return to Medata, her uncle's kingdom. Before leaving, she told the king's court :

"Govindnā guna gāshu Rānāji ame..."

I shall continue to sing Govind's virtues, I have vowed for the charanamrut and to visit the mandir everyday on awakening,

If the Rana is angry, he'll rob me of my kingdom, But if Bhagwan is angry, I will die.

The Rana sent cups of poison, which turned into nectar, I will row a boat of Bhagwan's name and cross the ocean of maya,

Mira has taken refuge in Giridhar and will remain at His lotus feet."

In Medata, her uncle provided all the facilities necessary to lead a life of bhakti. But political conflict caused him to leave Rajputana. She then left on a pilgrimage to Vrundavan, Mathura and other holy places. In Vrundavan she visited the sacred spots where her Beloved performed divine *lila*. Here she also revelled the company *(satsang)* of sadhus:

"Sing of Goving! Dear Govind! O my mind!

You have been lucky in this human life to get an occasion to sing of Him.

It is very difficult to get a human body and its span is too short.

To attend to discourses on matters divine, is verily to have a boat in which to cross the ocean of rebirth.

Dive deep into the Ganga of the sadhus' company.

My abode is at the feet of the sadhus, therein my mind finds rest forever, says Mira."

She finally settled in Dwarka, Saurashtra, where she spent her remaining years offering bhakti to Dwarkadhish (Shri Krishna). From her *padas*, it is evident that she also visited Dakor to have Ranchhodraiji's *darshan*:

Dwārkāthi   Prabhu   Dākor   padhāriā,
Dākorne kidhu Kāshi, morlivālo re Vrajvāsi.

Furthermore she cites *bhakta* Bodano's story; of bringing Dwarkadhish to Dakor.

From her bhakti literature, it is evident that she must have met on enlightened guru. His identity is not known or when she met him. On more than one occasion she uses the word 'guru', without citing the name. However in only one Gujarati *pada*, there is a possible indication:

Rahidāsni cheli Mirā boliyā, rākho charanomā vās

Mira worshipped Bhagwan wholeheartedly and sublime purity. Regarding herself as a Gopi of Vrundavan, craving for Shri Krishna, she sought no worldly comforts or happiness. She only yearned to unite with her Beloved, to attain constant union (*sākshātkār*) with Him. Until then, her bhajans reflected her pangs of sorrow and pain at being separated from Him. When she achieved *sākshātkār* she sang in a different light:

"All–pervading One, I am dyed in your colour. When other women's sweethearts live in foreign lands, they write letter after letter. But my Beloved lives in my heart, so I sing (happily) day and night."

Her fame spread through the land. In her words:

"I am true to my Bhagwan. Why should I feel abashed now since

I even danced (for the Beloved) in public? I have no appetite during the day, and no rest or sleep at night. Now the arrow (of love) has pierced me and come out (on the other side), ... family and relatives have all come and are sitting (around me) like bees sipping honey. Mira, slave of Giridhar, is no more a laughing-stock in the world."

Her famous Gujarati *pada*, reflects her joy and *mahābhāgya* – huge fortune – in having realised Bhagwan:

Mukhadāni māyā lāgi re, Mohan pyārā, mukhadāni māyā lāgi...

She was a born bhakta–poetess, using her talents to express her intense love for Bhagwan. She wrote in Marwari Hindi, her mother tongue, but some of her poetry is laden with Gujarati and Punjabi words. Her bhajans primarily depict *virah bhakti* – devotion arising from pangs of separation. Her descriptions are a yearning, a lament, a sigh, a tear from estrangement from her Giridhar Nagar, which she is unable to suppress and exudes forth in her exuberant bhajans. Her literary works consist of over 360 bhajans, of which 150 are in Gujarati.

The renowned Sanskrit scholar, K.K. Shastri, observes that she spent the major part of her latter life as a pilgrim visiting holy places. Her demise at the age of 67 was a miraculous phenomenon. Around 1546, the reigning Rajput in Chitor, Rana Udaysinh and Mewar's people, felt that their continual miseries stemmed from Divine intent, for having harassed a true *bhakta*. In repentance, Udaysinh sent brahmins to Dwarka to persuade her to return. Mira refused, not wishing to foresake Dwarka's tranquility. To force her to capitulate, they began to fast. This pained her. However only her Beloved would save her honour. She then entered the mandir's sanctum, and merged into the *murti* of Dwarkadhish. This is known as *sayujia mukti*.

Mira the queen. Mira the bhakta–poetess. To date, no queen in the world has renounced all her wealth and material comforts to sing Bhagwan's glory and attain an eternal place in the annals of bhakti and endeared the hearts of bhaktas, as has Mira.

33. Samarth Ramdas

It is nighttime. A bridegroom listens to the Brahmin pundits uttering, "The time is extremely auspicious. Beware (*savdhan!*)!" The groom, only twelve–years–old, is startled. "I have vowed to worship Ram. What am I doing here?" With these sentiments churning in his mind he flees the marriage *mandap*. His relatives look for him, but to no avail.

'Beware' is spoken during all Hindu marriage ceremonies. But so far, only this groom acted on the warning. His name was Narayan. Born in 1608 in Jaamb, a village in Maharashtra, his Brahmin parents were ardent devotees of Eknath. They often took young Narayan to Eknath for darshan and blessings.

From childhood, Narayan, like his elder brother Gadadhar, worshipped Shri Ram and his humble servant, Hanumanji. When Narayan was eight, he requested Gadadhar for the Ram mantra. Gadadhar declined, saying that he was too young. This hurt Narayan, who ran away into the forest. He came across a small shrine where he fell asleep. Shri Ram then appeared before him and awakened him to gift him the Ram mantra.

M – Mumbai
P – Puna

The power of austerities

Now a devotee of Ram, Narayan changed his name to Ramdas – the servant of Ram. He then sought out a cave near the confluence of the rivers Godavari and Nandini, not far from a village named Taakdi. Here he performed austerities for twelve years, during which he uttered the 13 letter (in the Sanskrit script) mantra Shri Ram jai Ram, jai jai Ram, 130 million times. The austerities endowed him with great spiritual powers. Hence he became known as *Samarth* – the great – Ramdas. Ramdas then set out on a pilgrimage throughout India.

During his pilgrimage, from Kanyakumari in the south,

to the Himalayas in the north, he performed puja of the presiding deities in all the sacred places. He believed that all deities represented Shri Ram. During his sojourns he noted the frightening decadence of religious values among the masses, who had been overcome by superstition and ignorance. He attributed this degradation to Brahmin pundits. Filled with grief and apathy, he decided to end his life. At that instant Shri Ram appeared, saved him and ordered him to, 're–establish dharma and uplift the world.'

After the pilgrimage, Ramdas returned to Jaamb uttering, *'Jai jai Raghuvir* (Ram) *the Great.'* He begged for alms at his own house. When his mother appeared, he bowed down at her feet – their first meeting after a period of 24 years.

For a while his mother kept him at home. He then requested permission to leave. She relented, save for one wish; to return during her final moments. Ramdas agreed and left.

Establishing Ramrajya

He now began his life's work. He established his centre in a village known as Chaafal. Here he built a mandir and consecrated the *murtis* of Shri Ram and Hanumanji. His incessant travels increased his following. Everywhere he established mandirs and *maths*. He often advised his disciples, "Use your wealth to serve others. Be happy in others' happiness. First practice, then preach." His following became known as the Ramdasi Sampraday and Samarth Sampraday. By offering worship to Ram, he enjoined people to establish Ramrajya – the kingdom of Ram. He urged his followers, "Gather together and be united." Whenever he wrote to someone, his first phrase would be, "Gather together."

His aim was to establish Ramrajya by reviving public interest in spiritual discourses, observance of dharma and the uplift of Brahmins. Spiritual discourses were his forte; but without the latter two, the former would not be effective.

Therefore, he first strived to gather people together. He had faith that his dream to establish such a kingdom would be fulfilled with the help of Shivaji, the Maharaja of Maharashtra.

Shivaji's Guru

Once in 1649, Shivaji bowed his head at Samarth's feet and begged for mantra of initiation. Samarth gave him the *Shri Ram, jai Ram, jai jai Ram* mantra. Shivaji then further requested the guru to let him serve like the other disciples. Samarth replied, "Your duty as a Kshatriya is to look after the citizens. Protect the land from foreign rulers and establish dharma. This is Shri Ram's command for you."

Samarth then handed him a coconut, a fistful of soil, two fistfuls of horse manure and four fistfuls of pebbles as *prasad*. He then blessed him, "O Shivaji! You are blessed. Shri Hari will take care of all your worries."

Shivaji easily gleaned the guru's wish. To his mother Jijibai, he revealed, "The coconut symbolises my moksha. The soil means Earth, pebbles mean forts and the horse manure means horses. I will become the king of the Earth, will conquer many forts and will amass countless horses in my army."

As Shivaji's kingdom increased in size, so did his devotion to his guru. Once he saw Ramdas begging alms from house to house. This pained him. He dropped a note in Ramdas's alms bag saying, "I offer my whole kingdom at your lotus feet. You are the master and I am your servant!" Samarth replied, "In that case take this bag and follow me to beg alms!"

Shivaji followed the guru to beg alms. After having food, Samarth said, "Since the kingdom is now mine, I command you to carry its burden on my behalf. Take this cloth (his saffron coloured upper garment) and make a flag from it. By Ram's grace, whatever you wish will bear fruit." Shivaji obeyed. From then onwards, the saffron flag fluttered over his kingdom. Since Shivaji was of a *sattvic* (pure) temperament, he tried to renounce samsara on three separate occasions. But he was prevented from doing so – twice by Samarth and once by Eknath.

Saintly virtues

As behoves a sadhu, Ramdas possessed the saintly

attributes of humility and forbearance. Once while travelling, his disciples cut a few cobs of *jowar* from a nearby field to satiate their hunger. As soon as the farmers heard of this, they mercilessly thrashed Ramdas. When Shivaji came to know of the incident he seethed with fury. He said to Samarth, "Tell me, what punishment should I inflict upon them?"

Ramdas replied, "Give them a prize of a *pagh* (turban) and *shelu* (upper garment). They are not to blame. We are."

On another occasion, some thieves entered the ashram awakening everyone. The disciples said to Ramdas, "Maharaj, thieves have entered the ashram."

"What will they steal? Whatever they take will be Ram's."

"Does that mean we should allow the theft?"

"Why not?"

"Theft in Bhagwan's house?"

"Does Bhagwan's house belong only to you and not them? Wealth either here or with the thieves will only be used for food and sustenance."

The thieves listened to this exchange with intereset. They then fell at Ramdas's feet and begged for forgiveness. Ramdas served them food and bade them farewell.

Swami Ramdas is respected as a stalwart among Marathi poets. In his poems there is no room for luck or apathy. He has forever extolled virtues such as boldness and initiative. His main work is *Dasbodh*. Once in the middle of the night, he composed a devotional verse of 205 lines known as *Manaache* Shlok. He ordered a disciple to pen it down there and then. After that, whenever the disciples begged for alms, they would utter one line of this verse at each house. In this way the verse gained popularity.

In the verse Ramdas addresses the mind:

"O mind, accept the Lordship of the almighty and compassionate Ram! Worship Ram! Sing Ram's glory! Ram is Brahman. Ram is the beginning and the end."

Another beautiful poem is the *Karunashtak Stotra*. In this, he divulges the glory of Shri Ram to the mind:

"O mind, why do you fear the cycle of births and deaths so? Raghupati Ram is sitting there (for us). Even if Yama (King of Hell) himself cometh, what will he be able to do? Who can even attempt to look at a Ram bhakta with a malicious eye?"

When the time arrived for him to depart, he stopped taking food and water. One day in 1681, he sat in front of Shri Ram's *murti* and chanted *'Har Har'* 21 times, followed by 'Shri Ram.' He then left his body. He was 78 years old.

34. Tukaram

The state of Maharashtra in western India usually conjures up images of the hero, Chhatrapati Shivaji. Also worth noting, is that he loved listening to sadhus and mystics sing bhajans. The most renowned of these was the bhakta–poet Tukaram. Though he did not take *samnyas diksha*, people revere him as a saint for his saintly disposition. One source does however, claim that he became an ascetic after his wife died.

The son of a Kanbi and therefore regarded as a lower *varna*, Tukaram was born in 1609 in Dehu, a village near Puna. The family ran a thriving business. Though details of his childhood are not available, historians note that as an adult, singing bhajans held greater interest for him than business. Added to this, he would be pained on seeing others suffering. Once, on returning to Dehu from a business trip, a wretched sight overwhelmed him. He saw a Brahmin walking in chains, dragging a plough tied to his neck, begging for food. Contemporary society inflicted this punishment on a person in debt. Tukaram gave him money to clear his debt and had him unshackled. In business, too, he was lenient. Whenever he weighed out an item for a customer, he made sure it was slightly overweight rather than under. As a result, he suffered losses. Soon, he was steeped in poverty and had difficulty supporting his family.

Like Narsinh Mehta, he left these worldly problems to Bhagwan. He remained engrossed in devotion, composing and singing bhajans, and serving sadhus. When he visited other villages to sing bhajans, he accepted neither any money nor any food as gifts. He considered it sinful to accept money for singing bhajans. Humility being the virtue of a truly pious bhakta, he felt extremely uncomfortable when devotees honoured him. He acknowledged this in his *abhangs*:

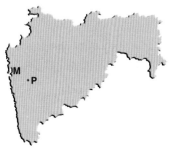

M – Mumbai
P – Puna

207

Tukaram's Abhangs

"This flitting wealth, wife and family are not yours. What remains yours at death is only Vitthal. Tukaram says go after Him only."

•

"One who wishes to attain Shri Hari should empty himself of all desires. Those who do chant Hari's name, yet are trapped in avarice, who tread the path of evil, injustice and immorality, send their ancestors to hell."

•

He is a true sadhu who is able to serenely bear all the upheavels of this world.

•

Attain victory over the senses, completely destroy all baser instincts and let not any delusive thoughts of the body enter the mind.

•

Only humility is the key instrument to cross the ocean of samsar.

•

One who keeps his indriyas under control is honoured the highest seat on every level.

•

The body is death's food. Then why do people crave for physical comforts and why do they believe it as the essence (of life)?

"I do not want such honour, but people do not realise this. What to do? This delicious sweet I regard as poison. People greatly praise me, but I cannot bear to listen. By listening my jiva flounders, O Pandharinath! Have mercy upon me. Save me from this fire! People gift me this horse, this parasol... but even in my good days I have never used them. So now, O Pandharinath, why trap me in such wealth? Pride and hypocrisy are a pig's excreta. So Vitthalnath, do rush and save me from this!"

As with Tyagraj, people flocked to Tukaram to listen to his bhajans. And as is usual in human society, jealous elements often arise. Unable to bear Tukaram's fame, a Brahmin named Mambaji maligned him. He informed people that being of a low *varna*, Tukaram had no right to deliver sermons. Therefore, they should avoid listening to his bhajans. Yet people continued. This so infuriated Mambaji that he arrived hotfoot with a cane. He then severely thrashed Tukaram. The latter bore the fury without uttering a word. In the evening, while Tukaram sang bhajans in the village mandir, he noted Mambaji's absence. He questioned the others about him. They informed him that Mambaji had suddenly fallen ill. Tukaram immediately visited Mambaji, prostrated and began to nurse him. Mambaji was so moved by Tukaram's humility that he asked for forgiveness. He then became the poet's disciple.

Another similar incident illustrates Tukaram's amazing humility. Once a Brahmin pundit named Rameshwar Bhatt ordered Tukaram to dump his bhajans into the nearby Indrayani river. He believed that composing bhajans in Marathi was sinful and they should only be composed in Sanskrit. Tukaram obeyed, flinging his bundle of *abhangs* into the river! When the disciples heard of this they were pained. They rebuked the pundit, saying that Tukaram had composed the *abhangs* by Vithoba's command. By discarding the *abhangs*, Tukaram realised that he had also inadvertently insulted Vithoba. For this, he grieved and sat disconsolately in the mandir for 13 days without food. Vithoba then gave him darshan in a dream, saying, "Do not lament. The *abhangs* are floating in the river." Tukaram related this to the disciples, who rushed to the river bank. Sure enough, they saw the bundle floating on the surface. On retrieving it, they discovered the manuscripts to be completely dry! Tukaram's eyes welled up and he resumed singing bhajans ecstatically. Realising Tukaram's glory, Rameshwar Bhatt wrote a verse requesting forgiveness. Like Mambaji, he too became Tukaram's disciple.

Around this period in Maharashtra, Maharaja Shivaji was establishing his reign. He venerated sadhus and mystics; offering them food, clothing and land. When he heard about Tukaram, he sent the poet a small pot of treasure as a gift. Although Tukaram barely had enough food for even one meal a day, he returned this uninvited treasure, with a bhajan. He wrote:

"By begging alms I fill my stomach. A rag covers me adequately. To sleep, I have the yard. The sky serves as a blanket. What more do I need? O Shivaji! You are a king. Therefore walk the path of truth. Observe a righteous morality. Care for your citizens justly. Protect the helpless. Offer devotion to Bhagwan. Lo! That is all the gift I require from you."

On reading this bhajan, Shivaji decided that he should meet such a mystic personally. With his ministers, he travelled to Dehu and was thrilled to hear Tukaram's bhajans. Thereafter, he often visited Tukaram. Being a noble–hearted *atma*, the bhajans profoundly affected Shivaji. They induced him to renounce. He discarded his royal attire to retire to the forest. His mother Jijabai was devastated. She then informed Tukaram that without Shivaji, the whole kingdom would be ruined by insurgents from Delhi. Therefore, he, Tukaram, should command Shivaji to return.

When Shivaji next returned from the forest to hear Tukaram, the latter gave a sermon, "A man who loses sight of his duties loses everything. A Brahmin should observe the duties of a Brahmin and a king, likewise, should observe his. He should please his subjects!" When the sermon ended,

Except for Bhagwan, everything else is superfluous, as is each individual's wish. One will never experience the taste of happiness by increasing desires. With great patience develop faith in Bhagwan who alone is the all-doer. Firmly bear this sentiment in mind. He will look after your welfare, without the slightest shortcomings.

•

The entire world is Devarup (Divine). This is my principle sermon. Firstly, renounce the 'my-ness' latent in you. Just by doing this you will pass all trials. Believe firmly that in this one sentence lies the storehouse of Brahmajnan.

•

If you show me that there is greater happiness in anything other than my Ram, then I will become your servant. No matter how much you run after fame and name, but one day these will all perish.

Shivaji re–adorned his royal garb and resumed his reign. It was Tukaram who advised him to accept Ramdas as guru.

Once, Shivaji called all sadhus to a town named Paradi for a bhajan festival. His guru, Ramdas, and Tukaram were also present. On this occasion, Shivaji decided to gift four villages to Tukaram. On gleaning this, Tukaram left. Shivaji then requested his guru, Ramdas, to persuade Tukaram to accept the gift. Ramdas replied, "O you fool! How can you try to entice a person, who has not the slightest desire for the three worlds *(trilok)*, with a mere four villages?"

In Sanatan Dharma, *namsmaran* *(japa)* is glorified immensely. It consolidates one's *bhava* (sentiments) for Bhagwan. Tukaram too experienced the effects of *namjapa*: "By uttering Hari's name, the body cools down, the senses become contented and lose their cravings. *Nam* is sweeter than *amrut*. *Namsmaran* increases devotional love. By this love, the body's lustre increases and instantly destroys the 'three pains' (*adhyatma*, *adhibhut* and *adhidaiva*). After uttering *nam* the base instincts do not survive." In another *abhang* he adds: "... (by *namjapa*) I forget even my existence. In this body I experience the state of *videha*. Because of *nam* I have become like the fire, *pap* and *punya* do not touch my body; as they come near they are burnt."

He inspired the whole of Maharashtra to utter *Ram-Krishna Hari*.

Tukaram also extolled the glory of sadhus and their association — *sant samagam*:

"Sadhus' proximity confers the joy of embracing *chidanand*. An experience of cosmic joy. One's *ahamkar* (ego) is destroyed. By meeting sadhus, samsar's pain is eradicated. They give more than what a wishing tree can give. In comparison to what they give, *chintamani* pales. There is nobody in the three *loks* more generous than sadhus. Not even parents, siblings, relatives or the closest friend. To one upon whom they shower their grace, they install him on the throne of *parampad* (moksha)".

> *"Nam (Hari's) reduces the most evil karmas to ashes and reveals the essence of atma's bliss. That I have realised and have become fully contented with beholding it (namjapa). Now there's no need for austerities or going into the forest. In the face of namjapa, Kaliyuga becomes a dwarf."*

Tukaram's sole desire in life rested in his devotion to Vithoba. On the sacred Ekadashi (eleventh) of Ashadh and Kartik, he regulary visited Vithoba's mandir in Pandharpur. On one such Ekadashi he was bedridden with illness. He therefore sent a bhajan with other pilgrims visiting Pandharpur. He requested them to offer and sing the bhajan on his behalf. The pilgrims duly offered the bhajan. When they returned, a week or more later – for Pandharpur is quite some distance away – they saw him slumped in the same position they had left him. Only when they offered him Vithoba's *prasad* did he regain normal consciousness.

One night in 1649, when he realised it was time to depart, he sang bhajans all night. In the morning, he bathed in the river and then sat meditating on Vithoba. Chanting Bhagwan's name, he left his body. He was only 40 years old.

Every year on Falgun vad 2, thousands of devotees gather in Dehu to sing his glory. Just as Jnaneshwar is regarded as the greatest Sanskrit scholar-mystic of Maharashtra, Tukaram is considered as the greatest bhakta-poet of Maharashtra. His bhajans number over four thousand. His *abhangs* are replete with analogies and imagery endearing them to devotees. The renowned Maharashtrian thinker and mystic, Vinoba Bhave observed, "His (Tukaram's) speech has that lustre, the power to attract and pierce hearts, which is unmatched in Marathi... Tukaram's speech is Marathi language's Ganga, which sanctifies everyone and is easily available to everyone. A mother does not need to learn language to teach her children. This is Tukaram's case" (Kalani 1991:183).

It is said that in Maharashtra, Jnaneshwar laid the foundations of Bhagvat Dharma. Namdev helped spread it. Eknath raised a flag over it. Finally, Tukaram became its pinnacle, which even today, remains standing in its ever attractive form by the divine grace of *Tribhuvansundar* Shri Krishna Vitthal.

35. Gauribai

In Sanatan Dharma, no barrier of age or gender exists for one who earnestly desires spiritual transcendence. Men and women, young and old, alike, have reached these sublime heights. Gauribai's life is a shining example of how sincere devotion to Paramatma leads one to the peaks of spiritual experience. Sadhus, mystics and poets, being of a humble disposition, generally do not encourage their followers to pen down details of their personal lives. In Gauribai's case, the poetess–*sadhvi* of Gujarat, we are not too far removed from her period and so we are able to procure reliable information about her life and work. When her biography was written in the 20th century, two members of her family were alive, who supplied facts about their saintly ancestor.

Gauribai was born in Samvat 1815 (1759 CE) in Giripur, also known as Dungarpur, on the border between Gujarat and Rajputana. She was a Vadnagar Nagar Brahmin. This community boasted one hundred per cent literacy, even among the womenfolk.

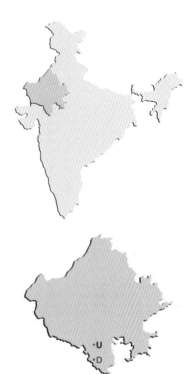

U – Udaipur
D – Dungarpur

Gauribai was married (betrothed) at the age of about six, as was the custom then. A week later, her husband contracted a mysterious illness and died within hours. When family members grieved and pitied her for her husband's loss, she replied philosophically, "Bhagwan is my Lord and I have dedicated my life to Him." As custom demanded, she stayed with her parents.

She then spent her time in worshipping the family deities (*kuldevata*), singing bhajans and reading shastras. She also composed a few bhajans praising Bhagwan.

As she grew up her fame spread. Raja Shivasinhji of Giripur heard of her purity and visited her for darshan. He discussed spiritual lore with her and was impressed by her knowledge and disposition. He therefore built a new mandir in her honour, together with an almshouse and constructed a step–well next to it. Gauribai then left her home, taking the *murtis* with her, which she consecrated in the mandir in Samvat 1836 (1780 CE). She was then 21–years–old. Soon the mandir's fame spread. Pilgrims, sadhus and pundits flocked here, inducing Gauribai to hold spiritual discourses. This further increased her spiritual knowledge and boosted her poetic gift.

Once, a learned sadhu arrived. He noted Gauribai's spiritual status and devotional yearning. He revealed to her, "You are Mirabai's incarnation. Though she was an ardent devotee, she did not possess as much knowledge as behoves a mystic. You are born to correct that defect. I will impart that extra knowledge." He then taught her *Brahmajnan* and *atmajnan*. Revealing the correct path of sadhuhood, he blessed her. He also presented her with a *murti* of Balmukund (the infant Shri Krishna) and then left.

As Gauribai's knowledge increased, so did her *vairagya* (detachment) from worldly affairs. It is said that she would attain samadhi which, at times, lasted a fortnight. Hariyan, an old female relative staying with her, once decided to check the nature of her samadhi. She pricked needles into her body. However, Gauribai never winced. Hariyan fled leaving the needles in place. Soon she was afflicted with leprosy. Realising that this was a punishment for her cruelty, she fell at Gauribai's feet begging for forgiveness. Gauribai forgave her and the disease disappeared.

After one such samadhi, Gauribai lived on milk alone. Later, she decided to visit Gokul and Vrundavan. When Shivasinhji heard of this he tried to dissuade her and offered expensive gifts, which she refused. Entrusting the worship of the main *murti* to a sadhu, she left for Vrundavan with her personal *murtis*.

When she arrived in Jaipur, the royalty came to have her darshan. The queen offered her 500 gold coins, which she declined to keep and donated them to Brahmins. This impressed the king. Yet he wished to test her proximity to Paramatma. He therefore ordered for the *murti* in his private shrine to be exquisitely decorated and then had the doors closed. He then invited Gauribai to the shrine on the pretext of listening to the Bhagvatam's *katha*. After the *katha*, he requested her to describe the *murti*, a test similar to Surdas's (see p.175). A trifle unnerved, she informed the king that she was just a lay devotee. But she would pray to Bhagwan to help her. She then meditated and composed and sang a prayer. She described the adornments and added, "The only flaw is the absence of the crown on the head." This astonished the king, for Shri Krishna's *murti* is never without a crown. When the doors opened, everyone present realised Gauribai's exalted status; the adornments were exactly as described and the crown had slipped off because the pujari had not placed it securely. The king was mortified and asked her to forgive him. She did. He then offered her the part of the palace where she was staying and requested her to live in Jaipur as his permanent guest. As before she declined, for she craved to live in Paramatma's sacred land. When the king persisted, she agreed to leave Paramatma's *murti*, which she worshipped daily, in the palace.

She lived in Gokul, Mathura and Vrundavan for a while. She then visited Kashi (Banaras). Maharaja Sundersinh, who had heard of her saintly disposition, offered her hospitality. He too was gifted in composing bhajans. And so the *sadhvi*–poetess and the king often composed bhajans together. She showed him how to meditate and he accepted her as his guru. He offered her 50,000 rupees. From this she used 20,000 to settle a community dispute and the rest she gave away in charity when she visited Jagannath Puri.

From Puri she returned to Kashi. Once, after remaining in samadhi for a week, she revealed to her disciples that her end was near. She wished to forsake her body on the banks of the Yamuna where Dhruv, the child devotee, had performed austerities. She prophesied that she would pass away on Ramnavmi. Raja Sundersinh arranged to send her there. After remaining in samadhi for a few days, she departed, on Ramnavmi, in Samvat 1865 (1809 CE) at the age of 50.

Her bhajans number in the thousands, the majority of which are in Gujarati, though many contain Rajasthani words. She composed a few in Hindi, the result of her stay in *Vraj Bhumi* and Banaras.

36. Tyagraj

Blessed with exceptional musical talent, Tyagraj spurned fame and riches and devoted his life to Shri Ram. His compositions have the capacity to instil devotion, joy and happiness in the hearts of all.

Along with the Alwars, Tyagraj (commonly spelt Thyagraj in south India) was a renowned bhakta–poet of south India. He was born into a Brahmin family in 1767, in Tiruvalur near Tanjore in Tamil Nadu. His father, Ram Brahmam, and mother, Shantadevi, had two other sons, Jayesh and Ramnath. Since both sons were of an unruly nature, the parents prayed at the local Tyagaraja mandir for a third son who would be a bhakta. One night Shantadevi had a divine darshan with the message, "I am pleased with your *seva* and bhakti. A great singer and a bhakta of Shri Ram will be born to you."

C – Chennai
T – Tanjore (Thanjavur)
S – Srirangam
M – Madurai

When the bhakta was born, Ram Brahmam named him Tyagraj, since he was born by the blessings of Tyagaraja. When he was five, his father began to teach him Telugu. Both parents also took him to Tyagaraja's mandir where the boy listened to bhajans. Often he would also join in the singing. The adult singers appreciated his sweet voice and singing style. Noticing his innate musical ability, Ram Brahmam arranged for him to learn music.

He became Shondi Venkatraman's pupil. The guru was a famous teacher at the raja's court in Tanjore. Tyagraj studied sincerely. By the age of 16, he had mastered many aspects of music, also composing and singing bhajans of Shri Ram. Simultaneously, he also studied Sanskrit.

After obtaining the guru's blessings, he returned home. Tyagraj never envisaged his musical abilities as a source of income. For this reason, his elder brothers often quarrelled with him. When 18, Tyagraj married Parvati. Soon Tyagraj's parents expired. Four years later, Parvati too, died. This increased Tyagraj's detachment from the world. However, at people's behest, he married Parvati's younger sister, Kamalaba. After marriage Tyagraj continued his deep devotion, singing Shri Ram's bhajans for hours at a time. This infuriated Jayesh, his eldest brother, who single–handedly supported the household. Jayesh scolded Tyagraj, saying that singing bhajans would not bring home food. How long could he support him and his wife? He should either start earning or else live separately. Tyagraj listened calmly and replied, "O elder brother, you are probably thinking that I will demand a share of our father's property. But you are mistaken. I do not want anything. You can have the house and all its contents. I will go and live in a hut somewhere. Sita–Ram's *murti* is my fortune, the *tanpuro* my boat to cross the ocean of samsara and Shri Ram's name is my moksha."

These words came as music to Jayesh. He quickly made Tyagraj sign a document, relinquishing their father's property to him. Jayesh then built him a flimsy hut on a distant hillock. Tyagraj left home with a tattered mat, a dented water–pot, old texts, a *mala*, a *tanpuro* (a stringed musical instrument) and his beloved Sita–Ram's *murti*.

Ram Ram

On settling into their new home, Tyagraj comforted Kamalaba, "Do not worry. In this isolated retreat it will be even more joyous to offer devotion. Shri Ram is here to care for us. He may awaken us hungry, but he will not let us go to sleep so.'

Being a true Hindu wife, devoted to her husband, Kamalaba had the grace not to demand perishable worldly objects from Tyagraj, who was totally immersed in devotion.

Once, while Tyagraj was engrossed in singing bhajans, an ascetic named Ramkrishnanand arrived on their doorstep. The couple welcomed him by offering the little fruit they had in the house. Pleased by their service, he offered them a boon. Tyagraj replied, "O Yogiraj! The stalwart ascetics never arrive without a purpose. All I ask is for a guru mantra to cross samsara."

Ramkrishnanand commanded Tyagraj, "Recite the Ram mantra ten million times and Shri Ram will redeem you."

Resolutely, Tyagraj commenced chanting the Ram mantra, 125,000 times every day. When he was 38–years–old, he completed the Ram mantras. By Shri Ram's grace he attained *vachan siddhi*. This meant that whatever he spoke would prove true. In addition, even in his sleep, while his lips remained closed, one could hear the incessant chanting of 'Ram, Ram.'

Yet a constant fear troubled him. By *vachan siddhi* one could not only do good to others, but curse them as well. What would be the outcome, he wondered, if an ugly incident arose and he cursed someone? He quickly held a *yagna* on completion of his *japa*. He offered back to Shri Ram the *vachan siddhi* he had been granted. By renouncing this *siddhi*, he also remained true to the meaning of his name – Tyagraj, king of renunciation.

At that moment he heard a knock at the door. On opening it, he witnessed an unbelievable sight – a teenage form of Shri Ram, accompanied by Lakshman and Vishwamitra rishi! Transfixed on seeing his Bhagwan, he forgot to welcome them. Divine rays emanating from Shri Ram entered Tyagraj's body and soon the divine darshan ended. Only then did Tyagraj come to his senses and repented for failing to welcome them. Deeply regretting this, the bhajans he composed thereafter, all pined for Bhagwan. These bhajans and his music spread his fame all over. People regarded him as a saintly personality and began to flock to his hut.

Rejecting royal riches

Once, an old man requested Tyagraj, "I have come to hear your bhajans. I have heard a lot about you. They say that Shri Ram gave you darshan. I have come to verify the truth personally."

"Fine. Please be seated," said Tyagraj, offering a mat. He then took his *tanpuro*, adjusted the strings and began to sing. As the bhajans soared, sung in the true classical style and metre, the old man started swaying in delight. At the end the old man blessed Tyagraj and left. That night, he appeared to the sleeping Tyagraj.

"Do you recognise me? I am Narad. I am extremely pleased with your singing. By your devotion, you have attained a unique *siddhi*. You are still to attain greater heights in this *siddhi*. For this I am gifting you this *Swavārnava* shastra. Study it."

At that instant, Tyagraj's eyes opened. He saw the shastra beside his pillow. By studying it, his knowledge and musical talents improved markedly. News of his unique musical talents soon reached the ears of King Sharbhoj. It was customary for him to hounour talented citizens with gifts. Soon a messenger from the court arrived carrying the king's invitation. This disturbed Tyagraj. He was worried; not about whether the king would like his singing, but that he may appoint him as the royal bard. Tyagraj wished to taste Ram's 'riches' rather than of royalty; to sing praises of the Almighty, rather than of a human overwhelmed by base instincts.

Therefore he sent a note with the messenger, "O King! Only Shri Ram's name plays on my tongue. Never will it sing a king's praises. My head which has bowed to Shri Ram will not bow to a king. By forsaking Shri Ram's *seva*, I will not adopt royal service. I only know Shri Ram's palace and if it is my good fortune, there I will go."

This is strikingly similar to the note written by the poet Ladudan Barot, who later became Brahmanand Swami, the *paramhansa*–poet of Bhagwan Swaminarayan. This was in response to the invitation of Maharaja Sayajirao Gaekwad of Baroda, who had offered him a lucrative post in his court in the early 19th century. Ladudan refused, because he had resolved to compose and sing bhajans of Bhagwan Swaminarayan only.

On receiving Tyagraj's message, the king was pleased. He realised the truth and decided to visit Tyagraj himself. When Jayesh heard the news that his brother had refused to visit the court, he was infuriated, since he craved for the worldly riches which the king would have gifted Tyagraj. He therefore grabbed Shri Ram's *murti* and flung it in the nearby river Kaveri. Loving this *murti* more than his own *atma*, Tyagraj plunged into the river. People on the banks watched aghast. Tyagraj swam to the bottom and somehow located the *murti*. Onlookers hailed him and scorned Jayesh.

Once, a music stalwart named Ayyar visited him. He sang in the *Anand Bhairavi* metre, which pleased Tyagraj. Ayyar then made a startling request. He said, "By singing this metre, I have been lauded as a maestro by people. But when they hear it from your lips, they will forget me. I request you never to sing this metre." Being of a saintly disposition Tyagraj, gladly gave his word!

Old age set in. Kamalaba soon died. This saddened Tyagraj. Henceforth, his poems reflected this sorrow and lamentations for Kamalaba. He then renounced to become a *samnyasi*. Soon after, in 1847, he passed away and joined Shri Ram in Vaikunth.

He composed hundreds of bhajans dedicated to Shri Ram. Bhaktas in south India have extolled him as the incarnation of Valmiki rishi, who composed the Ramayan.

37. The Pativrata

At the dawn of the 21st century, with promiscuity at the zenith, morality and cultural values at their nadir, a glance at Sanatan Dharma's glorious past, may inspire us to reinforce such values in our lives. These in turn will go on to inspire our children. One such value concerning morality is of the Pativrata.

Pati means husband. *Vrat* denotes vow. A woman who staunchly remains loyal to her husband is a Pativrata. The Ramayan mentions that an ideal Pativrata will not see another man other than her husband even in her dreams. In the Shikshapatri (159) Bhagwan Swaminarayan stipulates that a Pativrata should serve her husband as she would serve and worship Bhagwan, even if the husband is blind, diseased, poor or impotent. Sati is another synonym for Pativrata – one who preserves her *sattva* (purity) – physically, mentally and spiritually. It also denotes the widow who ritually immolated herself on the cremation pyre of her deceased husband. Sati also has a greater meaning. *'Sat'* means Paramatma, 'i' means *gati* – journey. Hence a woman who dedicates herself totally to attain Bhagwan is also termed sati. Mirabai, the bhakta–poetess and Zamkuba are two such examples.

In Sanatan Dharma the stalwart sati, Ansuya is well known. Sati Savitiri is another famed Pativrata. When she decided to marry Satyavan, Naradji tried to dissuade her. His reason was that Satyavan only had a year to live. Remaining resolute, Savitri married Satyavan. On his death, Dharmaraja, also known as Yama, the king of Narak (Hell), arrived to collect Satyavan's *jiva*. Savitri accompanied her husband. She told Yama, "It is my duty as a loyal wife to go wherever my husband goes." This pleased Yama, who granted her a boon and told her to return. She declined and continued to follow both. On two further occasions Yama granted her boons, then requested her to return. As before, she declined. Finally Yama sternly told her to return and granted her a final boon. She ingeniously requested for a hundred sons. Without thinking, Yama agreed and again ordered her to return. She calmly pointed out that this final boon could only be realised if he granted Satyavan life. She added, "My husband is my life, destiny, Lakshmi and happiness."

Savitri's true sentiments of fidelity and devotion forced Yama's hand, who granted Satyavan a lifespan of 400 years. As if arising from deep sleep, he awoke.

The shastras also proclaim another five women as *satis*:

Ahalyā Draupadi Sitā Tārā Mandodari tathā,
Panch kanyāhā smaret nityam mahāpātaka nāshinihi.

– the daily remembrance of the five Pativratas, namely, Ahalya, Draupadi, Sita, Tara and Mandodari eradicates great sins.

If sins are eradicated in remembering their names, this gives an inkling of the profound nature of and power latent in a Pativrata.

In this chapter we consider examples from a time period stretching half a millennium. These women remind us of the lofty value of and pride in maintaining *satitva* (chastity) rather than succumbing to *dehabhav*.

Around 1330, Raol Ratnasinh was the Rajput ruler in Chitor, Rajasthan. His queen, Padmini, was famed for her beauty throughout India. When Ala-ud-din Khilji, the Afghan ruler in Delhi heard about her, he ached to possess her. Therefore, he stormed Chitor. After a fruitless and protracted siege, he sent a message to Ratnasinh to allow him just a glimpse of Padmini, after which he would leave Chitor. All the Sisodia Rajput noblemen were against this, for it would be a violation of the woman's *satitva*. The Rajputs' strict morality allowed no man other than the husband to see his wife's face. However, to be free of the Afghan's relentless siege, the Rajputs agreed. They would arrange for him to see her image reflected in a series of ingeniously arranged mirrors. After he saw her image his base instincts ran riot. Day and night

Padmini's image seared his lecherous heart. He reamassed a greater army and reattacked Chitor. While the Rajput heroes prepared for battle inside the fort, their mothers, wives, sisters and daughters performed puja by lighting a huge fire in the fort's centre. As the Rajputs spilled out of the gate, Padmini was the first to jump into the fire, followed by several thousand females! This act, known as *jauhar* in Rajasthan, was valiantly performed on three occasions in Chitor's history to preserve the Rajput women's *satitva*.

Padmini was lawfully married to Ratnasinh. Yet an important feature of a Pativrata is to remain loyal even if she has betrothed herself to a man mentally.

During Akbar's reign, King Bajabahadur of Malwa had not bowed to him. Although he had many queens, he accepted Rupamati, the daughter of a dancer and singer. Probably being of a lower social order, Rupamati could not marry the king and mentally chose him as her husband. He in turn admired her expertise as a singer, archer, horserider and hunter.

In 1590 Akbar sent Ahmad Khan to conquer Malwa. He defeated Bajabahadur, who fled. Rupamati, too, fought in the battle and was wounded.

When Khan reached the queen's chambers he slew all the queens. He was then informed about Rupamati. Thereupon he sent her a deceitful message that he had captured Bajabahadur and that she could stay with him and recover in peace. When she arrived she realised his treachery. After she recovered, he pleaded with her to accompany him to Delhi where he would shower her with riches. Rupamati refused. Before he arrived again to forcibly take her she prayed to Paramatma. To protect her *satitva* she then drank a potent poison! Even today people in Malwa sing ballads extolling her as a Pativrata.

To uphold *satitva* demands profound moral and mental courage. Moreso when talent combines with beauty, as was the case with Rupamati. The allure of material riches, power or threat of political coercion are minor inconveniences, like flies to an elephant. The Pativrata regards her *satitva* as a form of devotion and every factor which may hinder or taint it, is ruthlessly excised from the root, even if it warrants suicide.

During Akbar's reign, his famous musician Tansen, once made a mistake while singing the *Deepak raag*. This resulted in an unbearable ailment. The only remedy was for someone to sing its 'antidote', the *Malhar raag*. Akbar despatched orders to his Subedars ruling the other states in the land, to search for experts of *Malhar*. They found none. Finally, the Subedar of Gujarat discovered two Nagar Brahmin sisters, named Tana and Riri Mehta of Vadnagar, in north Gujarat. He sent them to Delhi. Here they sang the *Malhar raag* and cured Tansen.

Their unmatched talent combined with beauty, caused many a general's heart to flutter at Akbar's court. These lecherous generals followed the sisters to Gujarat. Here they colluded with the Subedar of Gujarat and tried to coerce the sisters. They flatly declined. The generals then planned to kidnap them. When the sisters gleaned this, they drowned themselves in the village pond before the horde arrived.

The foregoing three examples, namely Padmini, Rupamati and the Mehta sisters, are of Pativratas who preferred to destroy their physical bodies in order to preserve their Pativrata dharma.

As mentioned earlier, there is also the Pativrata who dedicates herself totally to attain Paramatma – the *Param Pati* (Supreme Husband). During this endeavour, if her husband becomes a hindrance, she will forsake him. This is the greatest Pativrata in Sanatan Dharma. Of the many such women during the time of Bhagwan Swaminarayan, we consider three: Kadvibai, Rajbai and Rambai.

Kadvibai of Jetpur in Saurashtra was inclined towards bhakti from childhood. She had *vairagya* (detachment) and cared little for food and clothes. After marriage she discovered that her husband despised her offering bhakti. He began to cruelly harass her hoping she would renounce devotion to Paramatma. To prevent her from offering devotion at night, he would place one leg of his bed on her chest.

She then sought the help of her brother, Shivram. Both left Jetpur to visit relatives in a nearby town. Here they both heard Bhagwan Swaminarayan's voice, "One should not wear clothes and ornaments of a married woman. One should not keep the hair on one's head. Are you such a woman?" Shivram realised that Bhagwan Swaminarayan wished his sister to renounce samsara.

On returning to Jetpur, Kadvibai continued singing bhajans. Unable to tolerate this, her husband shouted, "From today you are not my wife. You are like a mother and sister to me! Do as you please."

This angry outburst came as a blessing. She could now legally leave her husband without social stigma. However, Brahmin elders decided to do away with her. The town's Kathi chief, being a Swaminarayan follower, came to her aid wielding a sword. The Brahmins fled. That night Bhagwan Swaminarayan appeared to her in a divine form and instructed her to hurl herself in the nearby river, at a point where she saw His *murti*. She would reach the opposite bank safely. From there she would be guided to Gadhada.

Events unfolded as prophesied. In Gadhada Bhagwan Swaminarayan initiated her as a *samkhyayogini* (a woman who has renounced all worldly ties). She then spent the rest of her life as a true Pativrata.

Like Kadvibai, Rajbai never wished to marry. She yearned to observe lifelong *brahmacharya* and offer devotion to Bhagwan Swaminarayan. Yet she was forced into marriage by her mother. On the first day after arriving at her in-laws, she prayed to Bhagwan for succour. When her husband entered her room and was on the verge of touching her, he screamed. Instead of Rajbai, he saw a lion on the bed! Scared stiff, he bolted out of the room and ordered his parents to get rid of her!

Rajbai requested to be sent to Gadhada to her cousin Jivuba, who had also chosen the path of *brahmacharya* and devotion. Later, the in-laws arrived to take her back. Bhagwan

Swaminarayan had no choice but to command her to go. Poleaxed with despair, she fainted. Blood oozed out of every pore of her body. This horrified the in–laws. Rescinding their demand, they requested Him to revive her. This He did.

Rajbai then spent the rest of her life in Gadhada. When she passed away to join Bhagwan in Akshardham, the firewood would not kindle. After all, being a male deity, Agnideva was hesitant to touch a *Pativrata*. Then Gopalanand Swami (see Ch.40), a senior *paramhansa* instructed the devotees, "Tell Agnideva that the sati has left. There's no harm now in touching her body." The fire then instantly kindled.

A celibate disciple of Bhagwan Swaminarayan, Alaiya Khachar, Kathi chief of Zinzawadar, Saurashtra raised an orphaned low *varna* girl named Rambai. When she came of age Alaiya decided to get her married. Politely, yet firmly, Rambai declined. Like Alaiya, she too wished to worship Bhagwan Swaminarayan by observing *brahmacharya*.

As the chief, the village would consider him to be uncaring if Rambai remained unmarried. Therefore he suggested to Rambai that he would write to Bhagwan Swaminarayan. Rambai agreed. In His reply, Bhagwan Swaminarayan wrote, *"Parnine prabhu bhajva"* – marry, then worship Bhagwan. For a moment this disconcerted Rambai, "Would Bhagwan allow her to wallow in the pits of samsara?" Praying earnestly for succour, an idea flitted through her mind.

Meanwhile Alaiya arranged the marriage. During the rituals, after circumambulating the *yagna* fire, the relatives offered gifts to the couple. Rambai joined them by removing her jewellery and offered them to the groom, "Here brother," she said, "my gifts to you too!"

Pandemonium ensued. Aghast, the in-laws wondered what she meant by addressing him as 'brother'? Hearing the uproar, Alaiya arrived. He noted Rambai's jewellery in the groom's lap.

"Rambai! What's this?" he growled.

Rambai remained silent. Alaiya had already gleaned her

intention. So he raised his arm to pacify the relatives. He then approached the groom, untied the *vivah* knot and whispered in his ear, "Consider yourself fortunate to have been graced with the hand of such a *samkhyayogini*. Now forget her and accept the hand which has truly held her's."

Alaiya then explained to the relatives that Rambai never wished to marry. She did so only to obey Bhagwan's command. "Now that she has obeyed half the command, she'll obey the other half by devoting herself to Him. You may return home."

Such examples of the Pativrata depict Sanatan Dharma's sublime values of morality. These apply equally to men too, for Pramukh Swami Maharaj often mirthfully points out in colloquial Gujarati that, "Just as there are ideals for the sati there are ideals for the *'sato'* (the male)!"

The Pativrata then, is not only a dharma but a lofty legacy of Bharatvarsh. She embodies all virtues associated with *satitva*, such as, purity, morality, fidelity, chastity, righteousness, goodness, duty, tolerance, service, devotion and many more. By imbibing these values, Hindus are inspired to mould purity of character and preserve and transmit this noble tradition to their offspring. The *shastras* support this:

In the Ramayan, Bhagwan Shri Ram asks Lakshman:

Pushpam   drushtwā   falam   drushtwā,
drushtwā   strinām   cha   yauvanam,
Trini rupāni drushtvaiva kasya no chalate manaha.

– whose mind is not deflected on seeing a flower, a fruit or a beautiful woman?

Lakshman answers:

Pitā   yasya   shuchirbhuto   mātā   yasya   pativratā,
Ubhābhyāmeva sambhutaha tasya no chalate manaha.

– his mind will not be deflected, who is brought up by a father who is pure and a mother who is a Pativrata.

38. The Jati

The virtue of *brahmacharya* is the stem from which many noble virtues branch out. *Brahmacharya* involves not only physical continence, but also the mind and *atma*.

Bharatvarsh's history is replete with examples of men who have achieved this ideal.

In this chapter we witness the determination with which some of the virtuous men upheld their vow of *brahmacharya*. Prior to India's independence, Maharaja Sayajirao Gaekwad of Vadodara often invited scholars from home and abroad to deliver scholarly lectures at his Lakshmi Vilas palace. Once he invited a German professor to talk on character. As the professor approached the dais, the palace spokesman gave a brief introduction of the listeners. He narrated a story from the Ramayan about Lakshman's character. He then added that the gathering belonged to such a lofty cultural tradition. When the spokesman finished, the professor thanked the Maharaja for inviting him and added that to such an audience he had nothing to say. He then returned to his seat!

The story that awestruck the professor concerned Lakshman's superhuman control over his senses. Such a person is known as *jati*. This facet of Lakshman's personality emerged after Ravan abducted Sita. While Ravan was flying to Lanka, Sita dropped her gold ornaments to leave a trail. When Shri Ram and Lakshman came across an earring, a bangle and an anklet, Shri Ram questioned Lakshman whether he could recognise any of them as belonging to Sitaji. Lakshman replied:

"Nāham jānāmi kundale nāham jānāmi kankane,
Nupure chaiva jānāmi nityam pādābhivandanāt."
— Valmiki Ramayan, *Kishkindha Kand 6–22*

— I do not know the earring nor the bangle. I do recognise the anklet for I bowed at Sitaji's feet everyday.

Such incredible control of the senses *(indriya saiyam)*

231

stunned Shri Ram. Incredible because the three of them – Ram, Sita and Lakshman – had roamed the forests in exile for fourteen years and yet the latter only had the darshan of Sitaji's feet. Hence, Lakshman is respected as one of the foremost *jatis* in the Sanatan Dharma.

Jati, with two synonyms, *yati* and *brahmachari,* comprise two types: the married, like Lakshman and Shri Krishna, and the *bal brahmacharis.*

Bal Brahmacharis

Bal means childhood. *Bal brahmacharis* observe *brahmacharya* from childhood. In ancient Hindu tradition such *jatis* include Hanumanji and Shukdevji – of the Shrimad Bhagvatam. Relatively recent examples include Bhagwan Swaminarayan, His *paramhansas* and Ramkrishna Paramhansa.

During His childhood in Ayodhya, Bhagwan Swaminarayan as Ghanshyam learnt wrestling from two young wrestlers; Bhuvandin, a brahmin and Dinasinh, a kshatriya. Ghanshyam was fond of their company precisely because both were *naisthik brahmacharis (jatis).*

During His Kalyan Yatra as Neelkanth Varni, from 1792 to 1799, the king of Vanshipur in Nepal offered Him his princesses, Ela and Sushila in marriage. Neelkanth left Vanshipur in the middle of the night.

Later, when His elder brother, Rampratap arrived with his family in Gujarat, his wife Suvasini was so overjoyed to see her beloved nephew, she rushed to hug Him. Bhagwan Swaminarayan instantly stepped back, cautioning her about His vows.

Once a man named Mathurbabu sent young prostitutes to Ramkrishna in a secluded room. As soon as they started behaving lewdly, he addressed them as *devis* in a beseeching tone, "Ma... Anandmayi Ma! ...Brahmamayi Ma!..." The young girls instantly regretted their behaviour, cried and begged for forgiveness.

In the 19th century many men resolutely renounced worldly enticements and marital opportunities to become

Bhagwan Swaminarayan's ascetic *jatis*. One notable example was of 33 year old Ladudan Barot, a bard genius who left home at a young age to study poetry in Kachchh and later enthralled Maharajas in Kathiawad. After Ladudan was initiated as Brahmanand Swami, a young woman named Mojbai arrived with Ladudan's family from Khan village, his birthplace in the Sirohi district of Rajasthan. She had betrothed herself to him when he was very young. In reply to her requests for him to return home, Brahmanand Swami instantly composed bhajans for eight consecutive days. Through these he informed Mojbai that the true, lasting wedlock in life was with Paramatma. Everything else was ephemeral. The rich imagery and powerful sentiments in these poems transformed her heart. She happily consented to his wedlock with Paramatma and returned home. Years later, an incident reflected the prowess of his *jati*–hood.

Once the Nawab of Junagadh warmly welcomed Bhagwan Swaminarayan in a grand procession through the city. One of his ministers, being a fierce dissenter of the Sampraday, set loose a full–blooded stallion, used as a stud in the Nawab's stables, in the procession. He hoped the stallion would cause chaos on seeing the mares ridden by the Kathi chiefs alongside Bhagwan Swaminarayan. The procession would fail and He would be publicly humiliated.

Brahmanand Swami instantly gleaned the grim outcome. Fearlessly, he approached the excited stallion and touched his forehead. The stallion calmed down immediately. He 'calmed' to such a degree that for the rest of his life he shied away from mares, and thus proved worthless for the Nawab's stud farm!

Similar to Ladudan, another *bal brahmachari* on his way to becoming a sadhu, encountered a similar enticement. A beautiful servant of a king, with a potful of gold coins offered herself to him. On the pretence of attending to a call of nature, he ran away. Bhagwan Swaminarayan initiated him as Govindanand Swami.

Brahmanand Swami and Govindanand Swami are just two

Brahmanand Swami calming the stallion in Junagadh.

among the three thousand ascetics initiated by Bhagwan Swaminarayan, many of whom were *jatis*.

Married Jatis

To those unfamiliar with Sanatan Dharma, the concept of *brahmacharya* for the married may sound paradoxical. However, the Hindu shastras assert that a married man who controls his senses and remains loyal to his wife is deemed a *brahmachari* – *ek nāri sadā brahmachāri*. In the Ramcharitmanas, Tulsidas eulogises the glory of this moral principle:

> *"Pardhan patthar jāniye parstri māt samān,*
> *Itnese Hari nā mile to Tulsidās jamān."*

– regard wealth other than your own as stone and a woman other than your wife as a mother. If then you do not attain Paramatma, Tulsidas will become your surety (to attain Paramatma).

This lofty tradition has been upheld sincerely over the ages in India both by Maharajas and the citizens.

King Vallraj of ancient Bharat appointed his son to manage the kingdom while he was on a pilgrimage. Once from his palace, he saw two brahmin sisters passing by carrying water pots. As a lustful thought crossed his mind he immediately admonished himself and thought, "Will the mind's sin affect the body? Better to die than live a polluted life." That night he hurled himself from a high window. The next morning, news reached the two girls that they were the reason for the prince's suicide. The two girls introspected, "If our looks induce lust in others, then we are at fault." That night both ended their lives.

Many Rajput Maharajas were renowned for their high morality and fidelity. Around 1670, an extremely handsome Rajput Maharaja named Chhatrasal, ruled Bundelkhand in Madhya Pradesh. Once, a prostitute named Pyaribai invited him to her house. As the ruler he could not refuse social invitations from his subjects. At her house, when she started behaving in an immoral manner Chhatrasal remarked, "Rather than crave for another son accept me as your son." Pyaribai fell at his feet.

A similar morality existed among the Kathis of Saurashtra. Sura Khachar, a tall, well–built, married Kathi chief of Loya, accepted the Swaminarayan Sampraday at the young age of 26. Once the chief of Jasdan village invited him on a social occasion. A fierce dissenter of the Sampraday, the chief decided to blot Sura's character. At night he sent a prostitute to his lodgings. When Sura opened the door he gleaned the women's intentions. Drawing his sword, he growled, "Take one more step and I'll behead you." The woman fled. Sura then galloped away to Gadhada. When he entered Dada Khachar's *darbar*, Bhagwan Swaminarayan commented to the assembly, "Here comes our *jati*."

Sanatan Dharma's avatars advocate such control over one's senses and desires. In the Bhagvad Gita (7/11) Shri Krishna declares, "I am that desire which is in accordance with the principles of dharma." Bhagwan Swaminarayan, in Vachanamrut Gadhada II–33, reveals that Bhagwan has a special benediction for those who observe *brahmacharya* and accepts their service. Amazingly, this seems to be true for those men whose behaviour at times may not conform to other social norms. We glean this from the lives of two Kathi leaders in the early 19th century.

Jogidas Khuman was a notable rebel, who harboured a grievance with Maharaja Wajesinh of Bhavnagar during the decade from 1820 to 1829. With his gang members he often raided, pillaged and looted Wajesinh's villages. Yet he never touched the womenfolk. Once, when he visited Gadhada to attend the mourning of Jiva Khachar, Dada Khachar's uncle, Bhagwan Swaminarayan questioned Jogidas Khuman about why he once flung chili powder in his own eyes.

Jogidas replied, "I once glanced at a beautiful woman. Later this pained me intensely, for my name is Jogidas – the servant of *jogis* (stalwart yogis). As such this behaviour tainted my name. To punish my eyes I flung chili powder in them."

Despite his warring nature and rebellious pursuits, his high morality pleased Bhagwan.

The second Kathi whom Bhagwan Swaminarayan considered a *jati* was Bhan Khachar, the chief of Bhadli, a village near Gadhada. He often harassed Dada Khachar, a stalwart amongst Bhagwan Swaminarayan's followers. Bhan Khachar occasionally harvested and stole Dada's crops growing on a patch of disputed land at Rampara, bordering Gadhada and Bhadli. Despite his malevolent behaviour Bhagwan Swaminarayan once visited him. When devotees requested to know the reason, He replied, "To have his darshan, since he observes unflinching *brahmacharya!*"

Being the omniscient Purushottam Narayan, only He could know for certain that Bhan Khachar was observing *brahmacharya*, which by definition, includes body mind and *atma*. More striking is that as Bhagwan Himself, He used the word darshan not only for a mere mortal, but a non–devotee. This reflects the importance of *brahmacharya* in Bhagwan's heart.

No matter where a person resides, if he sincerely observes *brahmacharya* Bhagwan will seek and bless him. Towards the end of His forest sojourns, Neelkanth Varni visited Jetha Mer and his wife in Madhada, near Mangrol in 1799. Without any prior acquaintance, Neelkanth Varni graced this *jati's* home. He revealed that He had arrived specially to give darshan and blessings to both, for they had been observing *brahmacharya* for one hundred births specially to have Paramatma's darshan!

Like the ideal *Pativrata*, the ideal *jati's* heart is wedded to Paramatma. When the call of the Divine beckons he eagerly upholds His commands. Once, Bhagwan Swaminarayan wrote a letter to test 18 married devotees to renounce instantly to become sadhus. They comprised Kathi chiefs, businessmen and prominent elders in society. Despite their eminence they promptly obeyed His command. On their way to meet Him, they passed through Kadu, a village near Methan, in Saurashtra to pick Aja Patel. Here young Kalyandas, Aja Patel's nephew, just happened to be on the verge of completing the final marriage rites with his bride. When he asked the group and his uncle where they were headed, they showed him the letter. To their astonishment he voluntered to accompany them, considering himself included in the list by the Gujarati word *vagere*, meaning 'etcetera'! Later Bhagwan

Shrine on site where Bhagwan Swaminarayan met 18 paramhansas, just outside Bhuj.

Swaminarayan sent all the 18 back to their homes. However, Kalyandas staunchly vowed to remain an ascetic. Pleased by his *vairagya*, Bhagwan Swaminarayan initiated him as Adbhutanand Swami, for he had performed an *adbhut* (fantastic) deed.

Similar is Govindram's case, another *jati*. He accompanied his wife Amrabai of Methan, near Dhangadhra, straight from their marriage to receive Bhagwan Swaminarayan's blessings. When the two knelt before Him, still in their marriage attire, He made an astonishing remark, "O you remembered Bhagwan first after *vivah*? Brother and sister have both come together for darshan! I am extremely pleased."

When the couple returned home they looked at each other with questioning eyes.

"You heard what Maharaj said?" asked Amrabai.

"He blessed us as 'brother and sister'," replied Govindram.

"Well?"

"So be it," asserted Govindram.

Henceforth they lived as siblings, observing *chheda vartman*. Literally, this means a vow of distance; not touching each other and hence observing *brahmacharya* while still living together.

Bhagwan Swaminarayan later lauded their marriage as "the open–doored marriage of Methan."

During Aksharbrahma Gunatitanand Swami's time, in the mid-19th century (see Ch. 41), Shivlal Doshi of Botad was a 33 year old, rich merchant devotee, whose *jati*-hood too is laudable. Despite his wealth, he remained engrossed in bhakti and detached from worldly pursuits. Once, his sister-in-law came to stay with the family. Everyday she served food to him. Once, she accidentally poured extra ghee in his plate. As he looked up, he realised that it was not his wife. He then inquired about how long she had been in the house. She replied, "Six months."

The *jati* then, has subjugated his mundane desires and is the embodiment of total control over his mind and ten *indriyas*. This renders him a sublime status as a sadhu, in the garb of a *gruhasth*. Even those who observe *jati*-hood as a mere dharma discipline, not necessarily to please Paramatma, receive His blessings, as did Jogidas Khuman and Bhan Khachar. Those whose goal is to please Him are the ideal *jatis*. Besides divine grace, *jati*-hood's most singular benefit is that it serves as a foundation for imparting sublime samskars to the offspring of the married *jati*. This universal truth, revealed by Shri Ram (in the previous chapter), is today propounded by Pramukh Swami Maharaj, himself a stalwart *jati*. By his grace and blessings, in an age when young people blindly languish in sensual pursuits, he continues to inspire hundreds of teenagers and young men to imbibe *jati*-hood as sadhus, to offer exuberant devotion to Bhagwan and serve society. Today he has over 700 such sadhus treading the path of *jati*-hood.

39. Zamkuba

India is the only country in the world with a proud legacy of kings and queens who renounced their royal riches to worship the Supreme Reality. Two such kings of ancient India, familiar to every schoolchild, are Gopichand and Bhartruhari. Sixteenth century India saw Mirabai, the queen of Udaipur forsaking the Udaipur palace for Shri Krishna. Three centuries later, another queen forsook the same palace to worship Paramatma.

A Rajput princess of Vaagad in Kathiawad, Zamkuba was married to the Rana (king) of Udaipur. However the Rana was not a pious man. He requested Zamkuba to eat with him from the same plate, like his other queens. Since he relished non–vegetarian foods, she refused. The Rana felt greatly insulted. Henceforth, he did not force her. Nonetheless, a rift began to develop between the two, inducing the other queens to taunt and harass her. For Zamkuba, the grandeur and glamour of a palace turned hellish.

U – Udaipur

Around this time, one of her maids, also from Kathiawad, divulged to her that a Brahmin named Mulji Brahmachari had arrived from Kathiawad. He so enthused with stories of Bhagwan Swaminarayan that she felt profound peace at heart. On hearing this, Zamkuba instructed the maid to summon the Brahmin to do *katha* in the queen's chamber.

Mulji Brahmachari arrived the following morning. He sat cross–legged on the floor, closed his eyes and first chanted the "Swaminarayan" *dhun*. His devotional chant wrought a divine vibration in the chamber which thrilled Zamkuba. He then narrated episodes of the young Bhagwan Swaminarayan, who had recently arrived in Kathiawad. Hours passed. Zamkuba was lost; engrossed in the divine glory of Bhagwan's *lila*. When Mulji Brahmachari stopped she felt pained, as if disturbed from samadhi. She wondered of a different way of life; a life of renunciation and devotion to Bhagwan. She recalled Mirabai, a queen in this same palace, who had severed the shackles of royalty. She felt the Divine beckoning her.

After Mulji Brahmachari departed, she yearned to flee to Kathiawad, to surrender at Bhagwan Swaminarayan's lotus feet. Meanwhile, she transformed her life. She performed puja and fasted more often. To ascetics and Brahmins passing by, she offered alms. Two thoughts constantly swirled in her mind – Bhagwan Swaminarayan and how to escape.

Ironically, the Rana provided the answer. Noting the change in her life, he suggested she go on a pilgrimage. He suggested that she visit the sacred rivers Ganga and Yamuna, Mathura–Vrundavan or even Jagannath Puri. She remained indecisive. A few days later when watering a pipal tree, she heard a voice, "Zamku, you need not go anywhere. I am your destiny. Strike off on your own. You will meet a gypsy caravan and at the pond in Vadnagar if you meet some pilgrims, consider this message to be true."

One dark night she stood staring out of a window high up in the queens' chambers. Again she heard a voice, "You are not meant to become a *Maharani*. Nor have you committed yourself to samsara. I have protected you so far. Now summon the courage to climb down. The fetters of maya will unshackle easily."

Escape from a well guarded fort would be impossible for even a soldier. For her, it was unthinkable. If caught, the Rana would have her whipped to death or plastered alive in a masonry wall. Nonetheless, being a spirited *atma*, she prayed to the Divinity who had guided her so far.

She knotted a series of saris. Using this 'rope' she slithered down from her chamber into a dry, storm water drainge tunnel under the palace. She then crawled along till she exited the fort. Not knowing the way to Kathiawad and deathly frightened of the army that the Rana would invariably send to capture her, she hid herself in a camel's decaying carcass! The next morning she heard hooves drum by. She remained in the carcass without food and water for three days, until the soldiers returned to the palace.

Emerging from the carcass, she walked southwards towards Gujarat. To avoid recognition, she had adorned the garb of a common Bhil (forest tribal). Along the way she met a gypsy caravan. Half the prophecy proved true! Her spirits soared. When the caravan reached Vadnagar, she met some women on the banks of a pond singing the Swaminarayan mantra! When they revealed their destination her heart fluttered; Gadhada! She thanked Paramatma for having constantly guided her.

A – *Amdavad*
G – *Gadhada*
B – *Bhavnagar*

In Gadhada her heart melted on having Bhagwan Swaminarayan's darshan. There was a story feeling of déjà vu! She felt the profound peace she experienced when Mulji Brahmachari was relating Bhagwan's *lila* at the palace. She fell at His lotus feet, praying to allow her to dedicate her life in offering bhakti. Bhagwan Swaminarayan readily consented and instructed her to live under Jivuba's care. Jivuba was the sister of Dada Khachar, the Kathi chief of Gadhada.

Mataji's room in Bhuj.

Though a Kshatriya, she was without ego, and a dedicated aspirant. Unaware of Zamkuba's royal background, Jivuba unknowingly allocated her menial chores, such as cleaning dung in the cowpen, fetching water from the well and sweeping the court compound. Zamkuba performed all these chores with zest and humility. For food she only ate one frugal item such as *rotlo* (thick chapati of millet).

Once while she was cleaning dung, Bhagwan Swaminarayan approached Jivuba.

"Do you know who she is?" He asked.

"No Maharaj."

"She has servants like you at her palace. She has renounced a great kingdom to worship Paramatma." He paused, then admonished her gently, "She's a queen of Udaipur! From now on do not give her such tasks."

He then had Zamkuba's head shaved and named her "Mataji" (mother). This was initiation as a *samkhyayogini*. Her vows were similar to those of sadhus; to observe *brahmacharya*, live an austere life and offer bhakti.

He instructed her to live with Ladhima, another *samkhyayogini*, in Bhuj and gave her a boon, "When the time comes, I will take you to Akshardham."

Zamkuba spent the rest of her life in Bhuj with Ladhima offering bhakti to Bhagwan. In turn, He always appeared to both in divine form when they meditated. He once visited them to have a meal in this small room.

Finally, He appeared in a divine form to take them to Akshardham. Both left their bodies together. Both were cremated on the same pyre.

The small room in which both lived and meditated in Bhuj, survived the January 2001 earthquake. Known as Mataji's Ordi, it is a pilgrimage spot in the Swaminarayan Sampraday.

Unlike Mirabai, Zamkuba did not compose any bhajans. She's probably not even noted in the archives of the Udaipur palace. Yet, unlike Mirabai, who could only offer devotion to

Paramatma's unmanifest (*paroksh*) form, Zamkuba was fortunate enough to offer devotion to His manifest (*pragat*) form. Audaciously renouncing her regal opulence for an extremely austere life, suffused with singular devotion, she attained an eternal place in the bhakti *shastras* and the Vachanamrut (Loya–3) of Bhagwan Swaminarayan.

For all those who covet wealth, opulence, possessions and crave for mundane objects, Zamkuba will forever remain an inspiring royalty.

40. Gopalanand Swami

Gopalanand Swami was born in a Brahmin family in Todla, a village in north Gujarat, on Maha *sud* 8 Samvat 1837 (1781 CE). He was named Khushal Bhatt.

At the age of four, Khushal learned Sanskrit from his father Motiram. Khushal then studied the Vedas, astrology, astronomy, Nyaya (logic) and Vyakran (grammar) from a pundit.

Precocious Khushal mastered Ashtang Yog and often meditated in a Shiv mandir nearby. Later, after completing his own studies, he set up a school in Todla and taught the village children. Not satisfied with orthodox methods of teaching, he also taught the children to sing bhajans extolling Bhagwan's glory. The children often attained samadhi (divine trance) due to Khushal's supranormal influence.

He also possessed miraculous yogic powers. At home, in secrecy, he often summoned and played with the *murti* of Shri Krishna from the famous, ancient mandir of Shamlaji, situated a few miles from Todla. Once the priest opened the mandir slightly earlier than usual and found the *murti* missing from the altar. Perplexed, he went to inform the villagers. When they arrived they discovered the *murti* in its usual position, undisturbed except for a missing anklet and a silk garment. The people naturally blamed the priest. They were about to flog him when they heard a mysterious, authoritative voice, "The priest is not to blame. I play with Khushal Bhatt everyday. But today, the priest opened the mandir earlier than usual and in a hurry to reach here, I left my garment and the anklet on the way. Go and search there." The listeners were stunned. They retraced the path to Khushal's house and found the two items and bowed down reverentially to young Khushal.

On another occasion Khushal's amazing power was painfully experienced by the king of the state and his palace

I – Idar
T – Todla
H – Himmatnagar
S – Shamlaji
A – Amdavad

staff. The king levied an unreasonable tax of three rupees per head on every Brahmin in the district. The Brahmins tried to persuade him to lift the tax, but he refused. They then urged Khushal to intervene in the name of justice. Khushal sat down and prayed. Soon there was an uproar in the palace. Everybody, including the king, could not pass urine or stool! This miserable discomfort continued for three days! All remedies failed to bring relief. Someone then suggested that the king apologise to young Khushal and remove the tax. Anxious to relieve his agony, the king complied. He summoned Khushal to the palace and gave a written declaration on a copper plate, freeing Brahmins from any tax for all time. Khushal forgave the king, rescinding the powerful spell.

Several years later, in a nearby village, Khushal met a *paramhansa* of Bhagwan Swaminarayan, Swami Sarveshvaranandji. After hearing Bhagwan Swaminarayan's glory, Khushal could hardly wait to meet Him. Some time later, when he did meet Him, it felt like a divine reunion and he yearned to become a sadhu. However Bhagwan Swaminarayan first sent him to Vadodara to teach in a school, as well as preach to people there. Finally, on Kartik *vad* 8, Samvat 1864 (1807 CE), Bhagwan Swaminarayan initiated him in Gadhada, naming him Gopalanand Swami. He then sent Swami to Vadodara to develop the Satsang.

During this period in the early 19th century, many pundits resided in Vadodara. Affiliated to various schools of philosophy, they resented the appearance of the Swaminarayan Sampraday. Their continual dissension and diatribe created a disturbing milieu for lay followers. A learned stalwart was needed to defeat the pundits. Therefore, Bhagwan Swaminarayan sent Gopalanand Swami to Vadodara. With his immense erudition, combined with yogic powers and saintliness, he cogently countered and defeated the pundits. He then firmly established and spread the ideals of Ekantik Dharma among the people. Ekantik Dharma comprises:

dharma, *jnan, vairagya* and bhakti with an understanding of the greatness, grandeur and glory of Purushottam, manifest as Bhagwan Swaminarayan. Swami's saintliness and wisdom inspired prominent state officials to enter the fold. Maharaja Sayajirao Gaekwad II, also became a disciple of Bhagwan Swaminarayan, to the extent that he invited and honoured the latter by a grand elephant procession in the city. After the procession, Sayajirao invited Him to his Lakshmi Vilas Palace.

Once in Vadodara, the participants of a Vishnuyag (ritual of the sacred fire invoking Vishnu) questioned the priest, "Can Yagnanarayan give darshan?" the priest replied, "Yes, if a Santpurush (realised sadhu) offers *ahuti* (oblations), then Yagnanarayan will indeed grant darshan." The question then arose about where to find such a sadhu. Somebody informed them that Gopalanand Swami, a *paramhansa* disciple of Bhagwan Swaminarayan was such a sadhu. They invited him to offer *ahuti*. Being compassionate, Swami offered *ahuti* of ghee in the fire. To everyone's astonishment, Yagnanarayan manifested from the fire.

Swami's compassionate nature and spiritual realisation is reflected by another event. In Saurashtra, Sarangpur is a village on the way from Botad to Gadhada. Vagha Khachar, its Kathi chief, was a pious devotee constantly steeped in penury. Though he wished to serve pilgrims on their way to Gadhada, he could not. When he divulged this to Swami, the latter had a *murti* of Hanumanji sculpted from stone. Then he touched it with his stick, as a ritual of pran *pratishtha* (image consecration). This infused such divine power in the *murti* that it began to vibrate. Swami then informed Vagha Khachar that Hanumanji would eradicate evil afflictions such as ghosts, *prêt,* etc., from people and fulfil their mundane desires. This Hanumanji's power and fame spread all over Saurashtra and Gujarat. With the increased inflow of people in the village, its economy improved. Vagha Khachar could then offer alms, etc., to pilgrims. Later, Shastri Yagnapurushdas, Bhagwan Swaminarayan's third spiritual successor, acquired more land around the small shrine. He developed and embellished the mandir campus, thus increasing the shrine's beauty and glory. Even today, people from all over Gujarat and Rajasthan visit this Kashtabhanjan Hanuman, to exorcise spirits and ghosts.

One of Swami's important contributions to the Sampraday was his commentaries on the Vedas, Upanishads, Brahma Sutras and the Bhagvad Gita.

His second and greatest literary service was in the compilation of the Vachanamrut, along with three other *paramhansas*. This is a text of 262 spiritual dialogues between Bhagwan Swaminarayan and His disciples. They occurred from 1819 to 1829. The Vachanamrut is an *adhyatma* shastra, one of the most enlightening texts on the path of realising Paramatma.

Thirdly, he realised and extolled the glory of Bhagwan Swaminarayan as Purushottam Narayan and Gunatitanand Swami as Aksharbrahma. The latter was a contemporary *paramhansa* of Bhagwan Swaminarayan, the incarnation of Aksharbrahma, whose glory is extolled in the Upanishads and Gita.

During his time, Gopalanand Swami visited Junagadh for one month every year to hear the spiritual discourses of Aksharbrahma Gunatitanand Swami, as commanded by Bhagwan Swaminarayan. From his group of 60 sadhus, he later sent three of them permanently to Gunatitanand Swami to attain *brahmavidya* and realise Paramatma. Prior to leaving his mortal frame, he instructed his own group of *gruhasth* devotees to henceforth associate with Aksharbrahma Gunatitanand Swami in Junagadh, who would mould them spiritually and take them to Akshardham, Bhagwan Swaminarayan's divine abode.

In recognition of his contribution in extolling the glory of Akshar and Purushottam, Shastriji Maharaj consecrated his *murti*, along with Bhagwan Swaminarayan and Aksharbrahma Gunatitanand Swami, in the central shrine of the BAPS Swaminarayan mandirs in Gadhada and Sarangpur.

Gopalanand Swami passed away at the age of 71 on Vaishakh *vad* 4, Samvat 1908 (1852 CE).

अक्षरब्रह्म
श्री गुणातीतानंद स्वामी

पूर्ण पुरुषोत्तम
ભગવાન શ્રી સ્વામિનારાયણ

અક્ષરમુક્ત
श्री गोपाળानंद स्वामी

Central shrine, BAPS Shri Swaminarayan Mandir, Gadhada, with Goplanand Swami's murti on the right

Rajasthani gemstone art craft using the following semi–precious stones: amethyst, calcedony, cornelian agate, garnet, green aventurine, red aventurine, metakite, red jasper, yellow agate & blood stone.

41. Aksharbrahma Gunatitanand Swami

The mystic of all mystics, the *siddh* of all *siddhs*, the yogi of all yogis, Aksharbrahma Gunatitanand Swami incarnated as Mulji Sharma on Aso *sud* Purnima, Samvat 1841 (1785 CE). His parents Bholanath and Sakarba, received blessings from guru Atmanand Swami, prophesying, "Bhagwan Purushottam will incarnate at Dharmadev's house in Sarvardesh (near Ayodhya) and four years later, His abode will incarnate at your place."

Bholanath's village was Bhadra near the river Und, not far from the port of Jodia, in north–west Saurashtra. Upon examining the child's astrological signs, Bholanath's astrologer revealed that, "He will be an eloquent speaker and spread Bhagwat Dharma."

During childhood Mulji often spoke to Sakarba about Bhagwan Purushottam's divine *lila* in Chhapiya, the village where Ghanshyam (Bhagwan Swaminarayan) incarnated. He could observe this from Bhadra. Once he requested Sakarba to sing bhajans about the *yagnopavit* samskar (the sacred thread ritual) since Ghanshyam was being invested with the *janoi* on that day in Ayodhya. When Mulji was given *janoi*, the 'guru' pundit advised him, as is customary, to go to Kashi to study. When Mulji refused, the pundit asked him the reason. Mulji replied, "Purushottam Narayan, at whose lotus–feet reside innumerable Kashis, will arrive here. Hence, what is the need for going to Kashi?" When Ghanshyam renounced home, embarking on His seven–year forest sojourns as Neelkanth, Mulji related this to Sakarba. During the next seven years he often described Neelkanth's travels. This always amazed Sakarba, reminding her of Atmanand Swami's prophecy, about Bhagwan's abode incarnating as her son. To his little brother Sundarji, Mulji often divulged, "I am going to become a sadhu and will also make you a sadhu."

A – Amdavad
B – Bhadra
R – Rajkot
G – Gondal
J – Junagadh

Shrine on birthplace, Bhadra

*Bhagwan Swaminarayan initiates
Mulji Sharma in Dabhan*

Mulji Sharma first had Bhagwan Swaminarayan's physical darshan on Kartik *sud* 11 (Ekadashi), Samvat 1857 (1801 CE), when He was given *bhagvati diksha* by Swami Ramanand, in Piplana. On this occasion when the two first met, Bhagwan Swaminarayan revealed, "This Mulji Bhakta is in constant rapport with me and in the future, will extol my glory. He is my very abode, Akshardham." Two years later, when Bhagwan Swaminarayan visited Bhadra, He revealed to Bholanath, "Mulji is constantly in my service, but you can't see that. He is my disciple since time immemorial. He has realised my form in all three states (physical, subtle and causal). He is Anadi Mul Akshar – the eternal Aksharbrahma."

In Samvat 1866 (20 January 1810 CE), Bhagwan Swaminarayan held a grand *yagna* in Dabhan near Kheda, specially to initiate Mulji as a sadhu. During this ritual He revealed to the devotees, "I am extremely delighted to initiate Mulji Sharma, who is My Akshardham incarnate, in whom I dwell alongwith numerous *muktas,* and who is limitless and is My Akshardham" (Harililakalpataru 7–17–49,50). He named him Gunatitanand Swami.

On many occasions during His life, Bhagwan Swaminarayan revealed Gunatitanand Swami's glory to His *paramhansas* and devotees. One such occasion was during the festival of Fuldol in Sarangpur. While playing *raas* and singing Kabir's verse (not the first Kabir, but a later one), Bhagwan Swaminarayan stopped at the following stanza and asked two of his *paramhansas*, Muktanand Swami and Anandanand, about the identity of such a Sadguru:

"Millions of Krishnas join their palms,
Millions of Vishnus bow their heads,
Millions of Shivs meditate,
Millions of Brahmās deliver knowledge,

254

And Sadguru celebrates the festival of spring."

The two *paramhansas* replied, "You are that Sadguru. Who else could it be?" Bhagwan Swaminarayan then pointed His stick at Gunatitanand Swami and revealed, "That Sadguru is this Gunatitanand Swami and I am the supreme Purushottam Narayan. The composer of this Holi *pada*, Kabir, worshipped and addressed Aksharbrahma as *Sadguru Saheb*."

During His lifetime Bhagwan Swaminarayan built six Vedic stone mandirs in Gujarat. In each He appointed stalwart *paramhansas* as *mahants* (heads), from His retinue of over three thousand ascetics. However, a question arose among the senior *paramhansas* about whom to appoint in Junagadh. Brahmanand Swami, a poet and senior *paramahansa* cautioned Him that conditions in Junagadh were very precarious and formidable, for it was a Muslim state managed by the Nawab, whose minions were Nagar Brahmins. The latter were absolutely averse to the Swaminarayan Sampraday and would pose great obstacles to the mandir's activities. However, Bhagwan Swaminarayan confidently replied that He would appoint just such a formidable sadhu – Gunatitanand Swami. After Nawab Hamid Khan honoured and welcomed Bhagwan Swaminarayan in his palace, he requested Him to leave behind somebody like Him in Junagadh. On that occasion, He replied, *"Ham jaisā rakhenge,"* (I will leave somebody like me) and pointed to Gunatitanand Swami.

Aksharbrahma Incarnate

Since antiquity, Mount Girnar has been the abode of ascetics and yogis performing austerities. During Swami's period, an ascetic performing *tapas* to please Dattatreya had the deity's darshan. The ascetic requested for the bliss of Aksharbrahma by uttering the shlok lauding Akshar in the Gita (8/11):

"Those great sages who have renounced the bondage of samsara enter what the Vedas proclaim as Aksharbrahma. To attain this (Akshar), aspirants strive and observe *brahmacharya*."

To the ascetic, Dattatreya revealed, "The bliss of Akshar that you wish is today manifesting as Aksharbrahma incarnate in Junagadh. Thousands of aspirants are flocking from afar for his darshan. Go to him for this bliss."

The ascetic then assumed the form of a lion. One day when Swami was meditating on the edge of the jungle outside the city with some sadhus, a lion suddenly emerged from the jungle and sat a few feet in front of Swami. Sadhus bathing nearby shouted to warn Swami. Swami opened his eyes and looked at the lion. In turn, the lion then bowed several times with tears in his eyes. Then he turned towards the jungle. Continuing to glance back a few times at Swami, he disappeared into the dense vegetation. The sadhus then rushed to Swami and inquired about the lion. Swami revealed the above story. Then he added, "The ascetic will now leave his body and take birth in the Satsang. After deeply associating with the Satpurush, he will attain Akshardham" (Dave 2000 I:239–40).

Another similar case was of Naranji, a Brahmin who worshipped Shivji. To earn his grace he retreated to the Ramnath Mahadev shrine in the recesses of Girnar, near Bilkha. Here he fasted for three continuous days, chanting *Namah Shivaay*. On the morning of the fourth day, Shivji graced him with his darshan. The deity instructed him, "If you wish to attain Bhagwan manifest (*pragat*), go to Junagadh. There is a Swaminarayan mandir there. Go and meet its mahant Gunatitanand Swami. He will grace you with Bhagwan's darshan."

Naranji rushed to Junagadh. After inquiring in the Swaminarayan mandir he bowed to Swami. Without uttering a word, Swami took him up to the mandir. Indicating Bhagwan Swaminarayan's *murti*, he divulged, "This is Sahajanand Swami, the Bhagwan that Ramnath Mahadev told you about and I am Gunatitanand Swami!" Swami's *antaryami* revelation of his past elated Naranji, to the extent that he decided to spend the rest of his life offering bhakti by accepting Swami as guru.

Swami's Katha

Though he was an eternal *siddh* (realised), Swami once asked Bhagwan Swaminarayan about which of the four forms of sadhana he should focus on: to imbibe *atmanishtha*, to meditate, to serve the ill or do *katha* – deliver spiritual discourses. Bhagwan Swaminarayan replied that he should do *katha*. He reasoned that by *katha*, both he and the recipient would benefit spiritually. Thereafter, Swami placed greater emphasis on *katha*. Wherever he went he delivered dynamic spiritual discourses, lauding Bhagwan Swaminarayan's glory as Purushottam Narayan. Moreover, his talks effectively castigated the mundane *panch vishays* (pursuits of the five senses: speech, touch, sight, taste and smell). His talks were noted by several *gruhasth* devotees and sadhus who accompanied him. These were compiled and published in the late 19th century as Swamini Vato. In the Swaminarayan Sampraday this text is considered as a commentary on the Vachanamrut of Bhagwan Swaminarayan. It contains the essence of the principles of sadhana, *Ekantik* Dharma and the glory of Bhagwan Swaminarayan. In his own words, Swami reveal that he had imparted *brahmavidya* to over 200 aspirants and nurtured the Satsang tenets to devotees numbering thousands. The British census of Saurashtra, in 1872, five years after Swami returned to Akshardham, testifies this and cites a total number of Swaminarayan devotees as follows: 151,399, divided in the following states: Junagadh (88,723), Bhavnagar (50,861), Dhrangadhra, Porbandar (47) and Jamnagar (11,768) (Source: Watson's *Statistical Accounts*). Such a large number was the fruit of Swami's *katha* in his incessant tourings during his 82 year lifespan.

His foremost disciple to whom he taught *brahmavidya* and graced realisation of Bhagwan

Aksharbrahma Gunatitanand Swami's murti first consecrated with Bhagwan Swaminarayan in the central shrine, in Bochasan, Gujarat, in 1907.

Swaminarayan, was Pragji Bhagat, a *gruhasth* tailor by *varna*. This was often spited upon and severely castigated – by senior contemporary sadhus in the Sampraday. However, Swami remained undaunted – *Sthitapragna* – in the words of the Gita (2/55). The societal shackles of *varna* did not play a role in Swami's choice of a spiritual successor.

In 1867, at the age of 82, he returned to Akshardham. Prior to that, he covertly revealed to followers that "he would now live in Mahuva." This meant that Bhagwan would now manifest through Pragji Bhagat of Mahuva. Thus, Bhagwan Swaminarayan's manifestation on earth continued through His spiritual successors. Today HDH Pramukh Swami Maharaj is Aksharbrahma manifest, the fifth spiritual successor of Bhagwan Swaminarayan and the head of BAPS Swaminarayan Sanstha.

At 12.45 a.m. on Aso *sud* 13, Samvat 1923, Bhagwan Swaminarayan appeared in divine from in front of Swami, who then circumambulated Him for some time. Then he sat in a lotus posture and returned to Akshardham. His body was cremated on the banks of the river Gondli, in Gondal, Saurashtra. A year later in 1868, Maharaja Sangramsinhji of Gondal State had a small shrine, named *Akshar Deri*, built on the spot. Since then devotees began to celebrate the Sharad Punam and Annakut festivals here. They witnessed and experienced many miracles and divine visions.

In 1934, Shastriji Maharaj built a beautiful, three–pinnacled mandir over the Akshar Deri. His successor, Yogiji Maharaj further increased the Deri's glory and importance by advocating its mahapuja and circumambulations to devotees and wrote a booklet, *Akshar Tirth*. It has since attained the status of the most miraculous shrine in Saurashtra. Its unique and aesthetic shape has rendered it the symbol of BAPS Swaminarayan Sanstha.

In the Sanatan Dharma, the principle of worshipping the foremost bhakta with Bhagwan, has prevailed since time immemoria: Uma–Mahesh (Parvati–Shivji), Sita–Ram, Lakshmi–Narayan, Radha–Krishna and Nar–Narayan. In the

Akshar Deri, shrine on cremation spot in Gondal, Saurashtra.

Harikrishna Maharaj, Bhagwan Swaminarayan's murti originally worshipped by Gunatitanand Swami, now worshipped by Pramukh Swami Maharaj

12th century Nimbarkacharya first introduced Shri Radha's *murti* with Shri Krishna (see p.102). Similarly, in Samvat 1962 (5/6/1907 CE) Shastri Yagnapurushdasji (Shastriji Maharaj) first consecrated Aksharbrahma Gunatitanand Swami's *murti* next to Bhagwan Swaminarayan in the central shrine of the Swaminarayan Mandir in Bochasan. Hence, the Sampraday became known as Bochasanwasi Shri Akshar Purushottam Swaminarayan Sanstha (BAPS).

Akshardham is the divine abode of Bhagwan Swaminarayan, who incarnated as Gunatitanand Swami. On 30 October 1992, His Divine Holiness Pramukh Swami Maharaj, consecrated the pink stone Akshardham monument in Gandhinagar. Another grander 'Swaminarayan Akshardham' was consecrated in New Delhi, on 5th November 2005. Both monuments are symbolic representations of the divine Akshardham.

The Need for Aksharbrahma in Sadhana

According to Bhagwan Swaminarayan, Aksharbrahma is needed for the *jiva* to identify with, in order to become like Brahman (*brahmarup*). Only when the *jiva* attains such a state does it become eligible to offer worship to Parabrahma (Shikshapatri 116). Shri Krishna also enjoins this principle in the Gita (18/54): one who becomes *Brahma–rup*, whose mind is always contented, who does not lament in any way, does not crave for any object, has equanimity for all living creatures, that person attains my supreme bhakti.

And to become *Brahma–rup* the *jivas* needs the manifest *Aksharbrahma*, who is the medium through whom they transcend maya, and who is also the medium to realise Parabrahma (Bhagvatam 1/1/1, Vachanamrut Panchala–7). And the manifest Aksharbrahma is known as the Param Ekantik Sadhu, to whom the *jivas* should resort, and in whom they should develop love and faith (*Shvetashvatar Upanishad 6/23,* Vachanamrut Vartal–3, 5, 11; Gadhada II–13).

Aksharbrahma in the Shastras

Isha Upanishad (5), Kath Upanishad (2/2/15), Mundak Upanishad (2/2/1,2,4,7; 11/3/2/1,9), Taittiriya Upanishad (Anandvalli 1), Chhandogya Upanishad (8/1/1,4), Bruhadaranyak Upanishad (3/8/1), Mahavakya Upanishad (3), Mahabharat *(Udyog Parva 44/28–30, Shanti Parva 44/31, 206/13–19),* Bhagvad Gita (8/3,11; 13/13–18; 15/6,16) and the Shrimad Bhagvatam:

"The cause of all causes, in which this universe looks like a *paramanu* (atom), and which comprises myriads of other universes, is called Aksharbrahma; which is the transcendent abode of Paramatma, the Supreme Reality in embodied form." (3/11/40,41).

Swami's talks

Aksharbrahma Gunatitanand Swami's talks were self–realised. They reflected his state of spiritual realisation, saintliness and detachment from maya. Stalwart *paramhansas* such as Brahmanand Swami, Shukanand Swami and Nityanand Swami often praised his unflagging zeal in delivering sermons, likening them to Bhagwan Swaminarayan's divine talks. A few short talks are listed below.

"Spoil ten million tasks but improve your moksha. But if ten million tasks are improved and moksha is spoilt, what has been achieved?" Swamini Vato (1/14).

"Whatever happiness there is in maya is not without misery. This, too, should be kept in mind." (1/25)

"If a true Sadhu is attained and one does as he says, then the faults that would have taken tens of millions of births to overcome are overcome today (in this very birth)." (1/119)

"We know that we have love for Bhagwan. But Bhagwan and His Sadhu have greater love for us." (1/196)

"That Bhagwan and Sadhu we wanted to attain through endless *tapas*, tens of millions of *japa, vrat,* donations and *yagnas*, we have attained today." (1/294)

"There are many things to understand in Satsang. Of these, the main is *upāsanā*. Otherwise, observe dharma and study Vachanamrut and other shastras." (2/166)

"One, *upāsanā*; two, *āgnā*; three, company; and four, addiction to the shastras – these four should be consolidated firmly." (4/22)

Shri Swaminarayan Mandir, Gondal, also known as Akshar Mandir, built over Akshar Deri.

Balaji Hanuman, Bhupendra Road, Rajkot – miraculous shrine consecrated by Aksharbrahma Gunatitanand Swami

Shri Swaminarayan Mandir, Junagadh,
where Aksharbrahma Gunatitanand Swami served as mahant for 40 years.

Akshardham monument, Gandhinagar, Gujarat.

Swaminarayan Akshardham, New Delhi.

Part IV - Heroes and Heroines

Introduction

The history of the world's nations is replete with great leaders, statesmen, heroes and heroines.

Yet rare are those whom people have continued down the ages to revere in their hearts; whose images continue to hang in the living rooms of homes, classrooms and public buildings. Such personalities possessed some unique virtues that had universal appeal; an appeal that was timeless and endearing.

In the final part of this book, we consider three personalities of medieval India: Maharana Pratap, Chhatrapati Shivaji and Ahalyabai. Their fame remains ever vibrant even today. This is less due to just great leadership. More importantly their greatest virtue, was their observance of dharma (righteousness) and their unflinching stance against *adharma* and oppression of the masses. This was exemplified by Maharana Pratap and Shivaji. Ahalyabai's laudable virtue was of simple living and piety. Despite possessing a rich kingdom, she never flaunted her riches, which she considered as belonging to the Deity and her citizens.

Among these virtues, the most singular, common for all three, was their intense *desh* bhakti for Bharat Mata – devotion to their motherland.

42. Rana Pratap

The Sisodia Rajputs of Mewar in Rajasthan are justly proud of their lineage. Over the ages, two of its stars have unequivocally scintillated in the hearts of Hindus. The first is Mirabai, -the staunch Krishna bhakta and the second is Rana Pratap, who is remembered even today for his successful struggle to uphold Sanatan Dharma and for the seeds he sowed of patriotism and freedom from foreign oppression.

Pratapsinh, the son of Maharana (King) Udaysinh and Rani (Queen) Jaywanti, was born on 10 May 1540 in Kumbhalgadh in Rajasthan. As a prince he received the usual training in warfare, weaponry, wrestling, horsemanship and war elephants. In his teens, his excellence in horsemanship won the hearts of the Rajput nobles. He grew up to be a tall, superbly muscled, formidable warrior. Udaysinh once sent him with an army to fight the Chauhans of Vagad. Pratapsinh humiliatingly crushed them. By his chivalry, dignity, integrity and noble–heartedness he became the people's favourite prince.

Around this period, except for his father, Udaysinh, other Rajputs chiefs had accepted Akbar's suzerainity and became his vassals. In the words of Akbar's court historian Badayuni, "these Hindus would wield the sword of Islam". When Akbar visited Khwaja Mohiuddin Chisti's tomb in Ajmer, its Rajput king, Bharmal Kachhawaha bowed to him and married his daughter to him. This catalysed a chain reaction which gave a detrimental turn to Rajput history; the other Rajputs, too, fell over each other to marry off their women to Akbar! At the root lay Akbar's craftily orchestrated diplomacy, killing two birds with one stone. He appointed the Rajputs as commanders in his army and so won them over on his side without shedding a drop of Moghul blood. Secondly, he gained their women without draining his coffers! However, Udaysinh

J – Jaipur
K – Kumbhalgadh
A – Ajmer
H – Haldighati
C – Chitor
U – Udaipur

of Mewar never capitulated. On his death, Pratapsinh ascended the throne of Mewar and became the Maharana on 1 March 1572, at the age of 31. Like his father, he too remained undaunted, vowing to continue the struggle to remain independent.

At this time, troubles in his court in Delhi kept Akbar from crushing this rebellious pocket, which incensed him to no end. He remained occupied for five years, from 1571 to 1576. Pratapsinh needed and made good use of this period. Being a man who upheld dharma, he won the support of his people and *Bhils*, the hill tribes. The latter's loyal support helped him to adopt guerilla warfare after the battle of Haldighati.

Rana Pratap was averse to the Moghul court's baseness; of uncontrolled drinking, laxity of character, rude mannerisms and treachery. He would rather face a gruesome battle than fall prey to *adharma* at the Moghul court. Akbar sent four envoys – Jalal Khan Qurchi (1572), Mansinh (1573), Raja Bhagwan Das (1573) and Raja Todarmal (1573) – to convince the Maharana to accept his sovereignty. These missions failed. Akbar insisted on the personal obeisance of Rana Pratap. The latter detested it, wishing to preserve the honour, dignity and nobility of the Sisodia dynasty. Failure of the four missions convinced Akbar that Rana Pratap would not concede willingly. War alone would break him. Therefore on 3 April 1576, he sent his vassal Mansinh of Amber with specially chosen commanders and 5000 troops to fight Rana Pratap. Mansinh also happened to be Pratap's maternal uncle.

Battle of Haldighati

Haldighati is a mountain valley in Mewar near Udaipur, with rocks of a yellow colour like *haldi* – turmeric. *Ghati* means valley. The famous battle of Haldighati took place on 21st June 1576. Maharana's army numbered 3000. Both armies had already arrived at Haldighati before 21 June. For a few days each side waited for the other to launch the offensive. Rana Pratap's army was sheltered behind the mountains while Mansinh's was in the open plain below. Pratap was continually informed of the latter's movements by the Bhils, who were secreted in the hills.

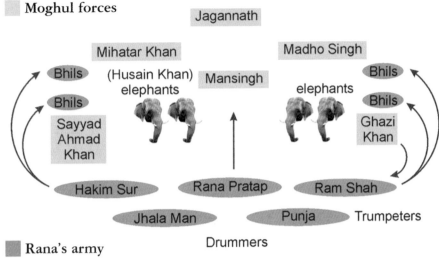

Battle formation at Haldighati

Moghul forces

Jagannath

Mihatar Khan

Madho Singh

Bhils

(Husain Khan) elephants

Mansingh

elephants

Bhils

Bhils

Bhils

Sayyad Ahmad Khan

Ghazi Khan

Hakim Sur

Rana Pratap

Ram Shah

Jhala Man

Punja

Trumpeters

Rana's army

Drummers

(Source: Sharma, *Maharana Pratap and His Times*. 1989:13)

Finally Rana Pratap took the offensive and charged out. So effective was the onslaught that Mansinh's frontline was thrown into disarray. Both his left and right wings "fled like a flock of sheep," noted Badayuni, Akbar's court historian, who witnessed and chronicled the battle. They kept their flight for about twelve miles beyond the river Banas !

Meanwhile riding Chetak, his horse, Rana Pratap valiantly stormed through the centre towards Mansinh. On reaching him, Chetak planted his forelegs on Mansinh's elephant, while Rana Pratap hurled his unusually long and heavy lance, weighing 1.5 *maunds* (30 kg), at Mansinh! The lance cleanly pierced the mahout and struck the palanquin. Mansinh ducked, avoiding injury. Meanwhile the elephant, wielding a sword in its trunk swiped at Chetak's hind legs, injuring a tendon. Many Moghuls rushed in to save their commander, showering Rana Pratap with arrows. Chetak then swiftly turned around. Despite the grave injury, he bolted from the field. Summoning all his strength, Chetak jumped across a stream beyond Haldighati and then buckled down dead. In memory of this valourous deed to save his master, a marble *chhatri* (shrine) was later erected on the spot. Down the centuries to this day, Chetak's heroic deed has endeared him to children all over India.

Since both armies comprised Rajputs, this created confusion about foe or friend. Hence Akbar's chronicler,

Badayuni asked Asaf Khan, one of Mansinh's commanders, "How are we to know in these circumstances between the friendly and hostile Rajputs?" Khan replied, "Just fire the arrows. On whatever side they may be killed, it will be a gain to Islam."

Rana Pratap gleaned this. Wishing to avoid needless Rajput casaulties on both sides, he signalled his men to retreat. The gallant Jhala Man snatched Rana's royal insignia, diverting the Moghul attack towards himself. Rana Pratap then attempted to divert the battle from the plains to the hills. Badayuni noted that both divisions of his army reunited before leaving the open ground. He also noted the casaulties: "nearly 500 men, of which 120 were men of Islam, the rest Hindus." The number of Moghul casaulties was greater than the Rana's, since the former were fleeing. Three factors contributed to their loss of spirit: confusion and disarray caused by Rana's sharp offensive, extreme heat and the sheer fright of getting ambushed if they pursued the Rana into the mountains.

His Rajputs fought fiercely till midday. With morale sagging low, Mansinh's soldiers shuffled off to camp in the fort in Gogunda. Even here, all paths leading to and from the town were blocked by Rana Pratap. During the night the Bhils continued to harass them.

Ever loyal to Rana Pratap, they provided efficient intelligence about every little movement of the enemy. During the battle, acting on his instructions, they attacked the Moghul camp from the rear. They plundered the store of provisions, carrying off what they could and destroying the rest. Later in Gogunda, this forced the Moghul army to survive on mangoes and slaughter its mules for meat.

When news of the battle reached Akbar, he was furious with Mansinh and Asaf Khan. He recalled them to Ajmer and censured Mansinh for failing to capture Rana Pratap, dead or alive. Such was his wrath that he forbade both to attend court for a few months.

Though the battle of Haldighati was Rana Pratap's first battle and a minor skirmish, it became a turning point in his military strategy against Akbar. For Hindus it became a milestone in the struggle against foreign domination.

In the period that followed Rana Pratap lived an austere existence. He resorted to guerrilla warfare in the mountain passes; a strategy which Shivaji later adopted. He instilled pride for dharma in his people and Bhils to such an extent that they remained wedded to dharma and loyal to him. Bhamashah, one of his ministers, was a shining example of such loyalty. He offered immense wealth to support the Rana and this army for twelve years.

Meanwhile, Akbar continued to send his commanders to seek and destroy the painful, independent 'spike' that relentlessly goaded him. Obtaining Mewar would not bulge his coffers. For him it was a matter of ego. For Rana Pratap it was to uphold dharma.

Once, Rana Pratap's son, Amarsinh, came across Mirzakhan's army returning from Gujarat. He defeated it and kidnapped the harem. When Rana Pratap came to know of this he ordered Amarsinh to return the *begums*. With honour befitting the Moghul harem, Rana Pratap returned them to Mirzakhan, with an apology. Thus Mirzakhan, developed great admiration for Rana Pratap. Akbar, too, was impressed by Rana's nobility.

Years passed. By 1589 Rana Pratap had recaptured most of Mewar. He spent the final eight years of his life in peace, leaving the administrative and military duties to Amarsinh.

He devoted this time in aesthetic pursuits. A connoisseur of stone architecture, he built many exquisitely sculpted mandirs. He was also a poet and a literatteur. He inspired Mathura's Chakrapani Mishra to write two texts: *Muhurtmala* and *Rajyabhishek Padhati*. He encouraged artists to develop their flair and the Chaavrund art style came into existence. Once while hunting tigers, he strung his bow with such strength that he suffered a painful disorder in his intestines. A few days later, on 19 January 1597, the Hindus lost their noblest leader.

When news reached Akbar, his bard lauded the Rajput. Akbar agreed with the sentiments. After much tribulation he had failed, while Rana Pratap had succeeded. Abul Fazl and

Badayuni, Akbar's historians, remained silent, having little sympathy for a gallant foe. Contemporary bards, poets and the entire extant literature in Rajasthani, Hindi and Sanskrit, lauded Rana Pratap for successfully upholding Hindu dharma and honour. He was an irrepressible lover of freedom, a beacon of single–minded determination and selfless sacrifice, a person who upheld lofty principles of dharma, and liberal and tolerant towards other beliefs. Like Shivaji he was never against Islam. One of his valiant commanders in Haldighati, Hakim Khan Sur, was a Muslim. Unlike Shivaji, who was fighting a declining Moghul power, Rana Pratap was confronting an empire whose sun was at the zenith; against the richest monarch in the world.

Rana Pratap maintained the traditional cultural values embodied in that chivalrous word, Rajput. Simultaneously he upheld all the values embodied in the word dharma.

on the way to Haldighati

Badshah baug, site of the battle of Haldighati

Chetak's memorial shrine near Haldighati

43. Shivaji

As one of the first crusaders for Indian independence, Chhatrapatiji Shivaji challenged the Muslim rulers of his time and won many courageous battles.

His valour symbolises his deep–rooted commitment to Sanatan Dharma and Indian Culture. During Islamic rule internal feuding among the Muslim rulers was rife. One such scenario was occurring in southern India in the 16th century. Malik Ambar, the Nizam Shahi Sultan, was at war with the Delhi Moghul, Jehangir. Ambar's most valiant commander was a Maratha nobleman named Shahji Bhonsle, who usually brought him victories. His wife's, Jijabai's second son was Shivaji. He was born on 10 April 1627 in Shivneri, a fort 50 miles from Puna.

Though Jijabai and Shivaji spent life in the midst of constant political strife and feuds, moving from fort to fort within the state, her duty as a mother did not falter. She was a woman of great earnestness and courage, of honour and esteem, with an inner yearning for independence from foreign oppression and the re–establishment of a Hindu state. It is said that the hand that rocks the cradle has the power to mould kingdoms. Thus, she constantly poured into Shivaji the valiant stories of his ancestral greatness the heroic achievements of the Jadhav's (her ancestors) and Bhonsles (Shahji's ancestors). She also kept a guru who instilled in Shivaji wisdom from the Purans, Ramayan and Mahabharat, emphasising the struggle of virtue and the ultimate triumph of good over evil. Shivaji revelled in listening to such scriptural recitals which strengthened his religious zeal and piety. Jijabai too, described the degradation of Sanatan Dharma by foreign insurgents, the desecration and destruction of mandirs and shrines, and the hideous slaughter of kins. This wrought in Shivaji a staunch thirst for liberty. He considered a servile allegiance to a Mohammedan ruler a gross and unacceptable

M – Mumbai
P – Puna

275

infringement on his independence. From childhood he decided to defy foreign domination even if it cost him his life.

From a young age, in addition to reading and writing, he learnt skills which would help him usurp his people's oppressors. He became a skilled archer, horse–rider, swordsman, marksman and an expert in the use of *patta* – the Maratha javelin. He learnt the art of examining horses and elephants. He frequented his father's military depots. As he grew up, he shunned vice and luxury. When he was 13, his father, Shahji, requested him to come to Bijapur at the Sultan's courts, where he was stationed, to get married. Shivaji declined. He replied that he preferred to get married in Puna where the ceremonies could be readily observed in the Hindu tradition. He then married Sayibai in 1640. Only then did he join his father at Bijapur.

Here, his precocity and respectful manners so fascinated the nobles that they sang his praises to the Sultan. This induced the Sultan to invite him to the court. He declined. He loathed bowing down to a non–Hindu ruler!

Later, Shahji and Jijabai tried to persuade him that his ancestors had risen to high ranks by serving the Mohammedan princes. And since they were the rulers of the land, what was the harm in serving them while still observing one's own faith? Shivaji politely replied that he would bow to the word of command, but could not bear the cruelty to his people and the desecration of Hindu shrines and priesthood. Finally he did accompany his father Shahji to the palace. Shahji had instructed young Shivaji, then 14, about the court etiquette of bowing down to the ground to the Sultan. On arrival, he only made a cursory *salaam*! Noting this slight, the Sultan asked Shahji whether the boy was his son. Shahji, replied that he was, and that this was his first occasion in the palace. The Sultan then presented jewels and robes of honour to Shivaji, being Shahji's son. When he returned home he discarded the courtly dress and had an expiatory bath! On every occasion thereafter, when he accompanied Shahji to the court, he defiantly continued his cursory *salaam*! Once the Sultan questioned him about this. Shivaji apologised and tactfully said that he'd always forget at the right moment, but that he regarded his father and the Sultan equally! This pleased the Sultan!

On his daily visit to court through the bazaar, Shivaji witnessed the slaughter of cows and the sale of beef. This constantly revolted him. Unable to restrain himself once, he beat up a butcher who was on the verge of slashing a cow's throat. This event became a point of public debate and reached the Sultan's ears. Yet he made no enquiry on account of Shahji's status. Wishing to avoid the hideous sight, Shivaji ultimately refused to accompany Shahji to the palace. His wishes were put before the Sultan by a Mohammedan friend of Shahji's. He said that it was the king's duty to honour equally the feelings of his subjects, both Hindus and Muslims alike. Pleased by Shivaji's lofty spirit, the Sultan decreed that cow slaughter and calf sale be shifted outside the city. Shivaji then resumed court attendance.

Once though, on exiting the palace he saw a butcher selling beef just outside the palace gate. Shivaji was so incensed that he cut the man down. When news reached the Sultan, he defended Shivaji's action as a just punishment for violating the decree. This caused great dissension in the Muslim community. Shahji tried to persuade Shivaji to curb such outbursts and humbly serve the ruler, without inciting him further. Shahji also requested Jijabai to talk to Shivaji. He listened respectfully, but requested to be sent away, for he would never change his inner feelings. Shahji then sent Jijabai and Shivaji to Puna.

During the period that followed Shivaji visited the surrounding mountains and forests. He surveyed and scrutinised the hill forts, the routes of communication, the by–paths and mountain passes. He met chiefs and men of position in every town and village. By his unique magnetism he won their hearts. They even idolised him. He listened to their woes and offered finance when necessary. By this he was forming deep bonds for the plan that was taking shape in his mind.

In Puna too, he invited and lavishly entertained the

neighbouring Maratha nobility and they left as fast friends and sympathisers. Gradually, he began to repair old forts and construct new ones on strategic mountains. He mustered an army and took complete possession of hill forts far away from Bijapur, without shedding a drop of blood. When news reached the Sultan, he questioned Shahji. The latter replied that he had no part in his son's activities.

When the Sultan sent armies to fight Shivaji, he'd disappear into the mountains and forests with which he was so familiar. Thus he came to be known as 'the mountain rat'. When outnumbered, as he often was, since he did not have the vast resources of the Sultan or the Delhi Moghul, he resorted to guerilla warfare. He'd strike from the flanks. He'd cut off units at mountain passes and wipe them out. And he'd also strike in the dead of night. On occasions, his forces would be fighting Muslim armies in three different areas of his kingdom. His successes and victories were due to his zeal for liberty, supreme administrative and military genius, efficient spy networks, dedicated commanders and forces, familiarity with the terrain which he knew like the back of his hand, and faith in Bhavani – the goddess he worshipped. She once manifested from the *murti* and gave him, hand to hand, the sword Bhujaly – meaning 'friend of the hand'. He also associated with and received the blessings of renowned mystics of Maharashtra such as Tukaram, Eknath and Samarth Ramdas.

Listening to sermons of such sadhus induced *vairagya* in him on three occasions, when he tried to renounce samsara. In 1649 (one biographer gives the year as 1672), he requested Ramdas to initiate him into the ascetic fold as one of his disciples. Ramdas gave him the *Shri Ram, jai Ram, jai jai Ram* mantra. He then commanded him, as did Krishna to Arjun, "Your duty as a Kshatriya is to look after the citizens. Protect the land from foreign oppression and establish dharma. This is Shri Ram's command to you." Shivaji obeyed implicitly. However, once he became proud about his victories. Ramdas gleaned this. To induce awareness in him about God's will rather than his own might, Ramdas told him to smash a large rock lying nearby. Shivaji pounded it. As the rock shattered, Shivaji was astonished to see a live frog, with some water in a hollow. Swami asked him, "Who sustains the frog inside the rock?" Shivaji gleaned the guru's import. His pride dissolved and he bowed at Swami's feet.

On 6 June 1674, he was invested as *Chhatrapati* (Lord of the Royal Umbrella), in Raighad. He continued his wars and skirmishes to free his people from oppression till he succumbed to illness on 5 April 1680, at the age of 53. He came to be known as the liberator of the Marathas and one of the proponents of independence.

Prior to his final campaign against the Moghuls, he wrote a stirring appeal to Aurangzeb, the emperor in Agra. This revealed his lofty outlook on religion. He reminded the Moghuls that even in the Koran God is described as the "Bhagwan of all men" and not only the "Bhagwan of Mohammedans". Further, "If it be a mosque, the call to prayer is chanted in remembrance of Him. If it be a mandir, the bell is rung in yearning for Him only. To show bigotry for any man's creed is really altering the words of the Holy Book." Whereas Shivaji was a soldier who respected dharma, Aurangzeb was averse to it. The latter not only oppressed Hindus and wantonly slaughtered men, women and children, he also waged war with Shi'ia Muslims, since he was a Sunni. His militancy stemmed from greed. Shivaji's valour arose from his noble commitment to restore the sanctity of his motherland, vilified by centuries of insurgence. Greed pitted against patriotism. *Adharma* versus dharma. Hence his fortitude. Hence his run away victories: *yato dharmaha tato jayaha.*

Shivaji is lauded in the annals of Indian history for his singular zeal to rise against foreign oppression. Considering the mighty armies and resources of the Muslim rulers, the odds were heavily stacked against·him. He neither possessed wealth nor a trained army.

He thus founded a new age. At a time when the Hindu heart bled from hapless inertia and mute oppression, he revived its pulsating rhythm for independence.

An incident during his life depicts his character regarding dharma. Once after raiding a town, his men came across several Muslim women fleeing. They noticed that one of them was very beautiful and would be liked by their master. They took her to him. When he learned why they had brought her, he was furious. He told them that he was a man of dharma. He then commanded them to return her safely.

44. Ahalyabai

When we look back in history to some kings and queens we find some interesting and often peculiar appellations – titles based on their appearance and character. Consider the following:

Louis I (814–40, France) – the Pious, Charles II (843–77, France) – the Bald

Karl III (877–87, Carolingian dynasty) – the Fat

Charles III (893–923, Saxon House) – the Simple

Edward (1042–66, England) – the Confessor

Alexander (Greece), Otto (Saxon House), Alfred (England), Frederick II (Prussia), Catherine, Ivan III & Peter I (Russia) – the Great

Ivan IV (1583–84, Russia) and Tanerkabe (1336–1405) – the Terrible. The latter, a Mongol warlord, once ordered his army to behead people. They piled 70,000 heads in a pyramidal heap outside a city in Isafan (modern–day Iran).

With a few exceptions, the appellations reveal the rulers' appearance, personality and often quirky nature, such as, greed, tyranny, snobbery and cruelty. Some of the more ancient rulers were famed for their wealth or beauty; for example, Solomon, Cleopatra and Helen of Troy. But rulers of saintly disposition were rare. The land of Bharat has had its lion's share of such saintly rulers. Dilip, Yudhishthir, Rantidev, Bhartruhari, Gopichand, Janak Videhi, were just some of the great rulers of ancient India. Those of recent history include: Ashok, Chandragupta, Rana Pratap, Sawai Man Singh and Shivaji.

Ahalyabai justly belongs to this galaxy of India's stalwarts for reasons which will become apparent.

She was born in 1725 in Maharashtra. Her father was Mankoji Shinde. Mankoji, a poor farmer, had well nurtured, the values of dharma and devotion in Ahalyabai, to add to her past samskars. Once, the Maharaja of Indore, Malharrav Holkar, saw her devotionally offering puja in a mandir. He

M – Mumbai
P – Puna

281

instantly decided to get her married to his son, Khanderav.

After marriage she won the hearts of her royal in–laws by her sincere service and care. Whenever Malharrav visited other places, including battles, he always took her with him. He also trained her in state affairs. This period was the acme of the Maratha empire, with frequent wars and feuds. In one such battle in 1754, Khanderav was killed. The aged Malharrav was shattered. He soon regained his courage and said to Ahalyabai, "You are now my son. I wish that you look after my kingdom."

With ease Ahalyabai took charge of the state's affairs. In 1766 Malharrav passed away. Ahalyabai's son, Maalerav then became the king of Indore. Being of an unstable and cruel disposition, he summoned Brahmins to give them alms and simultaneously arrange for them to be bitten by scorpions! Soon, he too died. Ahalyabai again resumed the kingdom's affairs.

Her minister, Gangadhar, then suggested that she adopt a son, and let them both manage the affairs. This would grant her more time for devotion to Bhagwan. Though Ahalyabai greatly enjoyed her periods of devotion and meditation, she did not wish to escape from the duties entrusted to her by Bhagwan to look after her people. Therefore, she rejected Gangadhar's proposal. Infuriated, he wrote to Raghoba, the Peshwa ruler, that since Holkar's treasury is overflowing, he should overcome this fickle female to usurp the treasure. Raghoba took the cue and asked Ahalyabai for the riches. Ahalyabai quipped, "This wealth belongs to the Deity and Brahmins. If you are asking as a Brahmin I will give it to you."

This angered Raghoba, "I am not a Brahmin beggar! I will take the riches with the strength of my arms." He then brought his army. Ahalyabai gathered an army of women soldiers! She stood at its head on horseback. She boldly challenged Raghoba, "Now I will show you how weak I am. If I lose fighting against men then I will have lost nothing. But if you men lose against women then you will be in the soup! And remember, that is exactly what will happen."

Raghoba cringed. Changing track, he said, "I have not

come to fight but to mourn Maalerav's death!"

He stayed as Ahalyabai's guest for a month. During this period he learnt enough about Ahalyabai's prowess in running her kingdom.

When Ahalyabai assumed the reign, she placed a tulsi leaf on the state's coffers, declaring, "This treasure and the kingdom belong to Shankar. On behalf of Shankar I will do my duty to manage the affairs for the benefit of the people." Whenever she signed state orders, she scribed, 'Shri Shankar' as her signature. She did not live in the palace but on the shore of the sacred river Narmada, at a pilgrim spot named Maheshwar. No member of the royalty, anywhere else in the world, has chosen such an austere place of residence. This was the same ancient spot where Shankaracharya and Mandan Mishra held their famous scriptural debate. Contemporary religious poets regarded Maheshwar as analogous to Kailas – Shivji's abode.

At the time, her kingdom was burdened with crime and theft. Learning that the root of all such evils was hunger, she managed to get people involved in trade and farming. She wisely appointed the Bhils, who looted travellers, to offer security on the roads. She used the state's riches for the people's benefit. Never did she use it for personal comforts. This form of detached and saintly rulership paralleled that of Raja Janak, of ancient Mithila.

Once, two widows offered Ahalyabai immense wealth, bequeathed by their husbands, and for which they had little use. Although the state had a right to unclaimed hereditary wealth, Ahalyabai declined to accept it. She advised the widows to use it for religious charity.

Ahalyabai's success in administration is especially laudable in light of the feuding that prevailed elsewhere. Raghoba, the Peshwa ruler in Puna, out of sheer greed, continually ordered his commanders to exact money from his dominions in northern India. These commanders carried out ruthless, predatory campaigns, leaving people in chronic penury. Further, the Peshwas, as rulers, did not even restore the Hindu shrines ravaged and desecrated by repeated Islamic insurgents.

Therefore Ahalyabai's noblest contribution to Hindustan, behoving a true ruler, for which we remember her today, was the repairing and construction of roads, wells, step–wells, ponds, *dharamshalas* (pilgrim resthouses) and mandirs. She even contributed to projects outside her dominion. From Rameshwar in the south, to Badrinath in the north, from Dwarka in the west, to Jagannath Puri in the east, she built *ghats* on the sacred rivers for pilgrims to bathe and opened almshouses and schools for the poor. She repaired the Kashi Vishweshwar Mandir, the Vishnupad Mandir in Gaya and reconstructed the Somnath Mandir. She also delighted in supplying holy water from the river Ganga to many shrines in the south, for bathing the deities.

Everyday she distributed food and clothes to the poor and the sadhus, regardless of *varna* or religious beliefs. She even had mosques built for her Muslim subjects to enable them to worship in peace. Whereas wars and feuds continued all over the land, only Ahalyabai's kingdom enjoyed peace for 30 years. Neighbouring rulers, including the Nizam of Hyderabad and Tipu Sultan of Mysore, greatly respected her.

As a person, Ahalyabai was humble and unassuming, shunning praises by court bards. She once flung a book, replete with her praises written by a poet, into the river Narmada. On another occasion, she refused to have her portrait painted. She exhorted the artist to paint deities rather than mortals. In dress, she wore only simple white, as befitting a widow, and never wore coloured materials often used by royalty. Neither did she wear jewellery. She would see anyone who wished to lodge complaints, from poor peasants to rich merchants, as truly behoves a *Rajmata* (Queen Mother). She attended court four to five hours each day. All the court's attendants dined with her in her kitchen. A staunch proponent of *ahimsa*, she remained a vegetarian throughout life. She only ate one cooked meal a day.

She maintained a high morality, leaving little room for fraud and deceit. Once the neighbouring Maharaja, Mahadji Sindhia, proposed an unethical deal which would benefit her kingdom. She flatly refused. This angered Sindhia, who threatened her, "Listen woman, remember that we are men." Ahalyabai replied acidly, "Do not consider me as a piece of *sopari* (betel nut), to be chewed up and swallowed! Go ahead, bring your army over to Indore. If I do not welcome you by tying you with elephant chains, I am not fit to be Malharrav Holkar's daughter–in–law!" Sindhia turned pale.

At the age of 70, in 1795, Ahalyabai passed away in Maheshwar.

Kings and queens of yore may have temporarily lit up like stars. Eventually however, they fizzled out; victims of their indiscretions, vices or *swabhavs*. However, a *bhakta*–ruler like Ahalyabai shines brightly in the firmament of history, for ruling her kingdom with piety and selflessness; sincerely devoting herself to her subjects while keeping Bhagwan in the forefront. Thus in *The Maratha Supremacy*, the historian, Majumdar, ascribes Morley's definition of a true statesman to Ahalyabai, "The distinctive mark of the true statesman is a passion for good, wise and orderly government" (1991:272).

Glossary

Abhangs	:	Devotional poems.
Amrut	:	Divine nectar which renders immortality.
Anu	:	Molecule.
Atma	:	The pure soul.
Avatar	:	Incarnation.
Avatarvad	:	Principle of Paramatma incarnating on earth.
Bhajan	:	Devotional poem.
Bhakti	:	Loving devotion.
Bhashya	:	Commentary.
Brahmachari	:	One who observes *brahmacharya* and whose *indriyas* are immersed in Parabrahma.
Brahmacharya	:	Eight–fold celibacy and being immersed in Parabrahma.
Brahmanisth	:	One who has realised Brahman.
Chaturmas	:	Four holy months of the monsoon.
Darshan	:	To see, sight, system of philosophy.
Dharma	:	A term which encompasses divine law, path of righteousness, moral duty, ethical conduct, justice, responsibility, religion and truth.
Dhun	:	Type of prayer in which a mantra is chanted melodiously.
Diksha	:	Initiation.
Dosha	:	Humour of Ayurveda, namely three: *vatta* (wind), *pitta* (bile) and *kapha* (catarrh). Also baser instincts such as: avarice, lust, anger, ego, etc.
Ekantik Dharma	:	Composite religion of Dharma, *Jnan,*

286

Vairagya and *Bhakti*.

Janmangal stotras	:	Bhagwan Swaminarayan's 108 names versified in Sanskrit.
Jati (Yati)	:	A supreme *brahmachari*.
Jnan	:	Knowledge
Jyotish	:	Ancient Indian science of astronomy and astrology.
Kalyan Yatra	:	Bhagwan Swaminarayan's pilgrimage to redeem (from 1792 to 1799 through India's sacred places).
Katha	:	Talk expounding Bhagwan's glory from a shastra.
Lila	:	Divine actions of Bhagwan and His Sadhu.
Mādhurya bhakti	:	Melodious devotion.
Maya	:	One of five eternal realities; ignorance.
Math	:	Monastery, ashram of ascetics.
Moksha	:	Liberation from maya and cycle of birth and deaths.
Mukta	:	Liberated *jiva*.
Mukti	:	Liberation, moksha.
Murti	:	Image.
Narak	:	Hell.
Nishedh	:	Don'ts. *See also vidhi*.
Nivrutti marg	:	Path of inaction.
Padarth	:	Substance.
Panch Karma	:	Rejuvenation therapy of Ayurveda, comprising five procedures.
Paramanu	:	Atom.
Pativrata	:	Woman who observes strict chastity.

Praman	:	Means of valid knowledge.
Prasthanatrayi	:	Three shastras – Brahma Sutras, Upanishads and Gita.
Prayashchitt	:	Atonement.
Pravutti marg	:	Path of action.
Premlakshana bhakti	:	Devotion with exuberant love.
Puja	:	Worship ritual.
Punya	:	Spiritual merit.
Raag	:	Tune (of a bhajan, poem).
Raas Lila	:	Traditional folk dance performed by Bhagwan Shri Krishna with the Gopis.
Sadhak	:	Person endeavouring, novice on the spiritual path.
Sadhana (saadhanaa)	:	Spiritual endeavour.
Sakshatkar	:	Realisation of the Divine.
Samadhi	:	Divine trance.
Samhita	:	Compendium.
Samkhyayogini	:	Woman who observes *brahmacharya* and dedicates her life in devotion to Paramatma in the Swaminarayan Sampraday.
Sampraday	:	A tradition handed down from a founder through successive spiritual gurus.
Samsara	:	Cycle of rebirths.
Samskar	:	To improve upon something, sacrament.
Sharanagati	:	Surrenderance at the lotus feet of Paramatma.
Shastra	:	A text by which self–governance and self–control are imbibed (e.g. Shruti *shastras*, Shikshapatri) and which truthfully throws light upon a

subject (e.g. Brahma Sutras, Vachanamrut) - *Shāsanāt shamsanāt shāstram* (*Upadhyay* *1976:3*). 'Scripture' is not an appropriate rendering.

Shlok	:	Sanskrit aphorism.
Shraaddh	:	Ritual of offerings to ancestors.
Siddh	:	A yogi endowed with spiritual power.
Upasana	:	To offer worship to Bhagwan.
Vairagya	:	Detachment from material objects and pursuits.
Vidhi	:	Ritual, acts, procedures, also the "do's" codes of conduct.
Yagna	:	Ritual of the sacred fire.
Yama	:	King of hell, also first step of Ashtang Yog.

Abbot, J.E. and N.R. Godbole (1996). *Stories of Indian Saints*. Delhi: Motilal Banarasidass.

Anon. (1995). *Gurvashtakam*. In *Sri Sankaracharya Stotras*. Madras: Samata Books.

Awasthi, J.P. (1981). *Swaminarayan and Tulsidas on Bhakti*. In *New Dimensions in Vedanta Philosophy. Vol. II*. Amdavad: BAPS Swaminarayan Sanstha.

Bandyopadhyay, P. (1991). *Shankaracharya*. Calcutta: United Writers.

Barz, R. (1992) *The Bhakti Sect of Vallabhacharya*. Delhi: Munshiram Manoharlal.

Behari, Bankey (1962). *Sufis, Mystics & Yogis of India*. Bombay: Bharatiya Vidya Bhavan.

Bhagvatsinhjee, H.H. (1998). *History of Hindoo Medical Science*. New Delhi: Logos Press.

Bhagwan Das (1976). *Caraka*. In *Scientists, Cultural Leaders of India*. New Delhi: Ministry of Information and Broadcasting.

Bhagvatsinhjee, Maharaja (1944) *Bhagvat Gomandal*. Gondal: Maharaja Bhagvatsinhjee.

Bhaktavatsaldas, Sadhu (1991). *Epistemology of Swaminarayan*. In *New Dimensions in Vedanta Philosophy. Vol. I*. Amdavad: BAPS Swaminarayan Sanstha.

Bhat, M. Ramakrishna (1997). *Varahmihira's Brhat Samhita. Vols. I & II*. Delhi: Motilal Banarasidass.

Bhatt, G.H. (1969). *The System of Vallabhāchārya*. In *The Cultural Heritage of India. Vol. I – The Philosophies*. Calcutta: The Ramakrishna Mission Institute of Culture.

Bhattacharya, A.C. (1981). *Bhakti Propounded by Swaminarayan and that of Alvars*. In *New Dimensions in Vedanta Philosophy, Vol. II*. Amdavad: BAPS Swaminarayan Sanstha.

Bhattacharya, S. (1969). *The Philosophy of Sankara*. In *The Cultural Heritage of India, Vol. I – The Philosophies*. Calcutta: The Ramakrishna Mission Institute of Culture.

Bilimoria, P. (1981). *Shri Swaminarayan and Shabda Pramana*.

In *New Dimensions in Vedanta Philosophy, Vol. II*. Amdavad: BAPS Swaminarayan Sanstha.

Bose, D.M., *et. al.* (1971). *A Concise History of Science in India*. New Delhi: Indian National Science Academy.

Brahmadarshandas, Sadhu (1996, 1997). *Bharatiya Darshan, Part 2 & 3, respectively*. Sarangpur: Shri Yagnapurushdas Sanskrut Vidyalay.

Brahmbhatt, Raghunath (1978). *Prachin Vibhutio*. Amdavad: Sastu Sahitya Vardhak Karyalay.

Burgess, E. and P. Gangooly (1997). *The Surya Siddhanta*. New Delhi: Motilal Banarasidass.

Chinmayananda, Swami (n.d.). *Bhaja Govindam by Bhagwan Shri Shankaracharya*. Madras: Chinmaya Publication Trust.

Chitrav, M.M. Siddheshwar Shastri (1964). *Bharatvarshiya Prachin Charitra Kosh*. Poona: Bharat Charitra Kosh Mandal.

Clark, W.E. (1930). *The Aryabhatiya of Aryabhat*. Chicago: The University of Chicago Press.

Crooke, W. (1920). *Annals & Antiquities of Rajasthan by Lieut. Col. James Tod. Vol. I*. London: Oxford University Press.

Dasgupta, Surendranath (1927) *Hindu Mysticisim*. New York: Frederik Ungar, 6th. ed. 1977.

—— (1975). *A History of Indian Philosophy, Vol. I*. New Delhi: Motilal Banarsidass.

Dave, H.T. (2000). *Aksharbrahma Gunatitanand Swami Vols. I & II*. Amdavad: Swaminarayan Aksharpith (7th ed.).

Dave, P. (1990). *Madhvacharyanu Tattvajnan*. Mumbai: Parichay Trust.

Dave, Ramesh, M. (2000). *Navya Visistadvaita – The Vedanta Philosophy of Sri Swaminarayana*. Mumbai: Aksara Prakashana.

Dave, R. & K. Dave (1987). *Swaminarayan Vedant Darshan*. Amdavad: Swaminarayan Aksharpith.

Deva, B.C. (1979). *Swami Haridas*. In *Composers, Cultural Leaders of India*. New Delhi: Ministry of Information and Broadcasting.

Devasthali, G.V. (1975). *Jaimini*. In *Founders of Philosophy, Cultural Leaders of India*. New Delhi: Ministry of Information and Broadcasting.

Dikshit, T.V.R. (1969). *Synthesis of Patanjali's Yogasāstra*. In *The Cultural Heritage of India, Vol. I – The Philosophies*. Calcutta: The Ramakrishna Mission Institute of Culture.

Diwakar, R.R. (1976). *Mahayogi Sri Aurobindo*. Bombay: Bharatiya Vidya Bhavan.

Dwarkanath, C. (1976). *Dhanvantari*. In *Scientists, Cultural Leaders of India*. New Delhi: Ministry of Information and Broadcasting.

Frawley, David (1991). *Gods, Sages and Kings – Vedic Secrets of Ancient Civilization*. Salt Lake City: Passage Press.

Ifrah, G. (1998). *The Universal History of Numbers from Prehistory to the Invention of the Computer*. London: The Harvill Press.

Ishwarcharandas, Sadhu (2001). *Gunatitanand Swami*. Amdavad: Swaminarayan Aksharpith.

Jaggi, O.P. (1986). *Indian Astronomy & Mathematics, Vol. 6*. Delhi: Atmaram & Sons.

Jani, A.N. (1981). *Philosophy of Swaminarayan and Vallabhacharya*. In *New Dimesions in Vedanta Philosophy, Vol. II*. Amdavad: BAPS Swaminarayan Sanstha.

Kansara, N.M., *et. al.* (1992). *Issues in Vedic Astronomy and Astrology*. New Delhi: Motilal Banarasidass.

Kalani, K. (1991) *Sant Tukaram*. Mumbai: R.R. Sheth & Co.

Kalarthi, M. (1957). *Sant Samagam*. Amdavad: Gujarat Vidyapith.

Keith, A.B. (1920). *Indian Logic & Atomism*. London: Oxford University Press.

Khurana, G. (1990). *The Theology of Nimbarka*. New York: Vantage Press.

Kirtan Muktavalli (2000) 11th. ed. Amdavad: Swaminarayan Aksharpith.

Lal, C. (1978). *India–Cradle of Cultures*. New Delhi: Oxford & IBH Publishing.

Lowe, W.H. (n.d.). *Muntakhabut–Twarikh*. Vol. II (Translation of Badayuni's chronicles).

Madhavananda, Swami (1974). *Vivekchudamani of Sri Shankara*. Calcutta: Advaita Ashrama.

Mahadevan, T.M.P. (1971). *Outlines of Hinduism*. Bombay: Chetana, 2nd. ed.

—— (1975). *Bādarāyan*. In *Founders of Philosophy, Cultural Leaders of India*. Delhi: Ministry of Information and Broadcasting.

Majmudar, R.C. (1991). *The Maratha Supremacy*. Mumbai: Bharatiya Vidya Bhavan.

—— (1984). *The Mughal Empire*. Mumbai: Bharatiya Vidya Bhavan.

Majumdar, S. (1969). *The Nimbārka School of Vedanta*. In *The Cultural Heritage of India, Vol. I–The Philosophies*. Calcutta : The Ramakrishna Mission Institute of Culture.

Mookerjee, S. (1969). *Nyaya–Vaisheshika*. In *The Cultural Heritage of India, Vol. III – The Philosophies*. Calcutta: The Ramakrishna Mission Institute of Culture. ed. Haridas Bhattacharya, rpt.

Munshi, K.M. (1990). *Krishnavatara (Vol. VI). The Book of Veda Vyasa – The Master*. Bombay: Bharatiya Vidya Bhavan.

Murthy, K.R. Srikanta (1997). *Luminaries of Indian Medicine*. Varanasi: Chaukhambha Orientalia.

Musalgaonvakar, G.S. (1992). *Mimamsadarshan ka Vivechanatmak Itihas*. Delhi: Chawkhamba Sanskrut Pratisthan.

Nayak, Champaklal C. (1983). *Ashtachhapiya Bhaktisangit (Haveli Sangit). Udbhav aur Vikas*. Amdavad: C. C. Nayak.

Ojha, G.H. (1998). *Maharana Pratapsinh*. Jodhpur: Rajasthani Granthagar, 2nd ed.

Pande, S.N. (1981). *Bhakti Propounded by Swaminarayan and that of Tulsidas*. In *New Dimensions in Vedanta Philosophy, Vol. II*. Amdavad: BAPS Swaminarayan Sanstha.

Parekh, M.C. (1969). *Sri Vallabhacharya*. Rajkot: Shri Bhagavata Dharma Mission.

Parikh, R. (2002). *Anandno Avishkar Part–I*. Mehsana: Shri

Harsaniji Public Charitable Trust, 9th ed.

Patel, Ambalal V. (1962). *Bharatiya Prachin Samskruti*. Surat: Samskar Prakashan.

Prabhavananda, Swami (1977). *The Spiritual Heritage of India*. Madras: Sri Ramkrishna Math.

Prakash, S. (1965). *Founders of Sciences in Ancient India*. New Delhi: The Research Insititute of Ancient Scientific Studies.

Prasad, G. (1956). *Bharatiya Jyotish ka Itihas*. Luckhnow: Uttar Pradesh Sarkar Prakashan Bureau.

Raghavan, A.S. (1985). *Vishishtadvaita*. Tirupati: Tirumala Tirupati Devasthanams.

Raghavan, V. (1979). *Tyagaraja*. In *Composers, Cultural Leaders of India*. New Delhi: Ministry of Information and Broadcasting.

Ramakrishnananda, Swami (1959). *Life of Sri Ramanuj*. Mylapore: Sri Ramakrishna Math.

Ramakrishna Rao, K.S. (1981). *Swaminarayan and Madhvacharya*. In *New Dimensions in Vedanta Philosophy, Vol. II*. Amdavad: BAPS Swaminarayan Sanstha.

Ramcharaka, Yogi. (1980). *The Philosophies and Religions of India*. Bombay: Wilco Publishing House.

Rau, S. (1969). *The Realism of Sri Madhvachārya*. In *The Cultural Heritage of India, Vol. I – The Philosophies*. Calcutta: The Ramakrishna Mission Institute of Culture.

Raval, C.V. (1974). *Shrimad Shankaracharyanu Tattvajnan*. Amdavad: University Granth Nirman Board.

Saraswathi, T.A. (1976). *Bhaskaracarya*. In *Scientists, Cultural Leaders of India*. New Delhi: Ministry of Information and Broadcasting.

Seal, B. (1991). *The Positive Sciences of the Ancient Hindus*. New Delhi: Motilal Banarsidass.

Shah, K.K. (1980). *Brahma Sutra ane tena saat Bhashyakarona sandarbhma vivechanatmak ane tulnatmak adhyayan*. Amdavad: Gujarat University, doctoral dissertation.

Shah, N.G. (1974). *Shad–Darshan Dwitiya Khand*: *Nyaya–Vaisheshik*, Amdavad: University Granth Nirman Board.

—— (1995). *Shad–Darshan Dwitiya Khand: Samkhya-Yog*, Amdavad: University Granth Nirman Board.

Sharma, B.N.K. (1970). *Madhva's Teachings in His Own Words*. Mumbai: Bharatiya Vidya Bhavan.

Sharma, G.N. (1978). *Maharana Pratap and the Battle of Haldighati*. In *Battle of Haldighati*, 4th Centenary Celebrations Souvenir. Udaipur: Maharana Pratap Smarak Samiti.

—— (1989). *et.al. Maharana Pratap and His Times*. Udaipur: Maharana Pratap Smarak Samiti.

Sharma, I.C. (1981). *The Philosophy of Shri Swaminarayan and the Pure Non–Dualism of Shri Vallabhacharya*. In *New Dimensions in Vedanta Philosophy, Vol. II*. Amdavad: BAPS Swaminarayan Sanstha.

Sharma, P. (2003). *Nimbark darshan ke pariprekshya mein ananta shrivibhushit Nimbark pithasth jagadguru Shri Radhasarveshwar sharandevacharyaji maharaj ka vyaktitwa evam krutitva*. Ajmer: Akhil Bharatvarshiya Nimbarkpith Shiksha Samiti.

Sharma, P. (1999). *Ayurveda ka vaijnanik Itihasa*. Varanasi: Chowkhambha Orientalia.

Shastri, K.K. (1977). *Mahaprabhuji Shri Vallabhacharyaji*. Mumbai: Vitthaldas Thakarsi Charitable Trust.

Shastri, N. (1995). *Pushti Pulin*. Nadiad: Vidyanidhi.

Shastri, Padmaprasad, H. Shukla (1970). *Nyaya Darshan – The Sutras of Gautam & Bhashya of Vatsyayana*. Varanasi: Chowkhamba Sanskrit Series.

Shukla, J.P. (1981). *Swaminarayan and* Yog. In *New Dimensions in Vedanta Philosophy, Vol. I*. Amdavad: BAPS Swaminarayan Sanstha.

Shukla, K.S. (1976). *Aryabhata*. In *Scientists, Cultural Leaders of India*. New Delhi: Ministry of Information And Broadcasting.

Soni, R. (1985). *Sant Sagar. Vol. I*. Amdavad: Rasikbala Soni.

Srinivasachari, P.N. (1969). *The Visishtadvaita of Ramanuj*. In *The Cultural Heritage of India, Vol. I – The Philosophies*. Calcutta: The Ramakrishna Mission Institute of Culture.

Subbarayappa, B.V. (1970). *India's Contribution to World Thought & Culture*. Madras: Vivekananda Rock Memorial Committee.

Sudarsanachar, J. (1996). *Andal*. Bangalore: Rashtrotthana Sahitya Trust.

Sullivan, B.M. (1999). *Seer of the fifth Veda–Krsna Dvaipayana Vyasa in the Mahabharata*. New Delhi: Motilal Banarasidass.

Swami, Acharya Shabar (1987). *Jaiminiya–Mimamsa–Bhashyam. Part I*. Vahalgadh: Yudhisthir Mimamsak, 2nd. rpt.

Tarkabhushan, P. (1969). *Purva–Mimamsa*. In *The Cultural Heritage of India, Vol. III. The Philosophies*. Calcutta: The Ramakrishna Mission Institute of Culture.

Telivala, M.T. (1980). *Shuddhadvaita Brahmavada*. Varanasi: Anand Prakashan Sansthan.

Thakur, A. (1975). *Gautama*. In *Founders of Philosophy, Cultural Leaders of India*. New Delhi: Ministry of Information and Broadcasting.

Thorwald, J. (1962). *Science and Secret of Early Medicine*. London: Thames & Hudson.

Trivedi, R. (1959). *Mira*. Amdavad: G. R. Trivedi.

Trivedi, K.V. (1908). *Charitra Chandrika. Part I*. Amdavad: Chandraprakash Printing Press.

Upadhyaya, B. (1976). *Bharatiya Darshan*. Varanasi: Chowkhamba Orientalia.

Upadhyay, Baldev (1956). *Shri Shankaracharya*. Allahabad: Hindustani Academy.

Vivekpriyadas, Sadhu (1998). *Apno Sanskrutik Varso. Vols. I & II*. Amdavad: Swaminarayan Aksharpith.

Viveksagardas, Sadhu (2000). *Zamkuba*. In *Kishore Satsang Pravesh*. Amdavad: Swaminarayan Aksharpith, 7th ed.

Watson, J.W. (1879). *Statistical Account of Porbandar*. Bombay: Education Society's Press.

—— *Statistical Account of Junagadh* (1880). Bombay: Education Society's Press.

—— *Statistical Account of Bhavnagar* (1883). Bombay: Education Society's Press.

—— *Statistical Account of Nawanagar* (1884). Bombay: Education Society's Press.

—— *Statistical Account of Dhrangadhra* (1884). Bombay: Education Society's Press.

Yamunacharya, M. (1978). *Ramanuj*. In *Philosophers and Religious Leaders. Part I, Cultural Leaders of India*. New Delhi: Ministry of Information and Broadcasting.

Zaveri, Nirmala (1991). *Mira: jivan ane kavan*. Mumbai: Navbharat Sahitya Mandir.

Shastras & Sanskrit Texts

Bhagvad Gita

Bhavarth Dipika (Jnaneshwar)

Charak Samhita

Devi Bhagvatam

Gopika Geet (Bhagvatam)

Gurvashtakam Stotras (Shankar)

Janmangal Stotras (Shatanand Muni)

Kapil Gita (Bhagvatam)

Karunashtak Stotra (Ramdas)

Mahabharat

Manaache Shlok (Ramdas)

Mimamsa sutras (Jaimini)

Mohamudgara (Shankar)

Narad Bhakti Sutras

Ramayan

Samnyasnirnayah (Vallabh)

Shikshapatri of Bhagwan Swaminarayan.

Shiv Puran

Shrimad Bhagvatam

Siddhantpradeep Tika (Madhva's disciple Shukdev)

Sushrut Samhita

Swamini Vato (Aksharbrahma Gunatitanand Swami)

Tattvadipika Tika (Vallabh)

Vachanamrut of Bhagwan Swaminarayan

Vaisheshik Sutras (Kanad)

Vivekchudamani (Shankar)

Yog Sutras (Patanjali)

Journals

Garg, P. (1959) *Sangit*. Hathras (U.P.): Sangit Karyalay.

—— (1959) *Swami Haridasji aur Tansen*. In *Sangit* (Feb. issue). Hathras (U.P.): Sangit Karyalay.

Datta, G. (1959) *Swami Haridasji*. In *Sangit* (Feb. issue) Hathras (U.P.): Sangit Karyalay.

Vaidya, R.V. (1997). *Some Controversial Dates Established*. In *The Astrological Magazine*, Bangalore.

Index